This book is dedicated to my wonderful family—you are the greatest bunch of people anyone could ever have around them! Thank you for your support, patience, understanding, hard work, and, above all, love.

This book is also dedicated to anyone who has had a bad time with a PC. If you've ever missed a tax deadline because of a system crash, had all your important email disappear, lost your precious family digital photos, had to use the old excuse that the dog ate your homework when it was in fact the computer, been sent an important document by your boss that you just couldn't open, or had to sit and look at an error message instead of playing your favorite game or surfing the Web, this book is dedicated to you!

About the Author

Adrian W. Kingsley-Hughes is a technical director and consultant for a U.K.-based computer company. He teaches many PC-related courses, including one entitled "Caring for Your PC." He has taught many thousands of people to fix their PC problems for themselves, and this inspired him to write this book.

Contents

V

Acknowledgments

No book ever gets written in isolation. Behind every good book is a good team. A lot of people have worked tirelessly to take this book from the initial idea through to print.

To start with, a big "thank you" is due to Scott Rogers and Jane Brownlow, who saw the potential of this idea in the first place. My sincerest thanks to you both.

Thanks also go to Agatha Kim for all the help, useful tips, timely prods, and for keeping the whole project moving along. Cheers!

Thanks also to Madhu Prasher and Judith Brown, who worked miracles and transformed my Word documents full of weird styles and markup into this polished final product that you see. Thank you!

Thanks also to all the other folks at McGraw-Hill/Osborne, who worked on this book but whom I didn't get the pleasure of meeting or talking to. Thanks!

A special thanks to Kathie for taking hundreds of photographs of components of all kinds for this book. I really appreciate your hard work and dedication to perfection in making sure that what I wanted in the shot looked great. Thank you very much!

Finally, thanks to all those around me who helped in many and varied ways with this project, from spotting my spelling mistakes or sloppy sentences to making sure that my mug always had tea in it. Thanks!

No electrons were harmed or mistreated during the writing of this book, but lots were terribly inconvenienced. Sorry.

Adrian W. Kingsley-Hughes
June 2004
www.kingsley-hughes.com/pcdoc

Introduction

If you are reading this, you probably have a computer. If I'm right and you do, then there's a very good chance that it's important to you, either personally or professionally, or both. Another thing I can safely assume is that you probably know what it feels like when your computer goes wrong.

Computers are all around us today, and they've become an almost essential tool of everyday life (in offices, homes, schools, businesses, and even carried with us when we are on the move). Yet frequently when they let us down, it is just at the time when we need them most, and this can be frustrating for people who don't know what is wrong or how to fix it. Wouldn't it be great to be able to do just that? And wouldn't it be really great to be able to upgrade your PC without shelling out a lot of money for somebody to do it for you? Or would you like to be able to set up your computer so that it's just the way you want it, as well as being safe and secure for you and your family?

In choosing a PC, we have a great deal of choice when it comes to what kind we want (desktop, laptop, tablet, handheld). We are also faced with a staggering array of hardware that can be connected to our PCs, such as a mouse, keyboard, speakers, microphone, and printer. You may additionally have already connected (or would like to connect) a digital camera, scanner, video recorder, cell phone, portable music player, GPS receiver, as well as a whole host of wireless peripherals (enabling you to interface and interact with other devices by using radio signals).

There is also an important choice to be made when it comes to what operating system (OS) you have loaded onto your PC. This can be mind-bogglingly confusing and scary for both the beginner and the experienced owner alike, and just about everyone around has an opinion to offer on which OS is best! But only you can appreciate your own needs, and it's important to make an informed choice.

 FIX-IT-YOURSELF HOME REMEDY *An operating system is no longer something that you necessarily have to pay for, and several free operating systems are currently available.*

After the OS comes the choice of what software you want to install. This can range from expensive off-the-shelf software to free downloadable software.

Once you've got your computer set up and started using it, you will no doubt begin accumulating data (such as word processor documents, photographs from digital cameras, web pages, downloads, email, and so on) that you will want to keep safe for the future. Storing your data on different media (CDs, floppy disks, DVDs, portable memory) is a snap these days if you have a PC. You can even create your own CDs and DVDs that can be played on your home entertainment system. Using these, you can easily and cheaply share huge amounts of video, photos, and other data with family and friends. (CDs cost mere cents, and DVDs start at around a few dollars.)

Add to all this the heady power we now possess to connect our own computer to other computers on a network or via the Internet, so that we can share both resources and information. We can send and receive information to and from anywhere in the world quickly and easily, without any fuss or huge cost. You can access information and resources on almost any subject you care to choose, as well as communicate with like-minded people from all parts of the globe.

There are several ways to connect to the Internet, depending on your geographical location, budget, and how much time you plan to spend online. For the vast majority of people, dial-up using a modem is still the way they connect to the Web, but some choose to access the Internet by high-speed DSL connections, or even satellite connections. For those on the move, the option exists to connect to the Internet via cell phone. If, however, you want to free yourself from your desk, you will want to go for the ultimate wire-free Internet experience, by tooling yourself up with a WiFi Internet connection. WiFi offers high-speed Internet access to those within range of an access point (charges may apply) and is becoming a popular option, especially for people on the move, with more and more access points being installed in restaurants, hotels, and cafés daily. But it's not just for people who want to surf the Web and check their email while on the move; a wireless network is fast becoming the easy, no-fuss, no-wires, no-holes-in-the-wall solution for creating home and office networks.

 PC DOCTOR'S ORDER! *Wireless networks and high-speed Internet connections are super, but it is vital if you have these in place, that you take much greater care when it comes to protecting your PC (or network of PCs) from attacks by viruses and hackers.*

So all in all, a PC is probably the most versatile and multipurpose piece of equipment ever made, allowing the owner unprecedented flexibility and scope. Computers seem like the perfect technology to accompany us all into the 21st century, and every day sees an increase in the faith and trust we place in them to solve our problems and manage our busy lives. They are seemingly without flaw or weakness.

But wait, that's not entirely accurate! They do have one major flaw that strikes owners and users alike the world over: they can go wrong, and go wrong often, in an almost infinite number of ways.

This defect comes as a direct result of having such a powerful, complex, and flexible tool.

NOTE *The complexity of a PC, both the hardware and the software, really is quite staggering. We went to the moon on far less computing power than you have at your disposal in the form of a home PC.*

Despite their obvious intricacy and processing power, computers are still incapable of looking after themselves in even the most basic of ways. If you compare a modern, top-of-the-line PC to even a relatively basic car, you will see many omissions relating to control and care of the system. Cars have simple, easily readable systems that are designed to give the user clear warnings relating to, amongst other things, dropping oil levels, insufficient coolant, broken fan belts, and defective brakes; they can even remind us when a service is due. Fire up a PC and you see nothing like this at all. No dials or gauges—even electronic ones—show you system speed, system temperature (even though, as you will see later, one of the most common causes of component failure in a PC can be directly linked to system temperature), not even a service reminder!

What This Book Has to Offer

Before we go any further, let me get one thing clear: no single computer book ever written is going to contain the solution to all possible problems that a PC can suffer. There are just too many ailments that can afflict your system. But that doesn't mean you are powerless to do anything about them! And this book aims to help you solve the most common problems as well as teach you how to find answers to the rest.

NOTE *Even if I listed only the documented ailments that can afflict an operating system such as Microsoft Windows XP, this book would be several volumes long.*

If every PC rolled off a production line, each identical to the previous one, each loaded with all the software, and you couldn't upgrade them or add more software or peripherals, it might be possible to come up with solutions to every possible PC problem. But things aren't like that. There is no such thing as a standard PC (although in the early days of the PC attempts were made to create standard PCs), and there are wide variations between different brands and models. The permutations are almost infinite:

- Different motherboards

- Different processors

- Varying amounts and types of RAM

- Different hard drives

- Different graphics cards

- Different mice/keyboards

- Different mousemats (only joking!)

Two PCs that are identical with regard to manufacturer and even model can contain vastly different components. One type of graphics card might have been replaced by another, or perhaps they ran out of hard drives from one manufacturer and bought drives from a different manufacturer that were of the same size and speed. No single book can even pretend to come close to listing every problem the PC owner may ever encounter. Add to this the wide variety of additional software and hardware most owners attach to the system after purchase, which further complicates the accurate diagnosing of a problem.

So, although this book will cover many common problems that affect PCs, my goal is to empower you with the skills and information you need to be able to track down the root causes of the issues you come up against and to give you the know-how to deal with the problems once you have correctly identified them. Until you understand what the real problem is, there is no point in trying to fix it.

Why Bother with Doing It Yourself?

Before you get a screwdriver out and set to work opening the case or go delving into the files buried in the operating system, I think you need to understand not only the advantages (and power!) of being able to deal with problems yourself but also the reason why you are taking charge of them yourself.

If you've read up to this point, I'm going to assume that you fall into one of the following groups:

- You are a computer owner and you have a problem (or problems) that you'd like to get rid of.

- You own a computer and so far your system is running great, and you want to keep it that way.

- Your computer is a few years old and you'd like to give it a new lease on life.

- You're thinking of building a computer and want a good grounding in what all the bits are and how they fit together.

- You bought this book by accident thinking it was a home health-care manual.

But before we get down to identifying and fixing problems, let's look at how PCs are usually sold and the safeguards that are in place to protect you when things go wrong. We'll also look at why so many PC owners don't realize their system needs any after-sales care—that is, until it goes wrong.

Imagine you want to buy a new PC. Now imagine walking into your local computer store or electrical retailer so you can take a look at what they have to offer. You've done quite a bit of research on the Internet and in computer magazines, and you've come up with the right level of specification for what you want.

 NOTE *We'll be deciphering everything you need to know about computer specifications later.*

Strolling around the store, you see a few systems that match your requirements. A salesperson notices that you are interested and sidles over to you. You exchange a few questions about performance and price, and perhaps the salesperson tries to sell you something a little more expensive than the one you'd planned on. (After all, they wouldn't be salespeople if they didn't try that!) You're not convinced that the more expensive system is worth the extra cash that the store wants for it, and so you stick with your planned budget and specification.

PC DOCTOR'S ORDER! *It's never a bad idea to stick with your planned budget and specification. If you do think that you want to change your plans, I'd suggest sleeping on it before you buy. Weigh up the pros and cons carefully.*

You're now sure that the system you are looking at initially, the one based on your research, is the right system for you, so you decide to buy it. The salesperson takes your order and tries once again to sell you some other things to go with your system, such as a printer. You think about this and remember that your current printer is a bit poor, and you decide to treat yourself to a new one to go with your new PC. You're happy, and the salesperson is also happy. As you get ready to pay, there's a chance that the salesperson will offer to sell you an extended warranty. Right on cue, you are offered an extended warranty on the system you are buying. You decline because you feel you've spent enough. You then pay for your goods, and you leave the store happy with your new PC all packed away in a few cardboard boxes.

Every day, thousands of PCs are sold just like this. (OK, not all are sold over the counter, with many nowadays sold by mail order or over the Internet or telephone.) But there is one common omission usually present in 99.99 percent of these sales. That one thing is rarely, if ever, mentioned. "What is that?" I hear you ask.

It's this. The buyer (you) is rarely, if ever, told that the PC he or she just bought will need at least a small amount of care and attention from the owner (you) if they want to get the most out of it. If you buy a car, you are routinely told how much and how often it will need servicing. If you buy a pet, you will undoubtedly be given quite specific "care and feeding" advice. The same goes for clothes, no matter what the cost. In fact, most things that you buy come with instructions as to how you can care for the product after you buy it.

Computers, it seems, don't need any after-sales care, or at least, none that you are usually told about. The salespeople certainly don't tell you that your new computer will need regular attention. OK, maybe it's buried somewhere in one of the many manuals supplied with a new system, but generally the manuals that come with systems rarely, if ever, make any mention of how you should look after a new PC system. It seems that you just set it up, plug it in, and run it. You keep on doing this until it no longer works right, at which point you wonder if you're supposed to go out and buy a new one and start on the cycle once again.

 NOTE *Maybe now you can understand why manufacturers and resellers don't supply any instructions for caring for your system.*

When most people buy a computer, they think very little about the kind of "care and feeding" that it will need. In fact, I'm convinced that most PC buyers (especially first-time buyers) think a PC is just like all the other home entertainment and electronic equipment found in their home and won't need anything beyond a quick wipe down with a duster every so often just to keep it looking fine.

This is simply not true!

The modern PC is without a doubt the single most complex piece of equipment that people have in their homes. (If you don't believe me, try finding something in your home that has more buttons and keys on it and is anywhere near as versatile.) This added complexity means that it needs *more* after-sales care than your stereo or TV, or even your car. Your new personal computer system will come with a warranty covering defects in parts, but it's important to bear in mind that this warranty is limited—usually 12 months—and I assume that you want your computer to last longer than that!

 PC DOCTOR'S ORDER! *Be clear about what sort of warranty your system comes with. Does your warranty mean that you have to get your system back to the store/manufacturer, or will they pick it up? Or will they send an engineer out? Do you get another computer while yours is being fixed? Warranties where you end up footing the bill to return a system can end up costing you a lot of money. Even calling tech support lines can be expensive.*

It is beyond this warranty period that taking care of your system really pays off. However, don't put off starting a good maintenance routine until your warranty is up.

Still not convinced? Well, here is just a small list of simple things that can affect the performance and ease of use of your system that are easy to remedy (as you will see shortly):

- Dirt stuck in the mouse causing erratic pointer movement

- Dirty keyboard causing sticky keys

- Dust collecting on fans causing noise

- CD-ROM drives not reading discs properly due to dirt on the laser

All of these are annoying. All are, however, easy to fix. To find out how, keep reading.

Protect Your Investment

Why should you be interested in taking care of your new PC? After all, modern electronic devices are pretty reliable, and when things go wrong you usually have a warranty to fall back on, don't you?

The first and most obvious reason for taking care of your PC is a financial one. Your computer system has probably cost you a lot of money, so it's wise to make sure you get the most out of what you spent.

Let's say you've bought your system and got it home and taken it out of the box. If you are lucky, you have set up your system, plugged it in, and gotten it going quickly and easily. (There is always a chance that you were unlucky and brought it home only to find it DOA—Dead On Arrival.) As the owner of a new PC, worries about its reliability and how long it will last are probably not paramount in your mind. You'll be too busy exploring it, discovering what it can do, and trying out new things. It's very easy to be lulled into complacency about how much care a PC actually requires.

Most PC manufacturers are very good when it comes to dealing with the early teething troubles that new PC owners experience. They are often happy to help with setting up the hardware and any software that came bundled with the system. However, this generally changes once you begin to experience problems that are unrelated to the original hardware and software supplied (such as software conflicts, problems with other peripherals, or connecting your PC to a network). There are many reasons for this, the most likely being that in order to sell computer systems at competitive prices, manufacturers and retailers need to cut their profit margins. This means a less-generous support package. It would also be unreasonable to expect manufacturers and retailers to have the knowledge and manpower to offer such a comprehensive package for every possible combination of peripherals and software that could be applied to their products.

 PC DOCTOR'S ORDER! *Be aware that you might be charged for support issues that arise from hardware and software you've added to the system after purchase. If you have any doubts at all about the kind of support you can expect, ask! If you still have your doubts, ask to have it in writing.*

Maybe It's All in the Manual?

You're always told to make sure that you read all the manuals and paperwork that come with anything you buy. Does any of this give the PC owner any "care" information?

No! The manuals and instruction leaflets that come with a new system don't mention much about how you should care for your system (beyond the obvious keeping it dry and not dropping it). What the manuals do give you is a rundown of your warranty rights along with all the telephone numbers, email addresses, and website addresses that you will need if you run into trouble. Combine this with the fact that modern electronic devices are pretty reliable, and there is a good chance that you will get many years of service from a computer, even if you don't perform any maintenance on it (in much the same way that you hear stories of cars running for hundreds of thousands of miles without an oil change or a service). It's also very easy to be drawn into a false sense of security by reassurances of telephone support and warranties. Why waste time and effort on maintaining your system when you have these to fall back on? Warranty and telephone support might sound good when you buy the system, but in the real world, all but the best (and most costly) support usually means lengthy downtimes and long, boring, expensive telephone calls.

 PC DOCTOR'S ORDER! *Check your documentation to see whether telephone support is offered on a toll-free phone number.*

Returning Your System—and Your Data!

Very often, a defective system will need to be returned to the manufacturer, which means you will be without it for some time. Returning the system also means being without access to all the data stored on it—work, photos, email and tax and financial records. How would you cope with this? What would you do if the worst came to the worst—you get your system back from repair, your data is gone, and the system is back to the same state that it was in when it first came out of the box?

 NOTE *Don't count on getting free help to recover your lost data. Few, if any, computer manufacturers or resellers will take responsibility for your data. They will assume that you have made copies of anything important before your computer went wrong.*

A common solution offered is to include a recovery disc that is designed to return your system to its original out-of-the-box state. While these can be quite effective solutions, any data stored on your computer will be erased (as will any additional software and hardware drivers that you have installed). So this should only be used as a last resort or if you have an up-to-date copy of all your data, which technical support may or may not tell you when they tell you to use the disc.

It's always a good idea to periodically think about the important data that's on your PC, and it's not always as obvious as you first think. It's easy to think about data as being the correspondence, emails, and tax records saved on your PC, but there might also be other data that's almost as important to you. For example:

- Game profiles

- Stills and video from digital cameras and camcorders

- Saved Internet favorite links

- Software that you paid for and downloaded from the Internet

- Music that you paid for and downloaded from the Internet

- Lists of recipes, plans, or hobby-related material that you've collected

- Anything else that you've created and saved on your computer that is important to you

 NOTE *Nothing beats having a sensible backup schedule. I'll show you later what you need to keep and the best ways to keep it.*

However, a little bit of maintenance goes a long way. Over the course of this book, I will show you that taking care of your system need not take up too much of your time (perhaps a couple of hours a month) and that this is time well spent on keeping the computer running when you compare the time, effort, and disruption you would be put through by a problem that could have been prevented.

Still Need Convincing?

Want another reason why you should take care of your computer? Looking after your system will also save you money. It's a fact. Not only will it mean that you suffer less downtime and support costs, but with regular maintenance, your system will last longer and hold its value better. It's great to upgrade a system or buy a new one if you need the extra power or resources that are offered, but upgrading because your current system is unstable or badly maintained is a poor reason. You didn't get the full value out of the old system, and you are unlikely to get full use of the next. By not taking proper care of a system, you are not only making room for a whole host of potentially expensive problems to come your way, but you are also, quite literally, reducing the effective life of your computer.

Unfortunately, there are also those problems that you cannot prevent, no matter how much care you take of your system. The two most common reasons for system failure are

- Old age: the system encounters a failure because a component has suffered a fault due to wear and tear.

- Defective components: the system encounters a failure because a component has suffered a fault resulting from a defect in its manufacture or installation. This may or may not happen within the warranty period.

It's Never Too Late to Begin

Don't think that just because you didn't begin a comprehensive routine of regular maintenance on your system as soon as you bought it from the store that it's too late to start. It certainly isn't! True, the earlier you begin a maintenance routine the better, but that's no reason to abandon a system to fate just because it didn't get the right kind of tender loving care straight out of the box. Whether your system is six days old or six years old, your computer will, without doubt, benefit from regular attention.

Do More—Quickly and Easily

Ask yourself these simple questions and make a note of the answers that you come up with.

- Why do I have a PC?

- What do I want to do with it?

- What software do I use most on my PC?

- What hardware do I use most on my PC?

- Do I have hardware/software installed that I never use?

These might sound like very simple questions, but answering them does give you the opportunity to consider how you make use of your computer and what things are on it that you really need. It also helps you to steer away from software and hardware that you don't need, since unnecessary additions often only serve to complicate matters.

PC DOCTOR'S ORDER! *Consider carefully when adding drivers onto more than one computer in order to access hardware such as a digital camera or camcorder. Do you really need to access it from both computers? If you really do, then that's fine, but don't do it if you think it won't be used. Every unnecessary piece of hardware added to your PC increases the complexity of the system as well as eats into precious system resources such as memory and processor time (sometimes even when the hardware isn't physically attached).*

One of the main advantages of a well-maintained system is that it works when you want it to. There is nothing more annoying and frustrating than going to your computer to do something and finding that you can't do it because the system crashes, is unstable, or the software or hardware you want to use doesn't work. You then either have to put aside what you were doing and fix the problem or abandon what you were doing altogether. This is the reason why you should spend some time setting up your system properly not only when you get it but also each time you add new software and hardware. Then carry out maintenance on the system regularly in order to keep it running at peak performance.

Having hardware or software on your PC that doesn't work properly can have a widespread effect on the reliability and performance you get from your computer. For example, if you have a mouse, scanner, or printer that isn't working right, this can cause you to have problems with other hardware or even software-related problems. These problems usually build up if not dealt with and then snowball until you have a PC that is crippled beyond usability.

Why Not Leave It to the Experts?

Many PC owners have had a problem that they can't see how to fix themselves or have had problems and had them solved by an "expert." It can be argued that taking any problems you have to an expert for attention is the best thing you can do. If you don't have the skill, knowledge, or know-how to solve the problems or issues you are having, then this might seem like the only option open to you, short of buying another PC.

There are five important reasons why PC owners would rather become their own "PC Doctors" as opposed to relying on other experts:

- Relying on experts is expensive, very expensive in fact. Just getting an engineer out to your home or office is not going to be cheap, and that's before they start tackling the problem! If you take the cheaper option and take your PC to them, you then have all the hassles of dismantling your PC, packing it into the car, taking it to a shop, and having to collect the PC and reassemble it once again.

- Normally, things have gone badly wrong by the time you call in the experts. There is usually a period that comes before calling out an engineer when one or more problems have been getting progressively worse. Just as running a car until something major breaks is a bad idea, because it's ultimately going to cost you more than if you'd serviced the car regularly, running a computer to destruction leads to the same kind of increase in repair costs.

 NOTE *PC problems rarely, if ever, just "go away." Quite the reverse, they grow in both scale and diversity and in annoyance level.*

- To most, a PC is a personal thing, and a great many PC owners really hate it when others use and modify their system. Also, when you let someone else loose on your system, you aren't always made aware of all the changes made. What was changed? What was deleted or moved? What was copied?

- You know the background story to your computer: what's been added to it or changed? What changes did you notice before the problem started? What was the last thing you did? Experts won't know (or necessarily ask) these things, so they won't know where to look for the problem. Once you take responsibility for maintaining your own computer, you will begin to take note of changes you make and also notice the subtle changes that occur as a result. You will then be better placed than the professional to solve problems quickly and easily before they ever become serious enough to need an expert.

- Experts don't always have the answers! Just as manufacturers couldn't possibly be expected to provide answers for every combination of hardware and software possible, neither can experts be expected to have specialist knowledge of your problem. What they do have is access to technical information, usually found freely on the Internet, and the confidence to use that information. Sometimes experts will merely return your system to its out-of-the-box state, similar to the recovery disc mentioned above, which is of little, if any, use.

Experts Are Never Around When You Need Them

The computer in the home is no longer looked at as the luxury that it was a few years ago. The home PC is now just as much a tool for getting things done as is the car, dishwasher, or oven, and more and more, we are beginning to rely on it to take the strain out of many mundane things that we have to do in our lives.

One of the reasons behind the PC becoming a useful tool is because it allows us to do things in so much less time than would be possible without it. Writing a report for work or term paper is so much quicker and easier on a word processor than on a typewriter. Filling in your tax return using a computer program that's designed for the job is substantially quicker and easier (and also a lot less prone to error) than doing it by hand.

We rely on being able to sit down at our home or office computer and get on with these things when we want to. Because computers give us the ability to do things a lot faster than previously possible, we have a tendency—some of us more than others—to leave more and more of the things that we have to do until the last possible moment before getting started.

 NOTE *Take filing a tax return for example: software is available that enables you to file your return in less time than it would take to fill out the paper forms. And once you've finished, you can then submit the form over the Internet easier and faster than you could print it out. PCs are paradise for procrastinators—that is, until they go wrong.*

But what if you switch on your PC and nothing happens, or when you load up the word processing or financial software, instead of being greeted by the application, you are presented with an error message? Well, if the task you were going to do wasn't urgent, then you are going to suffer some inconvenience, but no harm is done. But, what if it is a time-critical task? Your sales presentation is in the morning, or you have to get that homework in on time, but you can't print it out. These things are important and can even carry financial penalties if you don't get them done.

What do you do now?

It is at times like these that you will enjoy and fully appreciate the ability to be calm, take a deep breath, and see beyond the problem and begin looking for solutions yourself. Sometimes the solutions are simple. Other times they are not. However, by working through the problem methodically, the solution to the problem you're facing is likely to reveal itself to you; whereas if you take a random approach to problem solving, you are just as likely to make matters worse.

NOTE *Leaving things until the deadline is never recommended. The stress is just not worth it! If the problem you have is the result of some hardware defect or fault, there will inevitably be some delay before you can get replacement parts to fix the system.*

Benefits of "Fix-It-Yourself"

Huge benefits await those who choose to take control over their personal computer system and choose to solve the problems they encounter themselves.

Some of these benefits we've already looked at and are quite obvious:

- **Saving money**   Even the simplest of PC problems can be quite expensive to solve if you pay for technical support or use an expert.

- **Saving time**   By getting on and fixing the problem yourself, you can be back working a lot faster than having to wait for someone else to fix it.

- **Valuable learning experience**   If you take your PC to someone else to be fixed and you get the same problem again, it will cost you time and money to get it fixed again. If you fix it yourself the first time, the next time you get a similar problem, it will be quicker and easier to fix, as well as be more cost effective.

- **Satisfaction**   Successful problem solving can be very satisfying. Some problems are easy to solve, while others can be a bit more challenging. Either way, getting the system back into working order brings with it a great sense of satisfaction.

- **Making your PC better**   Because only you really understand the variety of tasks you undertake with your PC and exactly how you want to use it, you are the best person to be spearheading any upgrading you undertake. There's nothing wrong with getting advice from others regarding hardware and software upgrades, but remember that your needs might be different from theirs.

- **Privacy**   If your PC has personal or private information stored on it (names, addresses, financial information, passwords for online services, etc.), or it is used for business, then you might not feel comfortable allowing others to have access to it (especially if you have to leave the system with them). In situations like this, fixing and upgrading your own system might be the best option.

There are also a whole host of other fringe benefits of being the person in charge of repairing and upgrading your PC. By upgrading and repairing your own computer, you are sure of what parts are being added and that they are exactly what you asked for. You'll also be sure to get all the manuals and discs that come with the newly added hardware. Also, because you purchased the parts yourself, you have greater control over returns and warranty-related issues.

As you can see, there are a lot of compelling reasons why you should be taking care of your own system!

Benefits of Building Your Own System

Just as there are major benefits to caring for and fixing your own PC, there are major benefits to building your own system from scratch. Yes, in some respects it is a far bigger undertaking; many people feel overwhelmed by the sheer number of different parts they need to choose and assemble. Their most common worries generally revolve around getting parts that are compatible and what they will do if parts are defective.

 NOTE *By the end of this book you will have all the skills and information (and confidence) that you need to be able to choose the parts and assemble a PC completely from scratch.*

Briefly, here are some of the advantages of building your own system over buying one ready made:

- You save money: even at today's cut-throat prices, it is still normally cheaper to build your own system than it is to buy it ready made.

 NOTE *The reason why building your own system is cheaper than buying one "off the shelf" is because of the additional cost of company branding, manuals, discs, tech support, and so on.*

- You get what you want: one of the main advantages to building a system from scratch is that you know exactly what it contains. You can choose the parts that best suit the application you intend for your PC.

- You get complete information: you are sure to get all the manuals, discs, drivers, warranty cards, and other related bits and pieces that come with the components. These can be invaluable when it comes to solving hardware problems or dealing with warranty-related issues.

■ It is a learning experience: building your own system is a worthwhile learning experience, helping you to be more comfortable when handling PC components and allowing you to see exactly how all the parts fit together. It also gives you valuable experience in wiring and knowing which connectors go where, not to mention a great sense of pride and achievement!

 NOTE *Funnily enough, it's the wiring that scares most people. But wiring really isn't difficult, and it's pretty hard to get it wrong. You'll learn much more about the wiring inside a PC later.*

There are countless other benefits to building a system for yourself that will be personal to you. Needless to say, once someone has built a system for themselves, the quality that they expect from purchased systems increases dramatically.

Convinced Yet?

I am sure by now that you can see the immense benefits to be gained in both looking after a PC and building one for yourself. However, don't feel that you have to take on too much in one go. Caring for your PC is about taking small preventive steps regularly. While you are doing this, you are learning how everything works, and when something bigger (and scarier) comes along, trust me, you will be ready to handle it! You will have learned to look beyond the symptoms to the actual root causes of the problem, and the more hands-on experience you get before major problems strike, the better.

So, without further delay, let's move on and introduce you to the various parts that come together to make a personal computer.

Part I

Overview

Chapter 1

What's What—the Anatomy of a PC

Right, we've taken a quick tour of the main reasons why it's important to take care of your PC system, whether it's brand new out of the box or you've had it for years. You know what the benefits are in terms of system stability, performance, and its overall life span.

If you're still reading this in the bookstore, now is the time to take it to the counter, pay for it, and take it home because you're probably going to want to be near your PC while you read along. (The other option is that you put it back on the bookshelf, but I hope you don't do that!) Don't worry, the rest of us will wait for you till you get home.

OK, you're home. Great. Welcome back!

The reason I suggest that you need to be near your computer for this first chapter is that we are going to be taking a quick tour of its anatomy—that is, all the parts that come together to make up a PC.

Take a look at your PC. What do you see? Probably a half dozen or so bits all joined together to the main beige-colored box that sits on or next to or under your desk. I say beige because the majority of PCs are that color, although your case might be a different color. The point is that it's the main part of your computer, besides the monitor, and the part that you see! Other things are connected by wires (such as the monitor, keyboard, and mouse), although nowadays it's not uncommon to see peripherals (keyboards and mice in particular) connected via wireless radio transmitters, meaning fewer tangles and more freedom to move about.

Now take a look at the front of your PC. What do you see? Well, you're probably going to see buttons and lights. Something else that may attract your attention as you take a closer look is that, usually, none of these buttons or lights will be labeled. They may have a symbol or pictogram next to them, but often there's no writing associated with a light or button.

Next take a look behind your PC. Now you're going to see a lot of wiring back there—power cables, video cables, mouse, keyboard, sound, printers, network, peripherals—and chances are they are pretty tangled too.

 NOTE *If the wires behind your PC aren't tangled, well done! That's a good start.*

Let's now move on and take a deeper look at the parts that make up a PC.

ID the Parts

Follow me on a tour of the parts that make up a PC. Some of these parts you will be familiar with, others perhaps less so.

NOTE *This chapter of the book is concerned with desktops and not laptops, which are very different in construction, some requiring special tools for disassembly.*

We will divide the parts into two categories: essential and nonessential. Essential parts are the core parts, things that you absolutely need as part of a PC. Nonessential parts are all the bits that you can add on but that are not necessary to the PC itself.

 NOTE *You might not have all of the nonessential parts on your particular PC, but don't worry. Not many people will have all of these on one system.*

We're also going to break up our tour into two sections:

■ Outside the box

■ Inside the box

This distinction is pretty straightforward. Outside the box is what you can see while sitting by your PC, while inside the box is what you see when you open the case of the PC.

Let's begin our tour outside the box.

Outside the Box

Sit down in front of your computer. Take a look at the parts you can see. We'll discuss them one by one.

The Monitor/VDU

The monitor is the part of the PC system where everything seems to happen, making it an essential part of the system. Without the monitor, you would not get any feedback from the system so that you know what it is doing. Sometimes the monitor is called a VDU (video display unit) or even just a "screen."

 WARNING *A monitor holds a vast amount of electrical charge, even when switched off and unplugged. Never, ever open the case on a monitor. This job, in particular, should be left to the professionals. To prevent risk of electric shock, keep liquids away from your monitor, as well as items such as pins and paper clips that could find their way in through the ventilation holes. A simple paper clip finding its way into a monitor could destroy it or cause a fire.*

The monitor can have very few controls or quite a lot. Some monitors only have an on/off switch and a few basic controls to adjust the image brightness and contrast. Others have a great many controls to allow you to carry out all kinds of picture manipulation, for example, rotate the image, adjust the colors, control the shape and the sharpness of the image, as well as many other functions.

NOTE *Precise details of what your monitor can and cannot do are usually supplied with it at the time of purchase. Take a look at this manual.*

Monitors are usually measured in inches, and that measurement is taken diagonally across the screen, from corner to corner. So a monitor that's described as a "17-inch monitor" is actually 17 inches between the opposite corners.

NOTE *Actually the true corner-to-corner measurement of a monitor will always be slightly smaller than that stated because the measurement given refers to the CRT (cathode ray tube) inside the monitor. Some of this is always hidden behind the plastic frame around the PC, so the size you will see is slightly less.*

A monitor has two connections:

■ One connects to the video port on the PC; this connector is known as a 15-pin HD-DB-15.

■ One connects to power outlets.

Today you are also likely to find LCD (liquid crystal display) monitors making their way onto desktop PCs. These have the advantage over CRT in being smaller (flatter) and lighter, thus saving desk space. These LCD monitors can either connect to the standard 15-pin port of a graphics card or a DVI-D 24-pin port on an LCD monitor control card.

Keyboard

Another essential part of the PC is the keyboard. In fact, without a keyboard plugged in, many systems won't even start properly.

In spite of what seems like a standard layout, PC keyboards can vary a great deal. Most have the standard QWERTY layout, but the layout of the numbers and the other keys can vary dramatically. Many keyboards today also have buttons for controlling volume, playing media software, performing functions such as cut, copy, and paste, and much more. Some even have scroll wheels so that you can scroll up and down document windows while you work.

Most keyboards are the standard rectangular type, but if you want to break with tradition, you can choose one from the many different kinds of ergonomic keyboards available.

 NOTE *Before buying an ergonomic keyboard, if at all possible, try it out! Many have a dramatically different feel to them compared to ordinary keyboards, and that might not be what you were expecting. Make sure that what looks ergonomic actually works for you.*

Keyboard connectors can be one of three types:

■ A small round connector called a PS/2 (also known as a Mini-DIN-6): if you look at this connector, you will see the six little pins inside. This is normally color-coded purple. Here is the symbol used to mark the port.

■ A larger connector called a DIN-5 (also known as an IBM-PC connector): this has six pins inside. Note that this type is not often seen on PCs now.

■ USB connector: this is a small, flat, rectangular connector that usually has on it the symbol shown here:

Mouse

The mouse is the device that adds a second dimension to input. It allows you to move the cursor or pointer across the screen. There was a time when a mouse was considered to be an expensive luxury, but nowadays it is considered as much of an essential as the keyboard.

Mice vary in complexity, from simple mechanical, two-buttoned, corded types to versions that have optical sensors in them to detect movement and are linked to the computer by a wireless radio connection.

Mice can connect to a PC by several different connectors:

- Mice were originally connected via a COM port using a connector called a DB-9, a 9-pin connector that was once common.

- The DB-9 connector gave way to the PS/2 connector (the Mini-DIN-6). Using this connector freed up a COM port on the system for other devices. This port may be color-coded green. The symbol looks like this:

- Nowadays, the most popular connection type for mice is the USB port.

 NOTE *Many modern mice come with the adapter that allows them to be connected to either a PS/2 or USB port, increasing flexibility.*

Speakers

Speakers, while in no way essentials (although most modern operating systems and other software assume you have them), add a whole new dimension to the PC experience. Most PCs have a sound card capable of having a set of stereo speakers connected to it.

 NOTE *Some systems have stereo speakers built into the monitor, which saves on desk space.*

The quality of the output from PC speakers varies from pretty poor to fantastic, depending on the quality of the speakers used (the sound card makes little difference). It is also possible to equip a PC with a set of high-quality surround-sound speakers that can rival, equal, or even beat a home entertainment system.

Normal stereo speakers are usually connected to a sound card using a connector called a 3.5 mm (1/8 inch) stereo jack. On most modern sound cards this connector and the corresponding connector on the speakers are color-coded—the usual color being lime green (for audio out) or orange (for speaker output). You will see a symbol like the following for stereo speaker output:

Speakers can be powered in different ways:

- Many speakers are powered from the sound card and need no other power supply. The volume and quality of output from these can be quite poor.

- Larger speakers might require batteries to run. I don't recommend these, as the cost of running them is high.

- Speakers powered by the main outlet are very common nowadays. This allows the speakers to have a good output range and power. These are the best type to use.

Microphone

Like speakers, a microphone isn't an essential part of the PC but is quite useful. Along with speakers, microphones are becoming more and more common as people use their PCs to communicate with family and friends over the Internet. Like speakers, they vary tremendously in quality and price.

Microphones are connected to PCs using a 3.5 mm jack monaural connector (not stereo, it has fewer connection segments on the actual connector), and the connections are usually color-coded pink. Look for this symbol:

Printer

Although nonessential, a printer is connected to the majority of PCs. Even with the explosion in Internet use, paper output is still common and a widely used way to output material from your PC. Recently, printers capable of high-quality color output have become available, making printing pictures and images commonplace.

While there is a staggering array of choice available when it comes to printers, the connection choices are limited to two common types:

- The most common way to connect a printer to a PC used to be via a wide 25-pin DB-25 connector. This port was also known as a parallel port.

■ The parallel port has now been overtaken in popularity by the faster, easier-to-use, and more versatile USB port. This port is usually color-coded burgundy. The printer port symbol looks like this:

Many printers on the market can be connected to either a parallel or USB port, depending on your PC's capability, what cables you have available, and which you prefer.

 NOTE *If possible, connect your printer to a spare USB port. Not only will it print faster, but the setup is usually easier.*

Scanner

The ability to take text or artwork that exists on paper and turn it into a file stored on your PC can be very useful. Scanners can do just that. They work in much the same way as photocopiers, but instead of producing another paper copy, they can create an image of the item being scanned.

Scanners used to be found solely in offices, but nowadays, although not an essential, they are becoming commonplace in the home. Many people want to store their photographs on a PC for ease of printing and sharing, as well as saving on space, and some scanners enable you to scan photographic negatives and slides. This can be a useful way to protect your treasured memories on a CD or DVD. Most scanners allow you to scan a paper page and then, by recognizing the letters, will convert the text into text on your computer. Modern scanners can do this very quickly indeed and with a high degree of accuracy.

Scanners need to transfer a lot of data to the PC quickly, which used to be a problem. Because of this, scanners have gone through quite an evolution in terms of design and how they connect to the PC.

■ Many early consumer scanners connected to the PC via a SCSI (pronounced "scuzzy") port. The problem with this connection was that very few home or office PCs had a SCSI port, which meant that expansion cards had to be supplied with the scanners. This added to the cost as well as the complexity of the installation, because the PC had to be opened and a new card fitted before the scanner was connected. Your SCSI port will be marked with a symbol that looks like this:

- In an attempt to get around both the cost and the hassles of having to supply and support SCSI cards with scanners, manufacturers turned to the parallel port as a solution. The idea was that consumers could fit scanners on the parallel port and then daisy-chain, or link, the scanner to the printer so both could run off the same port. This method was a lot easier and cheaper for the consumer, but it still wasn't perfect, and many users found this setup unreliable.

- Again, the USB port has become the port of choice for most of today's scanners because of the high data transfer speeds of the port and the ease of setup.

- Another port that is available on many PCs is the IEEE 1394 port (also known as FireWire or i.Link). This is a high-speed port commonly used for linking video cameras to PCs, but it is also gaining ground for other devices that transfer lots of data to and from the PC. One advantage of the IEEE 1394 port is that it is capable of much faster data transfer rates than USB 1.1, but similar to that of USB 2.0. IEEE 1394 ports have their own symbol:

Web Cam

Not an essential by far, but something that is seen more and more on the standard PC is the web cam. The explosion in Internet use and the desire to communicate naturally with others, without resorting to text, has fueled an explosion in web cam sales. Web cams are basically low-quality (in terms of picture quality) video cameras designed specifically for sending real-time video (that is, video as it is happening) over the Internet.

Video, even low-quality video, involves transferring a lot of data about, which means that most web cams are connected to PCs using the USB port.

Joystick/Game Input Device

A total nonessential! If you are big into gaming, you'll already be familiar with a joystick or other form of game input device. Basically, a joystick acts as a second cursor, allowing you to steer around the game environment easily and naturally.

Joysticks come in all sorts of shapes and sizes and can vary enormously in terms of complexity and function. They connect to a PC by two means:

- A 15-pin games port (usually on the back of the sound card). This is usually color-coded gold; here is the port symbol:

- Any USB port.

Modem

Modems are not an essential, but since the Internet plays a key role for most PCs today, it's a very common item.

 NOTE *A modem need not be external to the PC but may be inside the case. However, with the surge in popularity of high-speed cable connections to the Internet, more and more PCs have an external modem now.*

The modem used to mean just one thing—a device that is plugged into the phone line, allowing you to dial out and make a connection to another device. That device might have been a fax machine, someone else's modem, or the modem of an ISP (Internet service provider), but it was simple and straightforward. There were many different modem speeds, from very low speed 9.6 kbps to the much faster 56 kbps modems.

 NOTE *The 56 kbps translates into approximately 7000 characters of text per second.*

Nowadays, with the widespread use of high-speed cable connections and DSL, modems are more complicated than they used to be. They can connect to your PC in several ways:

- External modems were traditionally connected to a COM port. This allowed modem connection speeds up to 56 kbps.

■ Modems can also be connected via USB ports. (There's not much you can't connect to the USB port!)

■ Cable or DSL modems can also be attached to a PC by an Ethernet (network) connection.

NOTE *Most external modems need a separate power connection, usually to an adapter.*

Inside the Box

That's the tour of the outside completed. While most of the devices and peripherals that we covered were probably already familiar to you, some of the information and background on them is going to be useful later. It also helps that as we move forward, we are all speaking the same language.

NOTE *Unless you've already done it before, don't start taking your system apart just yet! Refer to the chapter on safety first (Chapter 4) and also on how to take the case off (Chapter 7). Also, before you take apart your PC, check that this doesn't invalidate your warranty. Normally nowadays it doesn't, but if in any doubt, ask!*

Now it's time to move our attention from the outside of the box to what's on the inside (see Figure 1-1 for a sneak preview). If you've never had the case off

FIGURE 1-1   Sneak preview inside a PC

before, you might be surprised by what's actually inside. I usually find that people have one of two reactions:

■ You'll be amazed that there are so many different components inside the case, all working together to make your PC do what it does, usually without making themselves known.

■ You were expecting the PC case to be jam-packed with all kinds of weird, exotic electronic "stuff," spinning fans, and all sorts of whirring gizmos, so you'll be really surprised that there is so much empty space in there!

Let's begin the tour with the case itself.

The PC Case

The case on a PC seems pretty cosmetic, but in fact it carries out some vital tasks that might not be immediately obvious.

■ First, it acts as a box to keep everything else in—well, that part is pretty obvious!

■ It protects delicate components from the environment and from damage.

■ It is an important part of the PC cooling system. A well-designed case allows air to flow around all the vital components so that excess heat is carried away safely, prolonging the life of the components.

NOTE *More on the dangers of heat later, in the section "Processor/ Microprocessor/CPU."*

The PC case is also key to the actual structure of the PC itself. In fact, cases are made specifically for different motherboards so that the board actually fits into the case properly and all the ports, card slots, and wiring match up. (The motherboard, which we'll come to next, is the main circuit board.) The case also acts as the structure upon which the hard drives, floppy drive, and optical (CD or DVD) drives attach. Figure 1-2 shows the rear of a PC case complete with connectors.

The case isn't just a case either. Normally, if you buy a PC case, you get the case, the power supply (more on this a little later in the chapter), the switches (such as on/off and reset), a cooling fan or two, and a lot of the wiring that is needed. Also, you get other fixtures and fittings, such as case screws, rubber feet for the case, and so on.

FIGURE 1-2   Rear of case showing connectors

One important consideration beyond function when choosing a case, is finish. While this might seem to be cosmetic, some cases that are finished badly contain many nasty sharp edges that can and will draw blood when working inside the system, which I'm sure you'll want to avoid. While you are looking at the finish of the case, check the layout too. I've seen cases designed so badly that the cradle for the hard drive completely obscures the slots that hold the memory, making upgrading incredibly, and needlessly, difficult.

If you want to get fancy, you can get cases in shiny metal finishes, bright, fluorescent colors, containing eerie glowing fluorescent lights, windows, and much more. No longer do you have to make do with that boring beige box!

Motherboard

When you get around to opening your PC case for the first time and take a peek inside, the motherboard is probably one of the first things you'll see. It is the largest circuit board, either lying at the bottom or up along the side of the case.

NOTE *The motherboard is sometimes called a mainboard.*

The motherboard is the main circuit board inside the PC. Everything is connected to the motherboard in one way or another. Think of the motherboard as the nervous system of the PC, regulating basic functions and interconnecting more complex components together.

The most common motherboard design in desktop computers today is called the AT (now obsolete but still present in older systems) or the ATX (and MicroATX), which improves significantly on the AT design. In both the AT and ATX designs, the computer components included in the motherboard are

■ Microprocessor, or CPU

■ Coprocessors (optional)

■ Memory (RAM)

■ Basic input/output system (BIOS)

■ Expansion slots

■ Motherboard chipset and interconnecting circuitry that bring all the components together

 NOTE *Some motherboards also come fitted with built-in modems, graphics cards, network adapters, and sound cards too, which simplifies system setup.*

A key part of the motherboard is the BIOS, which stores the initial start-up parameters of the system. This information is used to bring the system to life when it is first switched on. Additional components can be added by using the expansion slots that are present on most motherboards. (The exception here is usually laptop motherboards.)

You might have heard the term *bus* or *busses* when reading techie material. A *bus* is the electronic interface between the motherboard and the smaller boards or cards contained in the expansion slots.

Processor/Microprocessor/CPU

If the motherboard is the nervous system, then the processor is like the brain. When faced with buying a new PC, one of the main features advertised by retailers is the type of processor that it contains. Two dominant questions that the buyer has to answer are

- Which manufacturer?

- What speed?

The answers to these questions are usually determined by:

- Budget: faster, higher-end processors cost more.

- How much power is needed: think about your current needs as well as your likely needs over the next 12 to 24 months. The power of the processor is usually measured in MHz (millions of cycles per second) or GHz (thousands of millions—or billions—of cycles per second). The faster the processor, the greater the number of instructions per second it can perform.

 NOTE *The term* processor *has generally replaced the term* central processing unit *(CPU).*

There are many different kinds of CPU, one type is shown in Figure 1-3:

FIGURE 1-3   CPU obscured by cooling fan

A processor (or more accurately, microprocessor) is the logic circuitry that responds to and processes the basic instructions that drive a computer. A microprocessor is sometimes also called a *logic chip* and is the engine that goes into action when you turn your computer on. It is designed and built to perform only basic arithmetic and logic operations on data held in small number-holding areas called *registers*. But what makes a microprocessor special is that it can do them very fast.

Typical microprocessor operations include

- Adding
- Subtracting
- Comparing two numbers
- Fetching numbers from one place to another

These operations are made possible by a set of instructions built into the microprocessor structure. In order to help the processor carry out these functions, it is now common for manufacturers to add small amounts of memory for the processor itself to use, either on a separate chip (known as L2—Level 2—cache) or, as is more often the case, onto the chip itself.

The microprocessor also plays a key part in PC start-up. When the computer is switched on, the microprocessor is designed to get the first instruction from the basic input/output system (BIOS), which comes with the computer on the motherboard. After that, either the BIOS, or the operating system that the BIOS loaded into computer memory, is controlling the microprocessor and giving it instructions on what to do.

There is one other thing that a microprocessor is responsible for that isn't good for the PC—heat! This heat, if allowed to build up, could destroy a microprocessor in minutes, so heat sinks and fans are used to keep the heat under control. A *heat sink* is a block of metal (usually copper or aluminum) designed to conduct the heat away from the sensitive microprocessor, while the fan circulates cool air around the heat sink to cool it down.

RAM/Memory

RAM (random access memory) is the PC's short-term memory and is where the operating system, application programs, and data in current use are kept so that they can be quickly accessed by the computer's microprocessor. RAM is much faster both to read from and write to than the other kinds of storage in a computer, such as the hard disk, floppy disk, or CD-ROM. Data stored in RAM isn't permanent though, and it is cleared as soon as the PC is shut down. When you turn your computer on again, your operating system and other programs are again loaded into RAM, usually from the hard disk. A RAM module is shown in Figure 1-4.

NOTE *RAM is called* random access *because any storage location can be accessed directly. It does not need to be written to or read sequentially.*

Generally the more RAM you have installed in a PC, the better and faster it will run and the more applications you can have open at once. Reliability and stability also increase. You do, however, have to stay within the maximums as laid down by the operating system and the motherboard you have.

There are many different types of RAM in use today. The two most common types are

- Single data rate (SDR) SDRAM is the older type of memory, commonly used in computers before 2002.

- Double data rate (DDR) SDRAM hit the mainstream computer market around 2002 and can be found in most new computers.

As the name suggests, the biggest difference between DDR SDRAM and SDR SDRAM is that DDR can transfer data twice as fast as SDR SDRAM.

Generally speaking, motherboards are designed to support one type of memory. That means you cannot mix and match memory types on the same motherboard in any system. They will not function and will not even fit in the same sockets. The only correct type of memory for your computer is the one that it was built to take!

FIGURE 1-4   RAM module

NOTE *If in any doubt as to the type of memory your system takes, consult the system manual or visit the website of a memory vendor (listed in Appendix B). They normally have online tools to help you identify the correct memory for a particular system.*

Adding more RAM to a system is probably the single quickest and best upgrade that can be carried out on a system. RAM is cheap, and adding more (especially if you currently have less than 512MB) makes things run a lot faster.

Hard Disk Drive

The hard disk drive, more commonly known as a hard drive, is the long-term memory of the computer. This holds all the files and applications, along with your operating system. Everything that your computer "knows" (apart from a tiny bit used to start it up, which is stored in the system BIOS) is stored on the hard drive. An IDE hard drive is shown in Figure 1-5.

FIGURE 1-5   An IDE hard drive

NOTE *You sometimes come across the terms* hard drive *and* hard disk *used interchangeably. While this isn't usually a problem, it is valuable to know that the hard disk is actually the physical part (a metal disk or disks) on which the data is stored.*

The hard drive is a very "mechanical" part of a PC in that it contains a lot of moving parts. Motors turn the disk platters and move the heads that write the magnetic information onto the disks. Hard drives also contain circuit boards and components to drive the logic of the drive.

There are huge differences between the hard drive and RAM with regard to speed of data access. RAM works out as being millions of times faster than hard drives for data access, but the major advantage of the hard drive is not speed (although they are getting faster) but the fact that the hard drive allows you to store data and retrieve it after the PC has been switched off and back on again.

Despite the very mechanical nature of hard drives, they aren't considered to be user serviceable. This means that if you have a problem with one, there is nothing you can fix inside, and you realistically have only one option: replace the defective drive. If you try to open a hard drive case, you will introduce dirt and other contaminants into it that will render it useless. However, despite being mechanical, hard drives are very reliable, theoretically capable of running for many hundreds of thousands of hours without problems. Although problems do occur, when you look at the numbers of hard drives in use today and how much use they get, and the fact that they are mechanically maintenance free, they are quite reliable indeed.

One thing that hard drives can be susceptible to is shock and impact. Because you have spinning platters with the read/write heads skimming very close to the surface, hard drives are particularly sensitive to impacts while in use. Never open a drive just to see what's inside; if you do, don't expect it to work again or to get it repaired under warranty!

NOTE *To give you an idea of how close the heads skim to the surface platters, it is equivalent to a supersonic airplane flying a few feet off the ground. A head colliding with even a tiny speck of dust can cause significant disk damage.*

There are two common types of hard drives (the types being based on the standard used to transfer data to and from the drive via the motherboard):

- IDE (Integrated Drive Electronics) is the most common type of drive found in desktop PCs.

NOTE *Actually, most hard drives sold today are an enhanced version of IDE, called, rather unsurprisingly, Enhanced IDE or EIDE.*

■ SCSI (Small Computer System Interface) is both fast and flexible in that it allows for more than just hard drives to be connected (scanners, CD driver, printers, and so on). It's not commonly used on desktop PCs but is more common on servers and high-end systems.

Hard drives are connected to the PC in two ways: data cable or power cable.

■ Data cables—the ribbon kind—connect the hard drive to the motherboard (via a channel). Now we also have the more modern serial ATA cables, which are faster and also thinner than the standard data cable, which means better case air flow.

■ Power cable connectors supply power directly to the hard drive.

Today, hard drive storage capacity is measured in gigabytes (GB)—thousands of millions of bytes, where a byte represents one character of text. Not long ago it was measured in megabytes (MB)—millions of bytes. It's hard to quantify what this means in realistic terms, but bigger is better, albeit also more expensive!

NOTE *Contrary to popular belief, hard drives aren't hugely susceptible to damage by small magnetic fields. Although powerful magnetic fields will damage or destroy the data contained on a hard drive, being near a speaker or monitor (both of which contain huge magnets) won't cause damage, which is why you can have a monitor and speakers next to your PC!*

Graphics Adapter

Without a graphics adapter of some sort, you're not going to be seeing anything on the computer monitor. There are a huge number of different types of graphics adapters on the market, designed for a wide variety of different applications, including gaming, CAD (computer-aided design), desktop publishing, and so forth.

Today's high-end video adapters have amazing power and performance, and they are capable of drawing (and very rapidly updating) highly complex screen images. This is made possible by the processing power built onto the graphics cards. They come with a large amount of onboard RAM, allowing them to display complex images using millions of colors. A few years ago the standard desktop PC might have come with 64MB of main system RAM; nowadays a graphics card can contain as much, or even more, simply for itself.

Choosing the right card for your needs can be daunting, but as a general rule you can use the following guidelines:

- If you use your PC just for word processing, spreadsheets, and so on, a low-end card will suffice.

- Gaming takes a lot of power, and depending on which games and how much you play, you may want to consider a midrange to high-end card. Here is where 3D cards come into play. In order to render game environments in the most realistic way possible, 3D graphics adapters have been developed. You don't get a truly 3D image (because it's displayed on a flat screen for one reason), but you do get an image that has fake depth and shadows that give the impression of 3D. This demands extra processing power, and modern graphics adapters aimed at gamers will incorporate these features.

 NOTE *Most games nowadays list recommended graphics cards, and this is always a good place to start when thinking about getting a new graphics card.*

- Specific applications such as CAD will mean that you might have specific needs, and you will have to choose a card accordingly.

In addition to make, manufacturer, and type of card, there is a fourth factor to consider—how the graphics card connects to a PC. There are three main ways:

- The graphics card can be built directly onto the motherboard. This is known as *onboard graphics*.

- A graphics adapter can be connected to an expansion slot, called an AGP (Accelerated Graphics Port) slot, at the back of a PC.

- A graphics card can be connected to another slot called a PCI (Peripheral Component Interconnect) slot. However, PCI slots are slower at transferring data than AGP slots, so the performance is reduced. PCI slots are physically different from AGP slots (AGP slots are smaller).

 WARNING *Cards designed for an AGP slot will not fit in a PCI slot, or vice versa.*

NOTE *Some older systems might also have a graphics card connected to the older ISA (Industry Standard Architecture) slot.*

Several graphics cards on the market also allow you to hook up two monitors (or even three, but using one of these, you will need two graphics cards—one PCI card and one AGP card—and one card must have dual-monitor capability). This problem has been solved now, by graphics cards that support three monitors, all on one card.

Floppy Drive

The floppy drive used to be the easiest method for sharing files with another computer user. Before the days of Internets and intranets, there were *sneakernets*— users would save files on a floppy disk and simply walk them over to another PC! But the old floppy drives and disks had many limitations:

- Floppy drives are painfully slow.

- Disk storage capacity is tiny by today's standards, and even simple word processing files have become too big to be stored on a single disk (which has a capacity of just 1.44MB).

- The disks aren't very robust and are easily damaged by exposure to heat or weak magnetic fields.

In an attempt to overcome these limitations, floppylike drives were developed, but these didn't really fill the gap because the media (disks) were expensive, and too many different types appeared. Eventually, CDs and DVDs killed off most of the interest in floppy drives and floppylike drives since the capacity is much greater and the media is cheap.

There was a time when every PC had a floppy drive, but now this isn't the case. With the advent of bootable CD drives, you can get a PC started up and the operating system loaded without the need for a bootable floppy disk.

Like a hard drive, a floppy drive has two connections: a data connection and a power connection.

Optical Drives

Optical drives are the collective name for CD (Compact Disc) drives and DVD (Digital Versatile Disc) drives. These discs offer amazing capacity (up to 700MB for a CD and 4.7GB for a DVD), and they are fast and robust. Add to this the ability to create your own discs with writable drives, and even write and rewrite discs many times over using rewritable discs, and it's easy to see how optical drives became so dominant.

Optical drives, like the one shown in Figure 1-6, are similar to hard drives in that they can be either IDE or SCSI, and they connect to the system using similar data ribbon cables and power cables.

Expansion Slots

You use expansion slots to add more circuit boards to your PC. These circuit boards can carry out a wide variety of functions that the PC itself might not be able to do without them. Popular expansion cards include

- Graphics adapters
- Sound cards
- Modems (shown in Figure 1-7)
- Network cards

FIGURE 1-6   CD-ROM drive

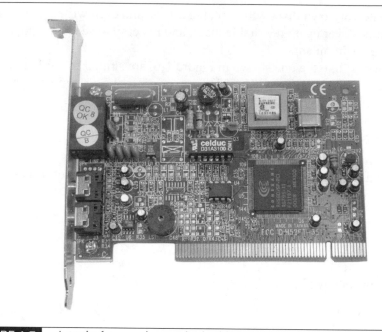

FIGURE 1-7   A typical expansion card—in this case, a modem

Expansion cards can be used to carry out other tasks too, such as adding more ports to a PC (for example, USB or FireWire ports).

Power Supply Unit (PSU)

The power supply unit (PSU) converts power into the correct voltages for running the internal components (motherboard, drives, and so on). The 120 volts (or 250 volts in some countries) delivered by the main power supply is too high for the delicate components that the system contains. A typical hard drive runs on 5 volts, CPUs on 3.3 to 5 volts, while a motherboard might run on 12 volts.

The actual power output of a PSU can range from about 230 watts to a whopping 500 watts and more. Power is an important element of your computer system because the more components you have (such as hard drives or optical drives), the more power you need.

Doctor's Notes

That rounds off our tour of the modern desktop PC. By now, we all should be using the same terminology. You should know your hard drive from your floppy drive and your graphics card from your sound card. This is a solid foundation from which we can progress.

PC Anatomy Checklist

☑ Familiarize yourself with the internal layout of your PC.

☑ Locate all the important components inside your PC.

☑ Trace the wired connections so you know where they start and end.

☑ Familiarize yourself with the connectors used, both outside the case and inside.

☑ Make a note of how many free drive bays you have. How many are available for CD/DVD drives and how many for hard drives?

☑ Make a note of how many free RAM module sockets you have.

☑ Similarly, how many free expansion slots do you have?

☑ What type of graphics adapter does your system use?

☑ How many free ports (such as USB ports) do you have?

Chapter 2

Files and Folders

Without any software on your machine, your PC would be no more than a beige (well, probably beige) box containing interrelated parts. It would switch on, and various lights would light up, but nothing much else would happen. It wouldn't actually do anything! To drive this hardware, you need to have software, and you can pick, choose, change, and tweak software a whole lot more than hardware. But what is software?

Files, folders, directories, applications, drivers, executables, BMPs, DOCs, JPGs … you're going to be reading about these and more a lot over the course of this book, and it's vital that right from the start you know what everything means. If you don't know your *.exe* file from a picture of your pet, then read on. (Even if you do know the difference, read on!)

NOTE *This book isn't a guide to your operating system or programs installed on your computer; there are plenty of books on those topics that give you the lowdown on the software side of things. The purpose of this book is to give you an overview of how things work on your PC.*

Files

A file is a single entity of data that lives on your computer. I've said "entity" and not "packet" or "bit" or anything like that because those terms mean different things and don't convey the true meaning of what a file is. What is meant by *entity* is that no matter what data is in the file, it can be manipulated as a whole. For example, you can change, copy, move, rename, or delete the entity as a whole no matter what it contains.

Maybe this sounds a little confusing, so an example might help. Let's say I launch my favorite word processor program (Microsoft Word) and type in a list of words. What I type doesn't matter, but I'll list my favorite foods, as shown in Figure 2-1.

I now take what I have written and save it as a file on my machine. In order to save it, I need to give the new file a unique filename (I'll come to this in a minute). In this case I'm going to call this file *favfoods.doc* (see Figure 2-2). Once you've saved the file, you can go looking for it. You can also easily cut, copy, move, rename, and delete that file at your leisure, regardless of the content of the file.

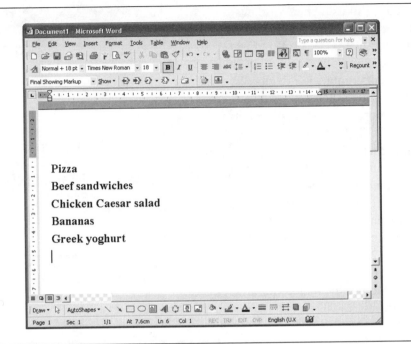

FIGURE 2-1   My list—favorite foods!

FIGURE 2-2   Saving the file

Because I'm using the Windows operating system (Windows XP), I'm using an application called Windows Explorer to manipulate the entities, but on a different computer or device, I would use a different application. For example, in File Explorer on a Microsoft Pocket PC 2002 handheld device, the saved file looks like this:

From within the Windows operating system, you can manipulate the file through the use of a context-sensitive pop-up menu that appears when you select the file and click the right mouse button (see Figure 2-3). *Context sensitive* means that the menu contains items that might be specific to the file in question.

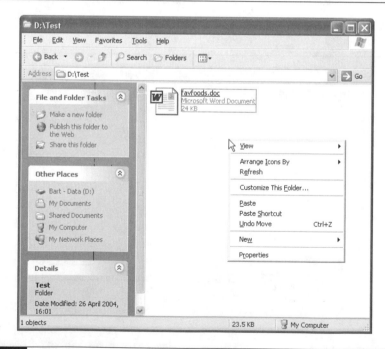

FIGURE 2-3   The file and context-sensitive pop-up menu as seen in Windows Explorer on Windows XP

FIX-IT-YOURSELF HOME REMEDY *If you have a newer-style keyboard, a quick and easy way to launch Windows Explorer is to press the Windows key (⊞), and while holding that down, press* E.

Filenames

When I saved the word processor file containing my list of favorite foods, I had to give it a filename. You cannot save any files on your system unless they have a valid filename. Valid filenames vary depending on the operating system you are running on your PC, but here is a rundown of what is and isn't allowed for filenames under Windows XP:

- You can have really long filenames—up to 255 characters long—so there is no need for me to be as concise as I was with the filename *favfoods.doc*. I could have quite happily named it *myfavoritefoods.doc*.

- Numbers are allowed (*myfavoritefoods1.doc*).

- You can have a mixture of upper- and lowercase letters (*MyFavoriteFoods.doc*), although two files with identical names that differ only in capitalization are not allowed in the same folder.

- Spaces are allowed, which make the whole filename a lot more readable (*My favorite foods.doc*).

- The characters / \ ; : * ? " < > | aren't allowed in filenames.

- Filenames must be unique in each directory or folder. (Read on for information on directories and folders.)

The File Extension

Take a look at Figure 2-4. It shows Windows Explorer in Windows XP and displays a few files. Each of the files is different and has a different icon and file type. If you double-click on the files, the operating system will fire up the appropriate application to use with that file. If you have the application installed, or another suitable one, you just have to double-click on the file.

Question: how does the operating system know what the files are? The answer lies with the file extensions. However, these are hidden from view in the screen in Figure 2-4 because of a default setting in Windows to prevent users from making drastic changes to the file extensions by accident. However, it's not difficult to

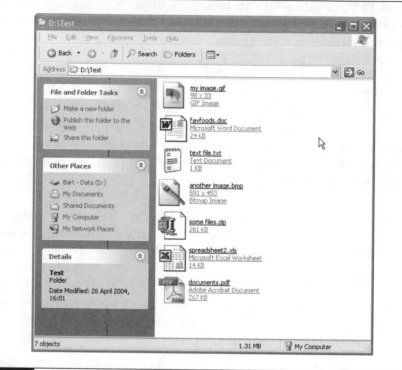

FIGURE 2-4 Displaying files in Windows Explorer

see them. Open Windows Explorer, click on the Tools menu and then on Folder Options. You will see this dialog box:

Click on the View tab if it is not showing. Now uncheck the Hide Extensions for Known File Types, and after making that change, click on the Apply button. A message will appear on the screen—click Yes and then click OK.

Take a look at the end of the filename. See the part after the dot, or period, in the name? That's called the file extension and serves an important purpose—to identify the file type (that is, the application that was used to create it or the format of the file). This tells the operating system what program to use to open it when the file is run. If I double-click on the word processor file I created earlier, the operating system knows that the *.doc* file extension is associated with Microsoft Word because that application registered that file extension (along with many others) with the operating system during installation of the program. Now, whenever I click on a filename with the *.doc* file extension, the Word application runs and opens the file.

FIX-IT-YOURSELF HOME REMEDY *The application that is loaded when you run a file depends on what you have installed on your computer system. If you don't have Microsoft Word installed, double-clicking on a file with a .doc file extension won't load that application.*

File extensions are normally two to four characters long, with three being the most common. Along with controlling what application is run when you double-click on the file, the extension can also control the icon used to depict the file and the contents of the context-sensitive menu that appears.

Renaming Files

From time to time you may find that you want to rename files. This is easily done through all file exploring utilities. The way you do it using Windows Explorer is to select the file, right-click on it, and select Rename. You can then type in a new name for the old file. Figure 2-5 shows a file ready to be renamed. Take care when doing this not to alter the file extension. By default this won't be an issue because the file extensions are hidden from view. However, if you have set the program to show extensions, take extra care, because if you make any changes to the extension, the file will no longer work properly.

PC DOCTOR'S ORDER! *If you accidentally make changes to the file extension, the quickest and best way to undo the changes you've made is to press the* ESC *key.*

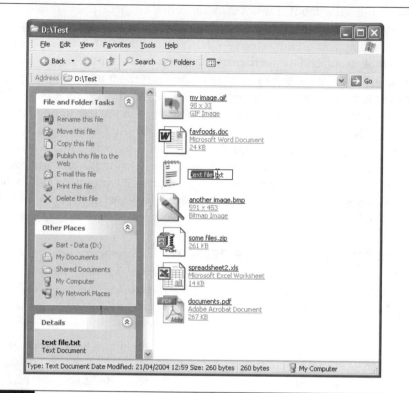

FIGURE 2-5   Renaming a file using Windows Explorer

This isn't the only way to rename a file. There are several ways to do it, but because you have to click on the file that you actually want to change, it's less likely that you'll make a mistake this way.

 PC DOCTOR'S ORDER! *Take great care not to rename any important system files or files relating to applications, as this could cause your operating system or installed applications to stop working. By default these are all hidden, so it's not a common problem. But if you make changes to the operating system that allow you to see them, take care.*

Files, Files, and More Files

So far, we've only looked at a word processor file as created by Microsoft Word. (If you create a file using a different word processor, it is likely to have a file extension other than *.doc*.) You've seen that different types of files have different file extensions, but it is important to remember that changing just the file type won't change the actual file, just what the operating system thinks it is. For example, say that someone sends you a file created with Microsoft Word, but you don't have Word installed on your machine. You have another word processor installed, say Corel WordPerfect, which uses the file extension *.wpd*. Changing the extension of the file from *.doc* to *.wpd* won't help at all because the structure of the file remains that of a Word document. The icon and context-sensitive menus, on the other hand, will change because they are controlled by the operating system and not the structure of the file.

 PC DOCTOR'S ORDER! *When faced with a file that you don't have an application for, probably one of the worst things you can do is change the file extension. This does not accomplish anything useful. Nowadays many applications such as word processors have import facilities that allow them to read files created by a rival application and convert them into their own format. Consult the help file or documentation for your application to find out more.*

There are a lot more files on your PC than just word processor files, and the way that you can distinguish between them all is by the file extension. Let's take a quick tour of the common types of files you will come across on a PC running a Windows operating system.

.exe

These files are the workhorse files of any system running the Windows operating system. Whenever you hear mention of applications, or programs, or executables, these files will have the *.exe* file extension.

Files with the *.exe* file extension all do something. It can be something small like a clock or something big and complex like a spreadsheet application. Whether you know it or not, you are using executable files on your system all the time. From installation, to running your favorite games, to using your word processor, files with the *.exe* file extension are involved. Double-clicking on an executable (or a shortcut to one) is all that is needed to run it.

A *shortcut* is a little file that acts as a convenient link to other files on your hard drive (see Figure 2-6). This means that you can have one original file but many shortcuts to that file in different places. Using shortcuts saves on disk space and eliminates the problems that you can end up with by having duplicate files on your system (applications not working, for example).

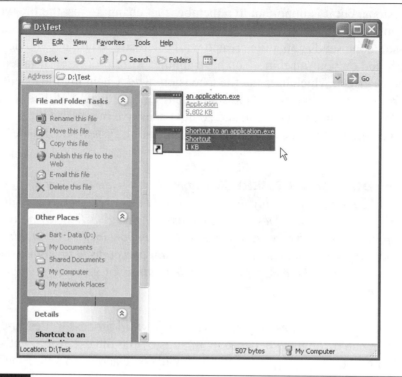

FIGURE 2-6   Shortcut to an executable file

.dll

Files with the *.dll* file extension are dynamic link library files that act as support for other programs (see Figure 2-7). The idea is that certain aspects of a program might not be needed too often. So, instead of bulking up the executable with the information and consuming unnecessary system resources, the application can load the additional features needed as required.

Take a word processor as an example of an application that uses *.dll* files. Certain features, such as spell checking or printing, won't be needed all the time and can be packaged into dynamic link libraries for access when needed.

.com

Files with the *.com* extension are command files, and while they are considered to be applications, they are a specific kind of application. Back in the old days of PCs running Microsoft DOS (Disk Operating System), they were very common, but with

Name	Size	Type ▲	Date Modifi
adsldp.dll	159 KB	Application Extension	29/08/2002
adsldpc.dll	137 KB	Application Extension	29/08/2002
adsmsext.dll	61 KB	Application Extension	29/08/2002
adsnds.dll	158 KB	Application Extension	23/08/2001
adsnt.dll	234 KB	Application Extension	29/08/2002
adsnw.dll	107 KB	Application Extension	23/08/2001
advapi32.dll	545 KB	Application Extension	29/08/2002
advpack.dll	89 KB	Application Extension	29/08/2002
alrsvc.dll	16 KB	Application Extension	23/08/2001
AM21E.DLL	96 KB	Application Extension	01/07/1999
AMN21E.DLL	135 KB	Application Extension	01/07/1999
amstream.dll	63 KB	Application Extension	12/12/2002
apcups.dll	101 KB	Application Extension	23/08/2001
apphelp.dll	113 KB	Application Extension	29/08/2002
appmgmts.dll	153 KB	Application Extension	29/08/2002
appmgr.dll	271 KB	Application Extension	29/08/2002
asapi.dll	19 KB	Application Extension	27/04/2000
asferror.dll	8 KB	Application Extension	11/12/2002
asfsipc.dll	15 KB	Application Extension	29/08/2002
asycfilt.dll	76 KB	Application Extension	23/08/2001
ATHPRXY.DLL	32 KB	Application Extension	22/01/2001
ati2dvaa.dll	370 KB	Application Extension	29/08/2002
ati2dvag.dll	198 KB	Application Extension	29/08/2002
ati3d1ag.dll	825 KB	Application Extension	29/08/2002
ati3d2ag.dll	900 KB	Application Extension	29/08/2002

FIGURE 2-7   A whole bunch of .dll files

replacement of the text-based DOS command screen and the widespread use of the graphical user interface of the Windows environment, *.com* files are now rarely used. (System recovery from problems that cripple the actual operating system are a common use for the *.com* file nowadays.)

Although command files aren't as common as they were a few years ago, they are still in use. If you search your PC, you will likely find a few on your system. I found one on Windows XP:

.bat

Files with the *.bat* file extension are another set of files whose roots go back to the days of DOS. The *.bat* stands for batch files, which are script files that can be written to carry out a variety of tasks. A batch file contains a sequence of commands entered from a file rather than interactively by a user. A common

.bat file on operating systems that predate Windows XP is the *autoexec.bat* (shown here):

This is a file containing specific DOS commands that are run when the computer is booted up. The commands contained in this file tell the operating system which application programs are to be automatically started and how memory is to be managed, and they set the parameters for other settings.

While the *autoexec.bat* file is pretty much gone these days, there are other *.bat* files that will be on your system. Some of these will be for administrative purposes, while others may belong to setup programs and the like. The *.bat* file might be disappearing, but it's not gone yet for sure. Here's a look inside a batch file opened with Windows Notepad:

```
@echo off
SET SOUND=C:\PROGRA~1\CREATIVE\CTSND
SET BLASTER=A220 I5 D1 H5 P330 E620 T6
SET PATH=C:\WINDOWS;C:\
LH C:\WINDOWS\COMMAND\MSCDEX.EXE /D:123
LH C:\MOUSE\MOUSE.EXE
DOSKEY
CLS
```

.ini

Files with the *.ini* extension are another of a dying breed of file types. The *.ini* files are used to initialize, or set parameters for, the operating system and certain programs.

In Windows, there are two common *.ini* files:

- system.ini
- win.ini

You can get some idea of what these files do by opening them using Windows Notepad. Figure 2-8 shows a peek inside one. These files were used extensively in the past. They contain statements that are used to set parameters for peripherals such as the mouse and keyboard, as well as to control screen colors and even things such as screensaver passwords.

PC DOCTOR'S ORDER! *Normally, no changes should be made to these files in the text editor. If Notepad gives you the option to "save changes" upon closing, click on No.*

Times change, and with the coming of Windows 95 (and then Windows 98, NT, 2000, and XP), most of the configuration is now done through values in the Windows registry, rather than through *.ini* files. However, many applications still use their own *.ini* files to store information about the setup and configuration of the program. The contents of these files are normally modified by changing the characteristics of a program through the user interface for that program, not by editing the files by hand.

.sys

Any files with a *.sys* extension are system files, which are used to control the system. These files are many and varied and appear all over the place. One example of a really big *.sys* file that you might find on your Windows system is a file called *pagefile.sys*. As you can see, mine is massive:

pagefile.sys
System file
1,310,196 KB

```
SYSTEM.INI - Notepad
File   Edit   Format   View   Help
; for 16-bit app support
[drivers]
wave=mmdrv.dll
timer=timer.drv
[mci]
[driver32]
[386enh]
woafont=app850.FON
EGA80WOA.FON=EGA80850.FON
EGA40WOA.FON=EGA40850.FON
CGA80WOA.FON=CGA80850.FON
CGA40WOA.FON=CGA40850.FON
msacm.l3acm=L3codeca.acm
[cineMac]
Password Value=0
[vicax]
msacm711=67989
msacm811=137765
msacm911=42405
```

FIGURE 2-8   Taking a peek inside an .ini file

The purpose of *pagefile.sys* isn't just to waste space on your system, so don't go deleting it! Windows uses the file as a way to expand on the amount of RAM in the system by taking some of what might be held in fast RAM on the PC and putting it instead on the hard drive in this file. This makes more memory available to the operating system, which means that more applications can be run with less physical RAM installed.

.hlp and .chm

With the complexity of software installed in a PC continually increasing, you might find that you need a bit of help every so often. This is where files with *.hlp* and *.chm* come in. Both of these are file extensions associated with help files. These are normally installed along with applications or the operating system and are placed along with the application in the programs section of the Start menu.

.txt

Sometimes there is a need for just a simple way of storing alphanumeric (text and numbers) information. This is where text files, which have the *.txt* file extension, come into play. These files are easily created or read with a word processor or programs called text editors, of which Windows Notepad is a good (and free!) example.

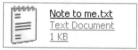

Text files are great for when you want to store text in a simple way free from formatting concerns (like font and text effects), or you need to exchange information with others and you don't know what word processor they might be using. They are also great if you just want to make little notes to yourself. In fact, you could make very brief notes to yourself without bothering to create a file with contents—just write the note as the filename itself:

.zip

Sometimes files take up more space than you'd like them to. You might be trying to cram some files onto a disk or CD to send to a colleague; or you might be sending some photos to a family member by email, but they are so big that sending them is a slow process. To help alleviate this problem, software utilities were created that allow you to compress files so that they take up less space.

FIX-IT-YOURSELF HOME REMEDY *Compressed files are also known as* archives.

There are many different utilities available to compress files, with many different types of compressed files possible. However, the most popular compressed file is, without a doubt, the Zip file, which has the *.zip* file extension.

my files.zip
222 KB

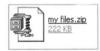

The advantages of creating a Zip compressed file goes beyond just simply making a file smaller. You can add many files to a single Zip file, which not only saves on hard drive space, but also gives you a way to keep related files together in one place. Figure 2-9 shows all the files in *my files.zip* on my system.

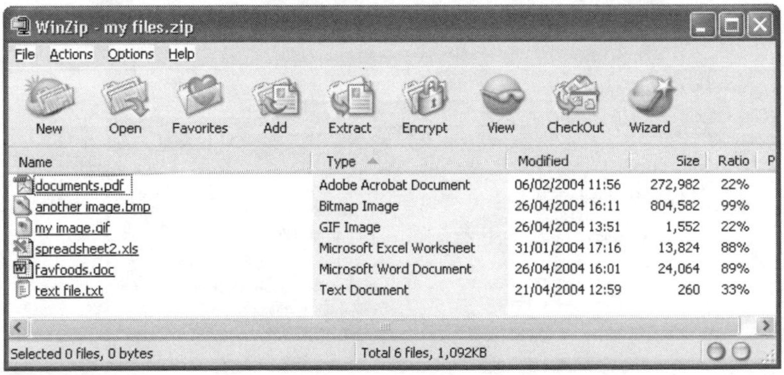

WinZip - my files.zip
File Actions Options Help
New Open Favorites Add Extract Encrypt View CheckOut Wizard
Name Type Modified Size Ratio
documents.pdf Adobe Acrobat Document 06/02/2004 11:56 272,982 22%
another image.bmp Bitmap Image 26/04/2004 16:11 804,582 99%
my image.gif GIF Image 26/04/2004 13:51 1,552 22%
spreadsheet2.xls Microsoft Excel Worksheet 31/01/2004 17:16 13,824 88%
favfoods.doc Microsoft Word Document 26/04/2004 16:01 24,064 89%
text file.txt Text Document 21/04/2004 12:59 260 33%
Selected 0 files, 0 bytes
Total 6 files, 1,092KB

FIGURE 2-9 Multiple files in a single Zip file

Zip files have become so commonplace that Windows XP now supports creating and opening Zip files automatically. It provides nothing more than rudimentary support, while a full-fledged Zip utility can offer much more—for example:

- Varying levels of compression depending on system performance
- Password protection of the Zip file
- The ability to make installation setup programs

WinZip, shown in action in Figure 2-10, is available from www.winzip.com. And more utilities are listed in Appendix B.

Other File Extensions

There are literally hundreds of other file extensions that you will come across. Some common ones are Internet pages that have an *.htm* or *.html* file extension, graphics file formats (*.bmp*, *.gif*, *.jpg*, and *.png*), and audio files (*.wav*, *.mp3,* and *.wma*).

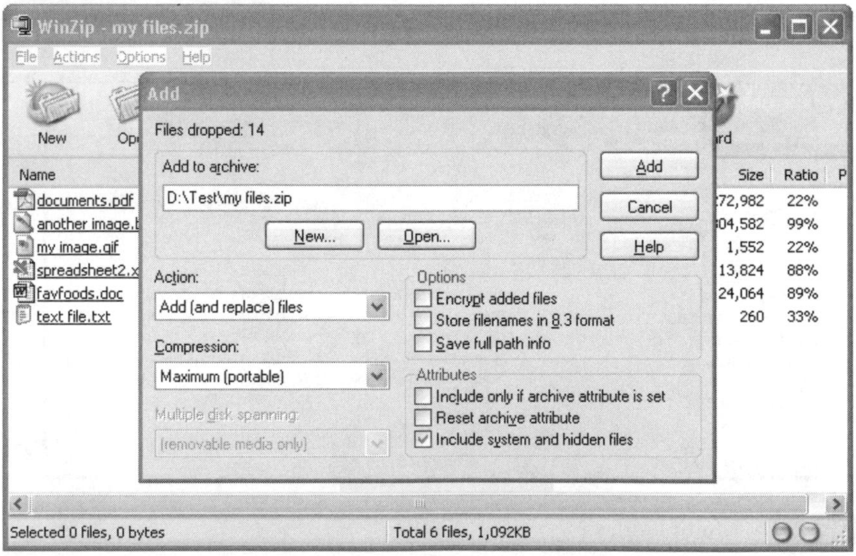

FIGURE 2-10   WinZip application in action

I don't have the space or time to list them all here, so I'll point you to Internet sites in the Appendix B that will list these for you.

Folders/Directories

We've looked at files, but you might have noticed something else when you were prowling through your file system with, say, Windows Explorer. See those little yellow things that resemble paper folders, like the ones in Figure 2-11? Well, that's exactly what they are—folders. But these folders don't hold papers, they hold your files.

The Right Term

Before we go any further, let's get the terms straight. We're going to be using the word *folders* here, but you might also hear them called directories, which was the original word used. However, as the more visual, graphical operating systems were developed, *directories* was gradually replaced by *folders*.

FIGURE 2-11   Folders galore!

NOTE *Actually, things are more complicated than this. The term folder (and for that matter, file) was chosen to be consistent with the metaphor that the user interface was a desktop. In some other operating systems (such as DOS and many Unix-based operating systems), the term directory is still used rather than folder.*

What Is a Folder?

A folder can be thought of as a way of storing related files in the operating system so that they are easy to find. The naming convention for folders is similar to that for files, with upper- and lowercase letters allowed, numbers, and many symbols.

PC DOCTOR'S ORDER! *The symbols / \ ; : * ? " < > | are not allowed in folder names.*

Folders are a collection of related files that have been assigned a specific name (see Figure 2-12). This collection can be retrieved, moved, deleted, and otherwise manipulated as one entity. They can almost be thought of as files containing files.

One important feature of a folder is that you cannot have two files with identical names in the same folder. Variation on the case of letters doesn't count as a different filename; so *lettertofred.doc* is equivalent to *LetterToFred.doc*, and you could only have one of these in a folder. Different file extensions do count as different

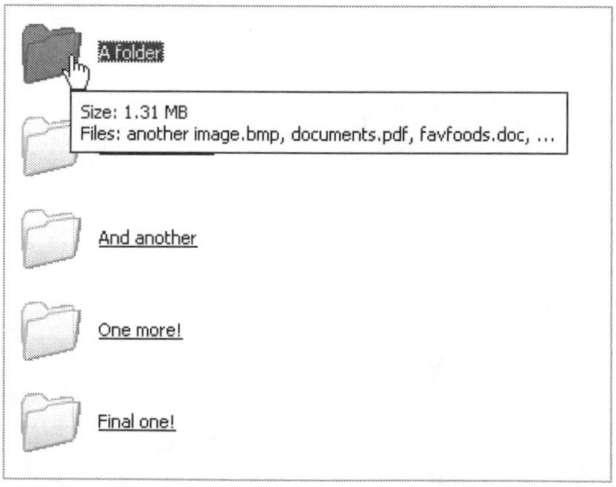

A folder

Size: 1.31 MB
Files: another image.bmp, documents.pdf, favfoods.doc, ...

And another

One more!

Final one!

FIGURE 2-12   Folders contain files

filenames, so *lettertofred.doc* is different from *lettertofred.txt*. You can, however, have a shortcut to a file that has the same name as another file in a folder. (The reason for this is that a shortcut has a different file extension that's hidden.)

Navigating Folders

Gone are the days of having to navigate folders by typing commands into a DOS screen (see Figure 2-13), which was both hard to remember and awkward. You had to know the folder names and type them in by hand. However, it's important to know how to do this because if you have to recover from a system problem, you might have to fall back on the old ways!

You can think of the folders on your system and the way that they interlink as a tree. At the bottom of that tree is the root. The root of your file system is where you store files on your system if they aren't in a folder. Each file system drive on your system will have a root. (I won't cover the technical details of this here; if you need to know more, consult your help manual.) So if you have one drive (say the C drive, represented as C:), this has one root. Normally you wouldn't store files in the root (especially the root of your main system drive—the drive that contains your operating system), as this will be used mainly by the operating system, and if you accidentally delete or modify a file there, you might render the system useless.

 PC DOCTOR'S ORDER! *It's not a good idea to use the root of any drive for storing files. Create folders instead, to place files in for safekeeping.*

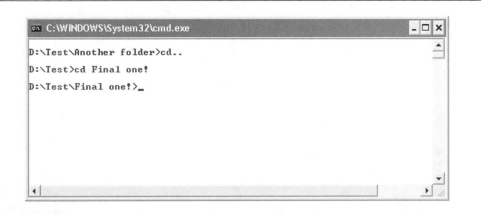

FIGURE 2-13   Navigating the file system using the DOS command prompt

Let's say that you have a folder off the root folder of the D drive called *MyStuff*, and inside that you have three more folders called *2002*, *2003*, and *2004*. If you wanted to navigate around these folders in a DOS command screen, you would begin at the root (D drive). To try this, click Start | Run, type **cmd**, and click OK. Your screen should look like this:

```
C:\WINDOWS\System32\cmd.exe                              _ □ ×
D:\>




                                                   ▶

```

If you are not in the root, type the change directory command:

```
cd\
```

Then press ENTER to get you there. Notice the backslash at the end, which signifies that you want to go to the root. (If you are not in the D drive at all, type **d:** and press ENTER.)

Now that you are at the root of the D drive, you want to go into the first folder, so you type

```
cd MyStuff
```

Press ENTER again, and you'll notice that you are now in the folder *MyStuff*:

```
C:\WINDOWS\System32\cmd.exe                              _ □ ×
D:\>cd MyStuff
D:\MyStuff>                          ▶




```

Note that if a folder name contains a space, you will need to enclose the name in quotation marks for things to work properly in the DOS command screen. So, if the folder is called *My Stuff*, you'd type the following:

```
cd "My Stuff"
```

To go into one of the folders that are contained in this one, type

```
cd 2004
```

And when you press ENTER you will be in the *2004* folder:

```
 C:\WINDOWS\System32\cmd.exe                          _ □ x

D:\>cd MyStuff
D:\MyStuff>cd 2004
D:\MyStuff\2004>_
```

You could have done all of these steps with just one command:

```
cd MyStuff\2004
```

This is quicker but harder to remember.

If you want to go back up one folder level, the easiest way to do this is like this:

```
cd ..
```

This command changes the directory to one above where you currently are. Your screen will look like this now:

```
 C:\WINDOWS\System32\cmd.exe                          _ □ x

D:\>cd MyStuff
D:\MyStuff>cd 2004
D:\MyStuff\2004>cd ..
D:\MyStuff>_
```

If you forget what folders a particular folder contains, you can use this command:

```
dir
```

(The command is a throwback because it stands for "directory.") The list of folders will be displayed:

```
C:\WINDOWS\System32\cmd.exe                                          _ □ ×
D:\MyStuff\2004>cd ..

D:\MyStuff>dir
 Volume in drive D is Bart - Data
 Volume Serial Number is C879-C57D

 Directory of D:\MyStuff

26/04/2004  16:54    <DIR>          .
26/04/2004  16:54    <DIR>          ..
26/04/2004  16:54    <DIR>          2002
26/04/2004  16:54    <DIR>          2003
26/04/2004  16:54    <DIR>          2004
               0 File(s)              0 bytes
               5 Dir(s)  51,334,721,536 bytes free

D:\MyStuff>
```

 FIX-IT-YOURSELF HOME REMEDY *If there are a lot of folders to display, they will scroll off the screen. To prevent this, add **/p** to the end of the dir command. This instructs the system to show only one page at a time. To look at the next screen (page), you press any key.*

Fortunately, there is rarely a need for navigating folders this way (although spare a thought for the days when this was the only way!). Nowadays there are far simpler methods, and all you need to do is point and click.

```
⊟ 🗁 MyStuff
  ⊞ 🗀 2002
     🗀 2003
     🗀 2004
```

To navigate through folders, either double-click on the folder or click on the + next to folders that have subfolders. To close folders, double-click on the parent folder, or click on the – icon.

Creating/Deleting Folders

There are two ways to create and delete folders. First, let's look at the command-line method. I'm going to go back into the *MyStuff* folder on the D drive and create a folder called *2006* (I future plan a lot!). So, first I navigate to the *MyStuff* folder, and to create the new folder I use the make directory command:

```
md 2006
```

To remove the folder, use the remove directory command:

```
rd 2006
```

Here is how your screen will look:

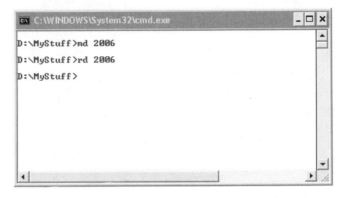

 FIX-IT-YOURSELF HOME REMEDY   *You cannot delete a folder from the command line if the folder contains files.*

Of course, you can also create and delete folders easily from within Windows Explorer. Open a drive or folder where you want the folder created, right-click in it, and choose New and Folder, as shown in Figure 2-14. A new folder will be created that you can rename. Deleting a folder is just a matter of right-clicking on the folder and choosing Delete, as you can see in Figure 2-15.

FIGURE 2-14   Creating a folder using Windows Explorer

FIGURE 2-15   Deleting a folder in Windows Explorer

Where Stuff Is Saved

Take a look at the structure of the data stored on your disk by the operating system and applications. You should notice a few things immediately:

■ **The *Windows* folder**   Normally, this is where the Windows operating system is installed. (On Windows NT and 2000, this folder is called *WINNT*.)

■ **A *Program Files* folder**   This is normally the default installation folder for applications.

■ **A *Documents and Settings* folder**   This folder is a mixed bag of different folders. It contains folders specific to each user that has a user account on the PC (the folder is named after the user). Inside these folders are more folders. If you look inside one of these folders, you see a bunch of other folders. These include *Desktop*, the folder that represents your system desktop, and *Favorites*, where your Internet Explorer browser favorites are stored. You also have *My Documents*, the default folder in which many applications save your information.

■ **A *Temp* folder**   This folder is used by the operating system for keeping temporary files that control the running of the operating system. (There may be more than one folder, depending on the operating system.) Files might build up in here over time, and you can delete them (although if they are in use at the time, you won't be able to delete them).

Doctor's Notes

In this chapter we've looked at the software side of your PC, in particular, the nuts and bolts of the software—files and folders. You've learned the details of

■ What files are

■ File naming and renaming

■ File extensions and different types of files

■ File compression and the benefits of using it

■ What folders are

■ Folder creation and deletion

If you've been using a PC for a while, most of this material will be familiar (although some of the DOS commands might be new to you), but it nonetheless makes all the terminology clear and gives you a solid basis from which to delve into the file system later on. Also, finding your way around the system will be important later when you come to making backups of your data, cleaning up after a virus attack, or installing new software. We've only covered the basics of file and folder manipulations here, but that will be enough to get you through the rest of the book.

Files and Folders Checklist

☑ Understand what makes one file type differ from another.

☑ Know how to manipulate files and folders.

☑ Know and be able to recognize the most common filenames.

☑ Familiarize yourself with the DOS command prompt and how it works.

Chapter 3

Improving on Perfection

There aren't many things in your home or office that you can take a screwdriver to and improve on. If you buy a TV, stereo, dishwasher, or microwave oven, you are stuck with what you left the store with. But if you buy a PC, with a little bit of know-how, you can take what you bought and improve it. In the same way that you can take a car and tweak the engine or the carbs, a PC holds much scope for the home Do It Yourselfer (DIYer) hungry for more power, speed, and the ability to run new, cutting-edge applications without buying a completely new system.

So, if you think you need a new PC, read on before you dig deep into your pocket!

Why Upgrade?

Why upgrade? It's a common question. After all, computers are now cheaper than ever and plentiful. We're encouraged to live in a throwaway world and continually buy new items instead of improving on what we already have.

Many times there are perfectly valid reasons to buy a new PC and either pass the old one on to someone else or dispose of it, but there are also times when, with a bit of know-how and a little time and money, an old system can be given a new lease on life.

 PC DOCTOR'S ORDER! *Dispose of an old system responsibly, following any local regulations that might be in force. Better yet, see if anyone else is interested in it. Your old computer might be just the thing that a local charity or school is looking for.*

Reasons for Upgrading

There are many reasons a PC owner should consider upgrading over buying a new PC. Here are three of the most common reasons for upgrading:

- Upgrading a PC is generally cheaper than replacing.
- Upgrading an otherwise stable system means a better system.
- You just want more!

There are hundreds of other more minor reasons why you should consider upgrading before replacing, but let's start with the financial one. The final cost, of course, depends largely on what you choose to upgrade or improve on. If you choose to replace most of the major components, the associated costs will naturally be higher than if you just replace one or two. Weigh up the cost. How much did the system cost you new, and how much does the upgrade cost compared to a new system? If the system cost you thousands and a new computer would cost you, say, $1000, then an upgrade costing $50–$100 is worthwhile. If you already have a good system, throwing it away and getting another is a poor choice when the upgrade you want might cost far less.

Second, upgrading an otherwise stable system means that the only thing you will notice will be improvements! Things will be faster, or programs will work better, or you will have more space to save files and data. Upgrading is also far less hassle than replacing a system, especially if you aren't upgrading hard drives. And even if you are upgrading the hard drive(s), there are programs available that allow you to move all the data, files, and programs from one hard drive to another.

 FIX-IT-YOURSELF HOME REMEDY *Using special software to handle the movement of your data from one hard drive to another is always recommended. It's nearly impossible to "do it yourself," and installing a blank drive and loading everything back on is a needless hassle.*

Finally, you just want more. More hard drive space. More RAM. Better, faster graphics card. Better sound. You might find that to run a specific application or game, you need, say, more RAM (see Figure 3-1) or a different graphics card. Getting rid of the old system and buying a new one in this case is simply not worth it, and an upgrade is just what the doctor ordered!

FIGURE 3-1   RAM upgrade is one of the easiest upgrades possible

FIX-IT-YOURSELF HOME REMEDY *Think carefully when replacing as to whether the new system will integrate with your existing hardware. A newer PC doesn't automatically mean that it's going to be fully backward compatible. Newer PCs can have fewer COM ports and even have fewer (and different) card slots than what you will need, so check carefully!*

Buying a new PC isn't always a straightforward experience. Even just researching the best PC to fit your needs can take more time than the upgrade. You would then need to make sure that it will integrate with all your existing hardware and run all your software. You could be one of the unfortunate people who receive their brand-new computer DOA ("dead on arrival"—a term used to describe a PC that doesn't work when it comes out of the box). An upgrade can be a far more trouble-free solution to your immediate problems and allow you to take more time to come to the right decisions about replacing a system at a later date.

 NOTE *Although DOA PC systems are not as common as they used to be, a significant number of new PCs arrive at the user's door with a defect. Laptops are generally more prone to this than desktops.*

Reasons for Replacing

Certain things might dictate to you that replacement is the best solution after all. Here are some reasons why you might be better off replacing a system:

- Your system is quite old.

- Replacement is more economical than an upgrade.

- You've already upgraded and will need further upgrades in the future.

These reasons are all related because they stem from having an old system— how old is a matter for debate, but if your system is over six years old, it might be more economical to replace it. The right parts might be expensive or difficult to find. An example of this is a type of memory used in older systems called EDO (Extended Data-Out, although the term isn't important here). Adding 64MB to a system that uses EDO will cost you nearly as much as adding an extra 128MB of memory to a newer system.

You might also be unsure about what parts your system takes. Again, memory is a good example. If you no longer have the manual, or your motherboard isn't listed on a website, you might find it hard to discover what kind of RAM it takes or how much it can support in total. Finding older processors or motherboards might mean trips to the smaller retailers to check out what they still have in stock. Finally, the older the system you want to upgrade, the less life span you might get out of the new parts you are adding. Is it worth spending $100–$200 on a graphics card for a system that might suffer component failure soon?

When you weigh up the cost of your system when it was new against the cost of the upgrade and the cost of a new system, is the upgrade economical? For example, if your system cost, say, $1000 new, and the upgrade you need to the memory would cost $150, but a new system could do what you want for only $500, you might want to consider replacing. There are many rules of thumb that businesses and accountants use to determine this, although these fall down for the home user or the small office user. However, if the total upgrade cost is greater than 50 percent of the total system value, the upgrade is probably not an economical one.

If you've already done some upgrading, how much have you spent on the system in the past three to six months? Don't forget what you've already spent on the system! Think about why you are upgrading and what else you will want to upgrade in the next three to six months. Make sure you take upgrades in the near future into account too. Also, be honest about the full cost of the upgrades— parts and labor if you aren't doing it yourself. Remember too that delivery charges can add significantly to the cost of parts if you're buying mail order—factor these in too.

If you are going to be building a new system as opposed to buying one, then some components from the old system might be usable in the new one, reducing cost. Good candidates for transplanting are hard drives and expansion cards (video cards, sound cards, and network cards). Also, you might be able to transfer the monitor and peripherals.

 FIX-IT-YOURSELF HOME REMEDY *Keeping the manuals for a system is important if you want to get the most out of it and keep it going longer.*

Upgrading

If you have a computer that's more than a year or so old, chances are there's something you'd like it to be able to do that it currently cannot. Maybe you want to be able to play the latest game but need a different, newer graphics card to do that. Or maybe it's the latest software package, and you need a faster processor, or more memory. Or maybe it's just that you loaded the latest operating system or filled your hard drive with photos from your digital camera, and it has simply run out of space to store any more data.

Whatever your circumstances, there will inevitably come a time in your life as a PC owner when something like this happens. This is the time when your computing horizons will really start to broaden!

 NOTE *Here we will be looking at upgrades from a generic standpoint in order to get you thinking about all the parts that go into your PC and what you'd like to change or improve. Specifics on upgrading individual components appear in Chapters 7 to 15.*

 PC DOCTOR'S ORDER! *If your system is under warranty, check with the manufacturer before carrying out upgrades in case that will invalidate your warranty. It is unlikely that it will, but remember your warranty won't cover any damage that you cause the system while performing the upgrade or to the new components that you add.*

Upgrading differs from repairing a PC in that the overall goal of repair is to get the system back up and running again. Upgrading is the betterment of a PC—changing parts so that it can now do tasks it previously couldn't. So already the goals are very different. Getting a system up and running again after a malfunction or defect is a clear goal, whereas changing parts in order for the system to be able to do something new is quite different.

 PC DOCTOR'S ORDER! *If you ever upgrade a CD- or DVD-ROM drive, remember to check that it doesn't contain a disc before getting rid of it!*

Not All Systems Are Upgradable

Before the screwdrivers come out again and you start ordering parts, it's vital that you realize it's not possible to upgrade every computer. Some, such as laptops, contain components specific to the system. Some items (such as hard drive and RAM) might be upgradable, but the rest isn't. Other PCs simply have been upgraded as far as they can be. They have the fastest processor and the maximum amount of RAM possible, and only a motherboard upgrade could give them a new lease on life. This, however, is usually a big, costly upgrade that might mean changing the case as well as the power supply.

Changing the motherboard also usually means a change in the number of expansion slots you have, and that means your existing hardware might not work.

You're then possibly looking at buying different hardware, making the upgrade far from economical.

Consider costs carefully. They are your best guide when it comes to deciding what to do. Sometimes replacing a few components in a system could cost more than a new system with a much higher specification altogether!

Decide on the Right Upgrade for You

If you are upgrading because you want your existing PC to do something that it currently doesn't do, it means you already have an idea of what you want. As mentioned earlier, you may want to play a game, and currently you cannot because you don't have the right hardware for the job (usually a graphics card, but it could also be RAM, or processor, or not enough free hard drive space). Perhaps you are upgrading the system, not by replacing parts, but by adding more, such as a USB expansion card.

Another possible reason for upgrading is that you simply want more speed out of your current system. Perhaps you're doing more with it now and need extra power, or perhaps you just want to make it faster so that you finish your work quicker. Either way, "speed" upgrades are a common reason for upgrading.

Speed Upgrades

Contrary to what you might think, the best way to achieve a speed upgrade is not by replacing the processor. This might seem like it goes against common sense since the speed of new PCs is determined by the speed of the processor; but when it comes to upgrading a system for more speed, the most common way to achieve this is by adding more RAM. The more speed you want, the more RAM you should add. The more RAM you add, the faster the system will go.

 FIX-IT-YOURSELF HOME REMEDY *The reason that adding more RAM makes a computer seem faster is because RAM is much faster than the alternative, which is using the hard drive as a temporary memory store. The more main memory can be used for temporary storage (rather than the hard drive), the faster your programs will work.*

There are only two limits to the amount of RAM you can add:

■   Your PC already has the maximum amount of RAM the motherboard will support. Consult your system manual for information on that.

■ Your PC already has the maximum amount of RAM that your operating system will support. Table 3-1 lists the maximum amount of RAM that the various operating systems support.

Usually, you hit the hardware limitation on the motherboard long before you get to the limitation imposed by the operating system.

Consider 128MB to be a good starting point for memory in a Windows 95, 98, 98 SE, ME, and OX 9.x machine, with 512MB being a good amount for Windows NT, 2000, XP (both Home and Pro), OS X, and Linux. RAM amounts beyond this are useful if you use very demanding software (image manipulation or 3D), but benefits to the average user decrease after this.

If your PC currently houses 64–128MB of RAM, it would certainly benefit from more RAM. Taking this to 256MB will give you enormous speed gains. Applications will appear to open and run faster, and animation and video will play far more smoothly.

In fact, a PC that has had a "speed" upgrade will feel and act like a new PC. Fresh and powerful. Crashes, application lockups, and hangs will be fewer, and waiting times will dramatically decrease.

 FIX-IT-YOURSELF HOME REMEDY *RAM is very cheap these days— take advantage of the great prices. Don't bother with "RAM doubling" software. Get the real thing. It's usually cheaper, better, and won't make your system unstable.*

Operating System	Maximum RAM (GB)
Windows 95, 98, 98 SE	1
Windows ME	1.5
Windows NT	4
Windows 2000 Professional	4
Windows XP Home and Professional	4
OS 9.x	1.5 (However, no single application can utilize more than 1GB.)
OS X	8 (Rather than being an operating system limitation, this is a hardware limitation.)
Linux	64

TABLE 3-1   Maximum RAM Supported by Various Operating Systems

Other Upgrades

Of the many other types of upgrades possible, none is as easy or as straightforward as a memory upgrade. Other possible upgrades, which are covered in detail later in the book, include

- Processor/CPU upgrade (Chapter 8)

- Hard drive upgrade (Chapter 9)

- Motherboard upgrade (Chapter 8)

Check the Specifications

When carrying out an upgrade, be sure that you know what you need and that what you walk out of the store with or get via mail is going to work for you. Never guess as to what might or might not work for your system. If you guess and get it wrong, several things could happen when you try to install it:

- At worst, the new component or your system could be seriously damaged, even to the point of being beyond economical repair. Get the right type of RAM, processor, and power supply.

 PC DOCTOR'S ORDER! *Don't forget to take all the necessary precautions to ensure your safety and the safety of the components from ESD-related problems. Check out Chapter 6 for full details.*

- The component may not fit. A common example of this is getting the wrong kind of RAM or graphics card (PCI/AGP).

- You might not have space for the component.

- Your system might not work once the component is installed, even though no damage occurs. If the PC is unhappy with your choice of component, the system usually won't start up. The main clues that you will have are the BIOS beep codes and the fact that the problems occurred only after you carried out the upgrade.

FIX-IT-YOURSELF HOME REMEDY *Although we'll be going into this in greater detail later in the book, I want to introduce you early on to the fact that things might go wrong after an upgrade. It's not something to fear or worry about; it's a fact of life! If your system won't work after you have replaced a component, always suspect the last component you added. If all the connections and fittings seem OK, the most likely problem is either an incompatible component or a setting that needs to be changed, either by a manual jumper on the motherboard—rarer on newer systems— or in the system BIOS. Try removing the newly installed component and replacing the old one, and see if the PC works. Now retry the upgrade.*

There are other problems associated with buying incompatible components. The store or mail order retailer will not accept them back, or they may charge you a restocking fee for taking them back. These fees can vary from 10 percent to 30 percent of the purchase price.

 WARNING *Read the company's terms and conditions carefully to check their policy on accepting returns.*

If the component is damaged because of an action you took, then don't expect a refund or replacement. Do remember though, that if you buy a component for upgrading from a retailer that gave you incorrect or false information (that the component would work in your system, when in fact it doesn't), you are entitled to your money back, and if damage occurs, you might also be entitled to compensation. If you rely on information from a retailer that you are unsure of, ask for that information in writing. If the retailer seems unwilling to do that, don't buy from them; there are plenty of other places that want your money!

These are the best places to get information about your system:

- The system manuals: all the information you want should be here. There may be more than one manual for your system, so if it's not immediately apparent, keep looking!

- The system manufacturer: they might need the system serial number, but they should have information available. Give them a call or drop them an email if you don't have the information you need.

 FIX-IT-YOURSELF HOME REMEDY *If you've lost the manual for your system, you may be able to download an electronic copy from the manufacturer's website.*

■ Reputable component vendors: most processor, hard drive, and memory vendors have extensive databases of information, and sometimes this is available on their website.

■ Computer magazines and Internet sites: these are also excellent resources, but remember they might not always be 100 percent accurate.

■ Family, friends, and other computer users: pretty much everyone with a PC has an opinion on them.

Take your time when planning an upgrade. Remember that an upgrade has different objectives from replacing a defective component and differs in many ways, urgency being the most obvious. When fixing a problem, you are usually either dealing with a warranty issue or buying a replacement for the defective product. It's not the best time to be thinking about upgrading. True, if you are in no rush to get the system back up and running, you might be able to spend the time needed to research the right upgrade. You may have been thinking of upgrading, in which case you will already have a good idea of what you should choose instead, although the chance of having researched the exact part that became defective is pretty slim.

Take your time, and bear in mind the golden rule: "If in doubt – Don't!" Never be pressured into upgrades, and take proper care that the component you are buying is suitable for your needs.

Check that You Can Physically Do the Upgrade

You don't want to get your component home, open up your system, and find out that it's not going to work. Here are the most common things to check for before buying, as well as before installing, new components:

■ Check that you actually have free slots available for a RAM upgrade you are planning (or that you are going to replace existing memory).

■ Visually check that the component fittings are the same before trying to make the connection. Luckily for the DIY upgrader, most connectors and slots are unique looking, and it is easy to spot differences. This is vitally important when upgrading processors, where the wrong socket could cause damage to the delicate pins on a CPU.

■ If you are going to add a new hard drive or CD/DVD drive, make sure you have the space for it in the case (some cases have limited space for drive upgrades) as well as free data channels and power cables available.

- If you are planning on adding new expansion cards, make certain that you have slots available and that they are of the right type.

- If you are adding new COM port/parallel port, USB port, or FireWire port components, make sure you have free space available. With USB/FireWire ports, you might have to add expansion ports or hubs.

- Check to see if you have all the screws and fittings you will need for the job. Some components (such as hard drives) don't come with the fittings.

- Check to see that adequate power connectors are available inside the PC. You might also need to consider whether the actual power supply is suited to powering additional devices inside the system (more on this in Chapter 7).

Trouble-Free Upgrades

Besides making sure you can physically perform the upgrade and actually have all the fittings you need for the job, you can take several steps to make sure that your upgrade goes as smoothly as possible.

PC DOCTOR'S ORDER! *If you've got any notes/tips on how to carry out the upgrade, print them out before beginning, as you might not have the chance later.*

1. Make sure you have all the documentation you need to carry out the upgrade.

2. Check for newer/updated drivers. The drivers you get with the hardware are unlikely to be the latest and best. (See the section "Upgrading Drivers" later in the chapter.)

3. Before carrying out the upgrade, check and then check again that the hardware you've got is the right thing. Check the specification again, and make sure that what is in the box matches the specification (not always possible, but it's worth looking). If you ordered a 512MB DDR PC2700 184-pin DIMM module, check that the sticker on the module matches and that you haven't received something different, such as 256MB.

PC DOCTOR'S ORDER! *Don't remove the stickers from memory modules. You will void your warranty.*

4. Before you start removing parts, give the system a quick clean inside with compressed air. (If you have a regular maintenance routine, it won't be that dusty inside anyway.) Doing this reduces the risk that dirt or dust will get into the electrical contacts, causing problems.

5. Uninstall old hardware first (unless it's core to the running of the system) and uninstall the drivers too. Uninstallation of drivers is carried out either from the Add/Remove Control Panel applet or Device Manager in Windows. On Linux, if you used a script, there is frequently an option to clean past installations. If you used **rpm**, then to uninstall, try **rpm –ev packagename**.

6. Handle components with care, and take all the necessary ESD protection measures (covered in detail in Chapter 6).

7. If you are in any doubt as to the original placement of wires or cables, make a note or draw a diagram.

PC DOCTOR'S ORDER! *Sticky labels are great for identifying wires and cables. Get a set of different colors, which will make the job of reassembly easier.*

8. Work carefully and methodically. Take your time and don't rush things.

9. Check all connections afterwards. Make sure that the connections are sound and firmly pushed into the connector.

10. Test carefully afterwards. Make sure everything works.

Finding Parts for Older Systems

If your system is older and you can't find the parts you need from your local retailers, you might still be able to get parts for upgrading, but you will need to be a little bit cannier in how you find them.

Local Retailers

Big retailers don't keep huge stocks. They buy little and often and send back old and unwanted stock to make room for new stock. This keeps costs low, as well as overheads.

Smaller retailers are different, and they might have old stocks. It's worth phoning around to all the computer stores in your area. You never know, you might get lucky!

Internet Retailers

Once you've exhausted local retailers, try the Internet for retailers. Again, you are probably more likely to strike it lucky with the smaller outlets that have slower stock rotation.

Use your favorite search engine and search for parts. If you are looking for an older Intel processor, such as the Pentium II, for example, be specific in your search. If you can be specific, such as the speed you are after (500 MHz, for example), then make sure you add that as a search criteria.

Once you've exhausted the Internet, try the newsgroups. They are not as good as a web search and far less likely to turn up what you are after, but you never know, you might be lucky.

Secondhand Systems

Another possible source of replacement parts is to look for a secondhand system that can "donate" parts to your system. This might also appeal to you because, while you may not be getting a brand-new part, if you know what you are looking for, you will be saving a lot of money!

Here are some suggestions for possible sources of secondhand systems:

- Garage sales

- Secondhand shops

- Classified ads

- Auctions (real-world auctions and Internet auction houses)

- Friends or relatives who have an old system gathering dust in a garage, basement, or attic

- If all else fails, try a wanted ad, not necessarily in a newspaper but on one of the many Internet forums dedicated to PC and PC repair/upgrading.

 FIX-IT-YOURSELF HOME REMEDY *Keep in mind that the farther afield you go for what you want, the more it will cost you in shipping, especially if you are talking about shipping an entire system.*

Someone, somewhere, is likely to have the exact thing you're looking for. There are literally millions of PCs out there either unused or looking for a new home (even if it is only to donate parts to another system). And by making use of an old system, you are recycling, so everyone wins!

More About Donor Systems   If you are buying (or acquiring) a PC that you plan on using as a donor system for parts, check out the following first (especially if you are paying for it):

- Does the system still work? If not, then what is on it that is of any value?

- Is the system a higher specification system than the one you have? Is it equal? If it's not, what parts can you salvage from it?

- Once you get the system, make a careful inventory of the parts — how much RAM, size of the hard drive, and so on. You can then either keep the system in one piece or dismantle it and store it as parts.

 PC DOCTOR'S ORDER! *Don't pay too much for a donor system unless you plan on using it before you take it apart. It is an unknown quantity, and there is no guarantee that you'll get much, if any, use out of it.*

Upgrading Drivers

Upgrading isn't always about changing hardware on a system. It can be about upgrading the software drivers that control the hardware.

Benefits of Upgrading Drivers

Although you might not give an old system a new lease on life through driver updates, and it might not feel like a new computer, making sure that software drivers are up-to-date has some significant benefits.

- Better performance: new drivers are usually better at what they do than older versions.

- Reduced system resource consumption: newer drivers usually take up less system resources (especially memory).

- More features: newer drivers usually have more features. Perhaps something you thought was missing in the old driver is available in the newer version.

- Increased stability: this is one of the major reasons to upgrade drivers. Newer drivers usually mean better system stability and fewer crashes. If you have a problem on your system, a driver upgrade is a good place to start.

- Better suited to new operating systems: if you upgrade the operating system, you might find that some hardware won't work until you get drivers that support it.

 PC DOCTOR'S ORDER! *If your system is running well and you are not experiencing any problems, it might be a good idea to leave the existing driver. While most of the time a driver upgrade results in benefits, on a well-running system, these might be insignificant, and the new driver could introduce problems. A case of "if it's not broken, don't try to fix it!"*

Finding New Drivers

Your first port of call for finding new drivers should be the Internet. Go to the vendor's website and see what they've got (look in the "drivers" or "downloads" section). If that doesn't turn up anything, search for the hardware name; you might find a driver elsewhere. For example, this sort of thing is common with graphics cards. Most graphics cards are built around chipsets from one of a handful of companies (Nvidia, ATI, and Hercules being the most common). These companies make generic drivers that work with third-party graphics cards built using their chipsets.

 NOTE *Get drivers from the actual manufacturer, as opposed to using generic drivers, if possible, as they can have features specific to the hardware.*

Another option is to run Windows Update (the updating application built into the latest versions of Microsoft Windows operating systems). This gives you access to hundreds of drivers for a wide variety of hardware.

If the Internet is not an option for you, or you can't find the driver you are after, try giving the manufacturer a call and see if they have updated drivers available. But be aware that some companies may charge for this service.

Doctor's Notes

Once you've carried out your first upgrade, it probably won't be the last time. When you stop looking at your PC as a static fixed tool and begin to look at it as a collection of parts, most of which you can replace easily, you will find yourself freed from limitations that you previously thought could only be overcome by replacing your existing computer setup.

The main thing to remember is to do the research beforehand and work through the upgrade methodically.

Have fun!

Upgrade Checklist

- ☑ Decide on the upgrade you require.

- ☑ Decide on an upgrade budget.

- ☑ Research your intended upgrades.

- ☑ Check that you have room for the upgrade (slots, drive bays, etc.).

- ☑ Find a good source of parts that you can trust.

- ☑ If you buy parts secondhand, try to get recommendations from others.

- ☑ If your drivers are old, think about updating them (it's a free upgrade!)

Chapter 4

Safe Computing

You're sitting at your desk using your PC. Perhaps you are playing a game or writing an email to a friend, colleague, or family member. You feel safe and secure. However, your PC might not be.

The Threats Exist

Each time you open a file, load a new program, or connect to the Internet, you are exposing your PC to other people and their work. You probably already know (and have experienced!) that installing a legitimate program can have an adverse effect on your computer, causing it to slow down, generate errors, or even crash because of conflicts with other programs or bad code. But there is a far more sinister side as well.

There are unscrupulous people out there, and they have written programs that are trying to gain access to your computer in an attempt to take it over. This can be for a variety of reasons. They might just want to cripple your system (their idea of fun) or play a prank on you, but most are not targeting you personally; they are aiming to spread chaos and disruption. Other reasons for trying to gain access could cost you financially, or damage your own or your company's reputation.

Here is a list of the most common ways that others gain access to your computer system:

- Dropping a destructive virus or worm on your system

- Installing a joke program on your PC (such as a screensaver or a program that generates fake error messages)

- Installing a program known as a *backdoor* so that your computer can be controlled by others

- Stealing the passwords you use for Internet banking, email accounts, or online stores you visit

- Stealing files from your computer. Word processor documents, spreadsheets, databases, and files relating to financial applications are common targets for this kind of attack.

- Altering your browser's home page or configuring it to visit alternative sites

- Using your email account to send viruses or spam email to others

- Using your Internet connection without your knowledge (a big problem if you are on a wireless network)

Let's take a look in detail at some of these threats and what can be done about them.

Viruses

The term *virus* is a broad one indeed, used to describe any program or code that can replicate or copy itself. This in itself isn't particularly harmful, but as you will see, besides containing code for replication, they also contain code that is purposely written to cause damage. In this sense, viruses are rogue programs that attempt to get onto your machine and run in a variety of ways. They can get onto your machine covertly (such as over the Internet, by email, on a disk or CD) or you might be tricked into inadvertently downloading and installing them, thinking that they are genuinely useful applications.

 NOTE *Some people mistakenly believe that computer viruses are just like real viruses, or think they spring into existence inside computers all by themselves. This isn't the case. They are all deliberately created by other computer users to cause nuisance or damage. Hence the reason another term commonly used for viruses is "malicious code."*

Viruses are normally small programs and can either be a stand-alone program (that is, a full, self-contained program of its own that has no other purpose), or they can be embedded in another host program. Some viruses aren't even confined to one host program and can move freely from one host to another.

Let's take a tour of the different types of code threats that you might encounter.

Types of Threat

Computer viruses, just like those in the real world, come in many varieties. And just as in the real world, different varieties do different things. Some are harmless, some give you a cold, some flu, and some of them can give you something much worse.

The following sections describe the types that you are likely to come across.

Adware

Programs that sit silently on your computer secretly gathering personal information about your Internet habits (such as the sites you visit and how long you view them) are known as adware. They then relay this information back to another computer, usually for advertising purposes.

This code typically finds its way onto your PC via websites (typically in shareware or freeware), email messages, and instant messengers. Adware sometimes even masquerades as legitimate programs, and it's not uncommon to find that the information about the tracking it undertakes is buried somewhere in the End User License Agreement you agreed to during installation.

Dialers

Programs designed to make money for someone—at your expense—are called dialers. They install themselves onto a system, without your permission or knowledge, and then attempt to use your modem to dial out to the Internet to a premium-rate 900 number or FTP site.

Hack Tools

Hackers use these programs to gain unauthorized access to a computer or network of computers. There are many kinds of hack tools, but a common one is the keystroke logger, which is a program that records all the keystrokes typed on the keyboard and then sends this information back to the hacker. This information can then be used to deduce passwords to the system or online resources.

Hoaxes

A hoax is typically an email that gets mailed as a chain letter. These emails usually predict or describe some new, stealthy, very destructive (and highly improbable) virus, or try to get you to delete a file on your system that it claims is a virus when in fact it isn't.

Hoaxes are usually easy to spot because they themselves contain no attached file, have no reference to any person or company that might validate the claim, and use a notably general tone and language in the message. They are usually unspecific (not making direct reference to, say, your username or a purchase or reference number) and vague when it comes to detail. (They have to be, to work on the maximum number of people.) Here is an example of the kind of language you might find:

```
Dear Friend
Here is the file you asked me for. Run it now!
Thanks you!
```

Social engineering is becoming a common factor in many hoax, malicious, and fraud-related emails. These emails pretend to be from a big company or organization in order to fool you into a false sense of security. Check the language for unspecific and vague elements.

```
Dear CUSTOMER

Your recent purchase at XYZ Auction House has not been cleared
because of problem with your credit card details. So that we can
deliver your product to you please reply to this email giving us
your USERNAME, PASSWORD and credit card information.

Thank you!
```

Another example:

```
Postmaster

We have had recent reports of SPAM email being sent from your
computer. Please run the attached file so that we can scan YOUR
machine for TROJANS. Failure to do this will result in the
SUSPENSION of your account!!!!!!
```

 PC DOCTOR'S ORDER! *If you get a hoax email, do everyone a favor and just delete it. Don't pass it on.*

Joke Programs

Some programs are designed only to cause distraction or nuisance. Joke programs are harmless programs that cause various annoying activities to display on your computer (for example, a fake error message).

Remote Access

Programs that allow another computer to gain access, information, or to attack or alter another computer over the Internet are referred to as remote access programs. There are many legitimate commercial remote access programs, and these may be detected by virus scans you run on your system. If you installed the program, great; if not, remove it!

Spyware

These stand-alone programs can covertly monitor activity carried out on your system (such as passwords and other confidential information), which they then transmit to another computer using the Internet or email. Spyware can come from a variety of sources, similar to those of adware applications.

 FIX-IT-YOURSELF HOME REMEDY *The moral here is to check the End User License Agreement carefully—even if it is filled with complex jargon and legalese. If in doubt, don't install.*

Trojan Horse Programs

A Trojan horse program is different from other viruses in that it doesn't replicate or make copies. One purpose of a Trojan horse is to damage or compromise the security of the computer (for example, by stealing passwords or disabling vital security software such as antivirus and firewall applications). Typically, you will be sent a Trojan horse program by email (as it cannot send itself), and it may come disguised as legitimate software or a joke program of some sort.

Virus

As you know, a virus is a program or piece of code whose main purpose is to replicate. Replication means it will infect another file by inserting itself or attaching itself to that medium. This might be a program, boot sector (the portion of data on the hard drive that begins the system boot-up process), partition sector (a portion of data on a hard drive that defines multiple drives on the same hard drive), or a document that supports macros (such as a word processor document or spreadsheet). While most viruses only replicate, many do a large amount of damage as well.

 NOTE *Even replication can cause big system problems. There may be hardware or software on the system that conflicts with the virus, or the virus may consume a lot of system resources (CPU and memory) while it replicates. A virus can make files bigger and also clog up email and Internet resources as it tries to continue to replicate.*

Worms

A worm is a program that makes copies of itself. It can do this in a huge variety of ways—for example, from one hard drive to another, by attaching a copy of itself to an email, and by spreading to other computers on a network. Worms can also contain code that might cause damage or even compromise the security of your computer or network. Like most other malicious code, worms can arrive in the form of a joke program, screensaver, or some other software.

What Malicious Code Is Capable Of

The nastiness or damage that a virus can cause is only limited by the imagination of its creator, the security features you have installed on your PC, and your vigilance. Viruses can be categorized by their threat level: low-risk, medium-risk, high-risk, or mixed/blended threats.

Low-Risk Threats

In the low-threat category we have jokes, hoaxes, and viruses that do nothing other than replicate. Hoaxes are false information that the hoaxer hopes you will act upon. While a hoax isn't itself harmful, if it tells you to delete an important file and you do it, that may well cause problems. The best way to deal with hoaxes is to simply delete them. Don't pass them on, and don't try to educate the person who sent them to you.

Jokes are mostly nuisance applications designed to annoy or irritate. (Well, some were initially designed to be humorous, but when you've seen the same joke error message several times in a row, the humor wears a bit thin!)

Don't feel that it's OK to live with joke programs on your system. Although they might not cause any harm or problems, they might conflict with other programs (or joke programs) to cause system instabilities and crashes.

PC DOCTOR'S ORDER! *Resist the temptation to send joke programs and hoaxes to other people; that way they are less likely to send them to you. Be serious about how you deal with security!*

Medium-Risk Threats

A medium-threat virus is one that isn't likely to do an awful lot of damage. Perhaps it looks for and deletes a certain file or application that can be easily recovered or reinstalled. A medium-threat virus may also try to send out copies of itself as an email attachment to others in your address book so that they too can suffer the unpleasant experience.

Bear in mind that a medium-threat virus might target a file or program that you didn't have a backup for. To prevent a medium threat from becoming a high threat, make sure you have a backup of important data and applications.

High-Risk Threats

A high-threat virus getting onto your system can cause you to have a very bad day (or several bad days). High-threat viruses can do a whole host of nasty things:

- Delete all the data stored on hard drives

- Alter files and documents on your PC (such as replacing certain words in word processor files or spreadsheet files)

- Capture your passwords and pass them on to others via the Internet

- Send your files to others (word processor, emails, spreadsheet, financial)

- Use your email system to send junk email to others

- Disable or make alterations to the security systems on your computer or network to allow others to enter and possibly take control

- Hijack your browser so that you can only visit certain sites

All these can be highly destructive. Even if you have an up-to-date backup of all your current files, rectifying the problem can be a time-consuming job if it happens on one machine. If you have a network of systems, the time and problems are multiplied.

When it comes to high-risk threats, prevention is a lot better than cure! We'll be coming to prevention soon.

Mixed/Blended Threats

Because a virus can be programmed to carry out more than one action, these types fall into a category known as mixed or blended threats. For example, a virus might initially carry out a low-risk threat activity (such as displaying some prank error messages) to lull you into a false sense of security. The virus might then send itself to other people listed in your email address book and to any other PCs linked to a network. After it has done this, it might, finally, delete all your files. This escalation of seriousness gives the virus time to spread, thus maximizing the amount of damage it can do.

Virus Myths

As with anything to do with computers and the Internet, there are plenty of myths surrounding viruses and their capabilities. Let's take a look at some of the most common myths that exist.

- **Myth 1**   You can only get computer viruses from the Internet. Viruses predate the Internet by many years. The first viruses (Apple 1, 2, and 3) were in the wild (that is, spreading between computers) during 1981. These viruses spread through the use of pirated games.

- **Myth 2**   You can get a virus from web cookies. Web cookies are merely text data that is meant to be read, not run in the same sense that a computer program runs.

- **Myth 3**   You can get a virus from image files on the Internet. Image files such as GIF files (.gif) or JPEG (.jpg or .jpeg) are only displayed, as opposed to being run like an application.

 PC DOCTOR'S ORDER! *Be careful though—sometimes image files are distributed with a viewer program, and that could easily play host to a virus.*

- **Myth 4**   You can detect viruses by checking file sizes or the time and date stamp for changes. Although it's useful sometimes to check the file size or the time and date stamps of your executable files for any changes, this is in no way a reliable way to prevent viruses. Many viruses are written in such a way that they do not change the time and date stamps when they infect a file. Some viruses can even hide the change in file size when they infect it. Add to this the fact that a PC can contain many hundreds of thousands of files, and you will see that this is really not a viable option.

- **Myth 5**   If you set all your files to read-only, a virus cannot infect them. This is one of the most misleading myths. A virus can easily be written to bypass this feature, and this is more than likely just to annoy you when you are trying to work.

- **Myth 6**   If you write-protect your hard drive, you are safe. There are tools available that claim to be able to write-protect your hard drive from any change. These tools are usually software based and therefore easy to bypass.

- **Myth 7**   Viruses pose the biggest danger to your data. Viruses do pose a significant risk to your data, but data loss through conflict, hardware failure, and accidental deletion by the user are far more common reasons for data loss.

- **Myth 8**   Viruses only come from pirated software, and if you stick to retail software, you will be safe. Viruses take many routes onto your system: email, web downloads, CDs and floppies, even retail software. Back in the days of retail software being supplied on floppy disks as opposed to CDs, it wasn't unheard of for a customer to catch a virus from retail software. How? A previous buyer returned the software after a virus found its way onto the disk, and the store subsequently re-shrink-wrapped the software and put it back on the shelf.

- **Myth 9**   Viruses only come from "unsavory" or "sleazy" websites. Again, viruses can take a variety of routes onto your system. Some websites are certainly more prone to having downloads that harbor viruses than others, but you should use commonsense protective measures for all of them.

- **Myth 10**   Antivirus software will protect you. As you will see shortly, software helps, but you certainly shouldn't think it is foolproof. New viruses are coming out all the time, and someone, somewhere, has to be the first to get it.

Hackers

You've probably heard the term *hacker* a lot over the years, but you might be surprised to learn the true meaning of it.

Hacker is used by some to mean "a clever programmer" and by others, especially journalists and editors, to mean "someone who tries to break into computer systems." The phrase "a good hack" used to describe a clever bit of programming, and "hacking" was the act of doing that. Nowadays the term has been hijacked by the press and other media and used almost exclusively to describe someone who tries to gain unauthorized access to a computer system. Typically, this kind of hacker is someone who is a proficient programmer or engineer with the right technical know-how to understand the weak points in a security system.

How Hackers Operate

We don't have the time here to go into the psyche of the hacker; it's too complex and ultimately doesn't help you protect yourself. However, we can break hackers down into two groups:

- **Group 1**   These hackers want to gain access to "high-value" targets. This might include banks, government computers, and those controlling infrastructure. The reasons for doing this are many and varied and range from personal satisfaction to theft.

- **Group 2**   These hackers are after much lower value targets, trying to gain access to the kind of system that you might run at home.

Group 1 hackers are unlikely to be interested in your home or office PC unless you store really important data there or it is of key importance. It's group 2 that you need to be on the lookout for. Group 2 hackers range from those interested in taking over someone else's system just to cause havoc on it, to those who will use the systems under their control to send email and carry out "denial of service" attacks on websites.

The group 2 hacker's main plan of attack is to get a program installed on your machine in order to gain control of it. They use three main types of programs:

- Hack tools

- Remote access tools

- Trojan horse programs that disguise a hack tool or remote access program

All these programs must be delivered to your machine and run—usually by you! Once this is done, they report back to say that they have been activated, and then the hacking begins.

Another way hackers gain access to a computer system is to exploit a vulnerability or flaw in an installed program or operating system. These kinds of hacks are getting more common because of the complexity of the operating systems and applications loaded onto a home or office PC and also because so many are connected to the Internet. Usually though, even when a vulnerability is being targeted, the system is taken over by sending the unsuspecting user a program or code that tries to take advantage of this, as opposed to being done by someone in person while you are online.

 NOTE *Being connected to the Internet does indeed pose the greatest risk of being hacked. There are other ways a hacker can try to gain access to your system (via your network or a fax/modem installed on a computer), but these techniques are now taking a back seat to hacking carried out over the Internet.*

It's important to understand that hackers aren't the same as email scammers. Email scammers try to fool you into believing that they are going to pay you vast amounts of money for the loan of your bank account details. A hacker might send out email that looks like junk mail, but this would contain hack tools or a Trojan horse program for you to run.

Hacker Myths

Just as with viruses, a lot of myths surround what hackers can and can't do. Here are a few of the most common hacker-related myths:

- **Myth 1**   There's no defense against a hacker. If you are truly worried about hackers, at the very least, disconnect your system from any network, a phone line, and the Internet, and you will be quite safe. However, for the rest of us, there are some simple steps that we can take to protect ourselves.

- **Myth 2**   Hacking is really hard and there are very few hackers. It's true that hacking is not a skill that everyone has, but the spread of the Internet has meant that the tools and skills needed are more widely available. We are also seeing a proliferation of *script kiddies*, who take an existing virus or worm and make small modifications to it to create a new version of an existing problem.

- **Myth 3**   Hacking can only happen over the Internet. OK, a lot of hacking happens via the Internet, but networks and especially wireless (WiFi) networks are also prime targets.

■ **Myth 4**   Hackers only hack big corporate networks and government computers. It's much easier to hack the standard office or home PC than a big government network if the hacker intends to launch a denial of service attack on a website or send out masses of junk email loaded with Trojan horse programs.

■ **Myth 5**   You have nothing a hacker would want. Yes you do! At the very least you have a computer that they can use and Internet access and an email account.

Your Defense Against the Marauders at the Gate

OK, so now you see that the Internet isn't the peaceful, orderly, well-behaved place you may have once believed it to be. You are now aware that the marauders are just outside of your digital fortress trying to get in. You may not know who they are or why they want to get in, but there's absolutely no point in burying your head in the sand and pretending they aren't there.

You're now also armed with information. You know that the attack doesn't have to be a fierce one, but that they are more than likely to wheel a Trojan horse up to you, than to attack outright.

But what can you do? What are your defenses? How do you protect your computer and others that it might be connected to? How can you protect your company's assets and image?

There are a few things you can do and use that will help you to harden your defenses and so make you too tough a victim for the hackers, who will move on to easier targets.

Here are the tools that you need:

■ Common sense

■ Firewall protection

■ Antivirus protection

Common Sense

The first line of defense when it comes to PC security is common sense, and it can protect you from many of the problems and security issues that seem to plague computers today.

When was the last time you heard about a big, widespread virus in the news? Probably not long ago, since there seems to be one almost monthly now. You're told about this or that virus that spread across the globe in a matter of hours and has infected many hundreds of thousands of systems all around the world. You might have also heard that this or that is to blame for it and that something should be done.

Do you know what you weren't told? It was this: at each point that the virus or worm spread, someone, somewhere, ran the offending program (usually attached in an email) in order for it to spread to the next victim. At each step of the way, people were fooled into running an application without knowing what it was. If everyone who got the virus initially had thought about whether they should run the program or open the file, the spread of the virus could have been prevented.

As mentioned earlier, virus creators are using what is known as social engineering to get their victims to run the attachments. They do this by making emails look like they come from colleagues or friends, as well as making the attachment appear to be a joke or images that you have to see. Sometimes the emails are written to make them sound like they contain important work documents or something from your ISP, online store, or perhaps even more official than that—the IRS.

Social engineering is a powerful tool, but it isn't perfect. Remember, the text of the email is usually a dead giveaway that it is a trick. The signs to look for are badly worded text or clumsy wording that sounds far too overenthusiastic about the content. Also, a hacker who might be on the other side of the planet cannot possibly know what your friends or work colleagues sound like in email and, as such, cannot imitate them.

Firewalls

A *firewall* is software or hardware that sifts through data being passed between the Internet and a PC (or PCs on a network), and it examines the data being transferred to and from the PC. Hardware firewalls are common in a corporate environment but not in the small office or home. Far more common on the SOHO (small office, home office) PC and on the home PC are software firewalls that are installed on the PC.

 NOTE *The term firewall comes from firefighting, where it is a barrier established to prevent the spread of a fire.*

Remember the golden rule: "If in doubt—Don't!"

Here are a few other commonsense rules you should follow:

1. If something sounds too good to be true, it usually is. Email that has an attachment saying you've won a prize, and all you need to do is run the attachment, is almost always going to be a fake.

2. Were you expecting a friend or colleague to send you an email containing an attachment? If not, ask yourself why they sent it. Also look at the text and ask yourself if it sounds like who they claim to be. If in any doubt, flash a quick email back, asking if they did actually send you something.

3. Don't automatically open and run attachments. Read the body of the email first at least. Do you really care to see the latest joke app anyway? Is it worth the problems it could cause?

4. Check the file extension of the attachment. If you are being told the file is an image, it will usually have the file extension .gif, .jpg (or .jpeg), .tif, or .bmp. It won't be a file with the extension .exe, .pif, .bat, .doc (or others—see the list later in the chapter), as these are either applications that can run or can contain or cause other programs to be run. Also check to make sure that the icon representing the file is the right one.

5. Remove suspicious file attachments from your emails automatically with one of many different firewall programs available (discussed next). (One example is Zone Alarm Pro, which removes suspicious file attachments before they make their way into your email inbox.)

The job of a firewall (whether hardware or software) is to look at all the data passing from an insecure environment (usually the Internet or another network) and decide whether the source is authentic and whether it's safe or not. On the home PC, a firewall is usually used to examine Internet traffic to the PC (data) for suspicious packets (bits of data). Packets are deemed to be suspicious if the address that they came from is not one that is expected, or if the packet has a signature that matches those previously determined as suspect.

There are many good software firewall options available, both free and for sale. Also, Windows XP comes complete with a firewall.

FIX-IT-YOURSELF HOME REMEDY *Firewall software and hardware can be challenging to set up, but the protection it offers far outweighs the time or effort of setting it up. It is usually updated regularly by the maker. Some will let you know automatically when there is an update, while with others, you will need to check the company's website regularly. Either way, it's important to keep it up-to-date so that you are protected against newly emerging threats.*

Antivirus Software

Antivirus software is the best defense against computer viruses. Back in the days when there were only a handful of viruses and no Internet, it was quite easy to keep an eye out for the various nasties that were about. Now, with tens of thousands of viruses and about a hundred new ones appearing monthly, you need a robust solution that can deliver program updates.

An antivirus program works by checking files for suspicious code. It can detect suspicious code in one of two ways:

1. The antivirus program contains complex code to search for any suspicious code.

2. Antivirus programs also contain a vast database of known viruses that they check against.

Modern antivirus software scans for viruses that come in via the Internet, email, on disks, and CD/DVD discs, or over a network. They can check inside compressed files (such as ZIP files) for viruses too. Add to this that they can usually remove viruses from most host files (executables, word processor files, and so on) without damaging the host file.

There are many possible antivirus solutions for PC users, ranging from free software to subscription-based software. Your choice depends on a few factors:

■   Is it for home or commercial use? Most free antivirus software is only licensed for home/noncommercial use.

■   Will you want tech support in the form of email/telephone support? Free software doesn't usually come with this.

■   Do you need fast response to new viruses? Going for the paid-for solution usually means you will get updates to the program to counter new viruses very quickly.

Whatever you choose, you really need to have a good antivirus solution in place. It's also a good idea to upgrade your antivirus software regularly (usually once a year). Even if program updates to detect new viruses are automatic, upgrades usually contain new features that are useful too (such as the ability to detect suspicious code in web pages, or inform you of joke programs or remote access programs installed).

Safe vs. Unsafe Files

Knowing which files you can run safely without risk and which ones can, potentially, carry an associated risk is vital. Generally, the distinction is simple:

- Files that are exclusively composed of data are safe.

- Everything else is suspect.

Listing every dangerous file extension would be difficult—far better to list the few files that are guaranteed to be safe. Here is a list of common files that you can open safely:

.gif	Graphics Interchange Format (CompuServe)
.jpg or .jpeg	Joint Photographic Expert Group
.tif or .tiff	Tagged Image File Format (Adobe)
.mpg or .mpeg	Motion Picture Experts Group
.mp3	MPEG compressed audio
.wav	Audio file
.txt	Text file

 WARNING *Remember that files such as word processor documents or spreadsheet applications (for example, those created using Microsoft Word or Excel or other applications) can contain harmful code (called* macros) *that can damage your system.*

Basically, if you want to stay safe, avoid any other files that you aren't expecting, as they could be hosts to viruses, worms, and other nasties.

Be careful to check that the files you are running aren't trying to hide their true identity by using a file extension such as:

```
suspectfile.txt.exe
```

This is actually an executable file masquerading as a text file. This is a common trick used to disguise harmful files as innocent ones.

Here are the most common types of files used to wreak havoc on a PC system:

.bat	.exe	.reg
.cmd	.js	.vbs
.com	.pif	.wsh
.doc		

If the Worst Does Happen...

You're using your computer, and, all of a sudden, a prompt appears telling you that a virus has been detected or that a hacker has been repelled!

What do you do?

First and foremost—*don't panic!* If you get a message telling you that a virus has been caught or a hacker blocked, the software you've installed is doing its job of keeping out the nasties. Follow the prompts and deal with the problem. Once the problem is cleared up, try to find out where the virus or hacker came from so that you can learn from the experience and perhaps tighten your defenses.

But what can you do if something like a virus slips through the net? Here are a few signs that you might have a virus on your system:

■ The system slows down.

■ You see weird messages popping up (greetings, insults, etc.)

■ The operating system or applications display unusual error messages.

■ You experience frequent data loss.

■ You notice odd graphic effects on the screen.

■ You experience frequent program crashes.

 NOTE *It's a fact of life that programs crash at times, but if applications begin to crash excessively, you should become suspicious.*

■ The operating system or other applications refuse to start.

The only reliable indication that you have a virus is when you are informed by an antivirus scanner, and you should see if you can detect it using the program on your system. Download the latest virus database for the application and scan the system again. (Consult your antivirus help program for information on how to do this.) If it still doesn't detect it, try another antivirus scanner if possible. (There are several free antivirus tools available on the Internet that you could try.)

So if this doesn't work, what do you do now?

Again, the first thing you should do is simple—*don't panic!* Why? Because while you are panicking, you are more likely to do something silly (such as wiping out your whole hard drive or deleting files and crippling your operating system). So don't panic. It might help to turn your PC off and walk away from it for a while. Go get a cup of coffee and come back later.

OK, once you are ready to come back, first thing you need to figure out is if you actually have a virus problem. Your antivirus software should pick it up and repair it automatically, but if it's slipped through, it might be something new.

What you are trying to do is isolate the virus. Once you can do this, you can deal with it. If you still don't turn anything up by trying a few different scanners, the best thing to do is wait a day to give the antivirus companies a chance to update their virus database so that you can find, isolate, and deal with the virus.

If you don't have any success in detecting a potential virus, then you might want to approach your antivirus software vendor for technical assistance. This is where using paid-for software helps!

Passwords

The keys to your digital kingdom are passwords. These are what allow you access, while other people are denied. The advent of the computer and the Internet has meant that many of us are called on to regularly create and assign passwords—passwords that will prevent access to financial records, business plans, and so on, which we want to keep away from prying eyes.

Increasingly, Internet users need to create and remember passwords that will allow entry to various parts of the online world, such as account details at online retailers, banks, and email and subscription services. If only we were all good at creating effective passwords and even better at remembering them! Some people are good at this, but most of us are not, and we give little thought to the passwords we choose—that is, until something goes wrong.

Good Passwords and Bad Passwords

Not all passwords are effective. There are good passwords and bad passwords. The difference between the two is that good passwords should be hard for someone else to figure out, and if you are going to create effective passwords, you need to be able to tell the difference!

Here are the most common reasons why a password is a bad one:

- The password contains less than eight characters. Below this level, a brute-force attack is feasible. (A *brute-force attack* is one in which someone creates a program to try out many thousands of passwords automatically.) At this level or above, most brute-force attacks would take a very long time, maybe months or even years.

- The password consists of a word or words that appear in a dictionary. Hackers and fraudsters can very quickly search against entries in electronic dictionaries built expressly for this purpose.

- The password consists of sequences like 000000, 1111111, abcdef, abc123, and so on. These are, unfortunately, quite commonly used, and fraudsters try them out early.

- The password is a name, a special date, or a place name. These are all bad choices and can be easily guessed, or they may appear in electronic dictionaries.

 NOTE *Dictionary attacks on passwords are a common method of attack. A search through 220,000 words in all upper- and lowercase combinations could be carried out in as little as a few days.*

Rules for Creating Good Passwords

It's not hard to choose a good password. All you need to do is follow a few simple rules:

1. A good password should be a minimum of eight characters long.

2. A good password should contain both letters and numbers.

3. Letters should be both upper- and lowercase.

4. If possible, integrate symbols and punctuation into the password.

5. Add something random to the password. A couple of characters at the beginning, middle, or end are ideal. This adds an extra random element to the password you create.

FIX-IT-YOURSELF HOME REMEDY *Recommended symbols to add to a password are* !@#$%^&*()_-+=[]{}:;'"\|<>,.?/. *But note that some systems may restrict some of these characters. Try them out and see if you can use them.*

So, by following the simple rules laid out above, we can observe the evolution of a good password:

1. Start off with a word or a phrase. This won't be the actual password, just a handy starting point:

```
password
```

2. Mix into this a few numbers. It's handy for remembering a password if the numbers you use resemble the letters you are replacing.

```
9a55w0rd
```

3. Change the case of a few of the remaining letters:

```
9a55W0Rd
```

4. Sprinkle in a few symbols:

```
9a$5W()Rd
```

Notice here how we substitute (and) for the 0, adding an extra character to the password, making it even better!

Even though we began with a pretty poor starting point (the word *password*), by applying the four simple rules to it, we end up with quite a good password.

PC DOCTOR'S ORDER! *Identity theft is on the increase. Victims of this crime stand to lose an awful lot. If you don't currently make use of passwords to secure data on your computer, you might want to reconsider. A computer contains a lot of personal information about you and your dealings. By not securing it, you are making it easier for criminals and fraudsters to target you.*

Sensible Password Use

Having a good password is only part of having a good defense. There are a few simple rules you have to follow to make sure your data or finances are safe.

- Never use the same password for two different things. Have separate passwords for securing files (preferably a different password for each different application that needs one) and one for each online site that needs one. Reusing passwords weakens your security, and if your password is compromised, you'll have a lot of work to do in changing it everywhere.

- Never disclose a password to anyone, either verbally, on the phone, or by email, not even if it appears to be a genuine request.

- Change high-value passwords at regular intervals—at least every six months. A high-value password is one which, if compromised, would result in a loss to you or to your company.

- Never write down a password. This may seem obvious, but people do it often. Worse still is seeing passwords taped to the front of PCs or on sticky notes around monitors.

- Be careful about copying a password to the Windows clipboard. If you do this, copy something else afterward, to make sure the password isn't easily available to the next user.

- Never store passwords as plain text (in Notepad files or as word processor documents). Don't trust the password protection offered by word processors to protect valuable passwords either.

- Never rely on any default passwords you have been issued. Change them as soon as possible.

- When using your passwords online, make sure you are using a secured website. These web addresses will begin with https:// instead of http://.

- If you have many passwords, it may be a good idea to get a program to store them in. If they are to be safe, you need to make sure that you can trust the encryption that the application employs, and you'll still need to remember the password to open your password file!

NOTE *Many password storage applications are also capable of generating strong passwords made up of random characters.*

Securely Deleting Files

When you delete files from your hard drive, they're gone … aren't they?

No, they're not gone. To begin with, if you run Windows (from 95 through XP), files that you conventionally delete end up in the Recycle Bin. In fact, the files aren't actually deleted at all, just moved to the Recycle Bin. You might decide that you don't like this feature and that you want anything that you've chosen to delete, well, deleted. This isn't difficult to do:

1. Right-click the Recycle Bin icon on the Windows Desktop and click Properties.

2. Check the box for Do Not Move Files to the Recycle Bin, and then click OK.

Now files will be deleted instead of being moved to the Recycle Bin.

Now they're gone, aren't they?

No, afraid not!

Your initial thought that when you delete the file, the data is gone, is not really an illogical one at all. After all, what else do you expect it to do? But, when you delete a file, the operating system doesn't really remove the file from the disk (not even if you bypass the Recycle Bin); it only removes the reference to the file from the file system table on the hard drive. The file, and all the data it contains, remains on the disk until another file is created and written over it. Even after it has been written over, it may still be possible to recover data by studying the varying magnetic fields on the disk platter surface of the hard drive (the surfaces that hold the data inside the hard drive).

Before the file is overwritten, anyone can easily retrieve it with a disk maintenance or an undelete utility. This is great news if you deleted a file by accident and want it recovered, but it's not such good news if you delete a file because you want it gone!

So how do you really delete files? You use a tool called a secure deletion utility. These tools overwrite the file with patterns of data a number of times. How many times you choose to overwrite depends on two things:

- How fast you want the process to be: the more times you overwrite, the slower it will be.

■ How securely you want the file to be deleted: the more times it is
overwritten, the more secure its deletion.

Also, there are generally different patterns of overwrite to choose from. Before
you are in a position to know what to choose, let's take a few minutes to look at
how data is stored on the hard drive.

The Anatomy of Data

Data on the hard drive is stored in binary, consisting of just 0s and 1s, called *bits*.
Each character of text is represented by eight such bits. The string "Here is my
data" would look like this:

```
0100100001100101011100100110010100100000011010010111001100100000011
0110101111001001000000110010001100001011101000110001
```

01001000 - H	01101101 - m
01100101 - e	01111001 - y
01110010 - r	00100000 - {space}
01100101 - e	01100100 - d
00100000 - {space}	01100001 - a
01101001 - i	01110100 - t
01110011 - s	01100001 - a
00100000 - {space}	

If you just think of a simple overwriting, it doesn't matter what pattern you
choose. However, the problem is that it is possible (although not easy) to read
the varying magnetic fields on the hard drive. This is where a good pattern of
overwriting comes into play. There are a lot of patterns, but the most secure level
of data overwriting calls for 35 overwritings using a variety of patterns, combining
random patterns with preselected patterns. The purpose of this is to "scrub" the
magnetic fields laid down when the data was written and create fresh, meaningless
patterns.

 FIX-IT-YOURSELF HOME REMEDY *For most applications, 35
overwritings are excessive, and for normal usage, 3–7 are enough,
both of which, by the way, are standards set by the U.S. Department
of Defense.*

Doctor's Notes

PCs are amazing repositories of information and data, and unscrupulous computer users out there want to either steal your data for financial gain or damage it in order to cause you trouble and hardship. The steps you take to protect your data depend on how much it is worth to you. It's also vital to realize that even if you don't feel you need to protect your data or Internet connection, your computer can be taken over and used to cause mischief, mayhem, or even computer crime elsewhere—all stuff that could be traced back to you, even though you are innocent!

Having firewall and antivirus programs installed on your computer is like having insurance: you might never need it, but if you do, you'll be glad you had it! You might never need it (unlikely), or you might be deflecting hackers and viruses all the time (equally unlikely!), but either way, it will make your PC experience a much better one.

Safe Computing Checklist

☑ Get and install an antivirus program.

☑ Same with a firewall—get one and install it!

☑ Familiarize yourself with the manual for both. (If you don't know how to use it, how do you know it's protecting you?)

☑ Update both regularly to combat new threats.

☑ Scan any media (floppy disks, CDs, and downloads) before software installation.

☑ Be wary of unsolicited attachments arriving via email—delete!

☑ Beware of hoax emails. Don't reply to them, just delete.

Chapter 5

Helping Yourself

You're doing something, and *bang!* a problem strikes completely out of the blue. You're faced with an error message that you've never seen before. You know that it surely must mean something (they usually do, although there are some that manage to be completely unhelpful!), but how do you find out? Where do you turn? To books? Tech support? The Internet?

No single book, person, or website, or any other resource, could possibly list every ailment that a PC can experience. There are far too many! Every possible combination of hardware and software leads to an absolutely staggering array of potential troubles and pitfalls.

A typical home PC can have dozens of bits of hardware attached and possibly hundreds of applications on the hard drive. All of this has to work together and be compatible. One thing out of place, and problems await you. Add to all this the scope of problems arising from improperly installed hardware and software or even damaged devices and files, and you might now begin to realize the levels of intricacy that a PC can achieve.

All this might dishearten you and make you think that you have no hope whatsoever when it comes to fixing problems and getting your PC running again. After all, the odds of your actually isolating the problem and coming up with a solution seem to be so great that it puts Las Vegas casinos to shame! This might be true if you were choosing to tackle problems in a random fashion and just taking shots in the dark, but you won't be doing that.

If You Have a Problem, Chances Are, Someone Else Has Had It Too

Misery likes company, but there are times when it can work in your favor. One thing that makes solving PC problems easier is that there are so many PCs in use, and even though the odds are against two PCs being the same, the odds are good that someone else has had the same problem, because usually only two or three things have to come together to cause that problem. For example, if all your word processor icons have changed to different icons, chances are that it's caused by what you installed last. The chances that this has happened to someone else are quite high, and even if you didn't realize that it might have been the last thing you installed, someone else might have!

But how do you tap into this? How do you gain access to other people's problems and the solutions that they have come up with? The answer is simple: the Internet!

Helping Yourself on the Internet

When it comes to PC problems, the Internet is a valuable tool to have in your toolkit. It's not the same as a screwdriver or multimeter, but it is just as important. The Internet has allowed people to network and form communities, and because the computer is core to that, it's not surprising that communities have sprung up around PC problems and possible solutions.

 NOTE *Here I'm concentrating on computer problems, but Internet resources can also be used to do research on the best components and software to buy as well as how to make your system better.*

 FIX-IT-YOURSELF HOME REMEDY *If you are having Internet connection problems or your system is completely unusable, you might still be able to access the Internet to do research from a friend's house, at work, a library, or in an Internet café.*

There are hundreds of such support communities on the Internet. Generally they are places where users have posted a question or problem in the hope that someone, somewhere, has the answer. But there are also millions of web pages hosted on the Web that list problems along with potential solutions. Many of these are put up by the software makers, but there is also a lot of information put up by individuals who just want to help others.

 NOTE *Don't dismiss "unofficial" solutions to problems. Usually they are based on official solutions that users have learned from tech support phone calls or websites. Other times, the solutions have been discovered by users through trial and error. Be open to all possible solutions!*

But the Net is a huge place, containing millions of websites and billions of pages. How do you find your way around?

Support Websites

Sometimes you don't have to search the whole Internet to look for solutions to your computer problems. Sometimes the best place to begin your search is at the digital doorstep of those who made your hardware or software.

Nowadays pretty much every company has a website, and I can almost guarantee that a company selling something to do with computers will have one.

(If you're not sure, check the packaging, manuals, or the help files of the software; failing that, do a search on the company name or product name using a search engine.) On the surface, the websites will appear to be mostly a sales and advertising tool, but dig deeper and you might find gold in the form of a tech support section or knowledge base. By freely offering technical information about their products, companies can save money because users solve their own problems and get answers without the hassle and expense of long telephone support calls. Everyone wins!

 NOTE *Checking support sites is also a good way of evaluating products before you buy.*

Website Tips

Navigating manufacturers' and vendors' websites can be tricky because the main purpose of the site is advertising, and making the support section or knowledge base too obvious might send out the wrong message! Here are a few top tips for making your way around a manufacturer's or vendor's website:

■ If you don't know their web address, check the manuals and help files supplied with your hardware and software. They might tell you exactly where to go.

■ Look for a site search page or a search box on the front page that allows you to enter search criteria for finding pages on the site. This can be invaluable and reduce time spent searching.

■ Failing a search box or search page, look for a support section. These are normally identified as "Support," "Tech support," "Knowledge base," or sometimes more ambiguously marked "After sales" or "Customer area."

■ If there isn't a clearly defined support area, perhaps the support area is accessed from the product pages. Go to the pages that list the product you have (or the nearest one you can find), and see if you can find a link from there.

■ Still can't find it? Look for an area marked "Site map." Site map pages usually list all the main sections of a website.

■ If all else fails, try the "Contact us" section, as there may be an email address or web form you can use.

If you don't find what you are looking for this way, you'll have to resort to other methods of contacting the vendor.

Search Engines

The Internet is an invaluable tool in solving computer troubles, but search engines are your guide, allowing you to find your way around. Which search engine you choose is up to you and your personal preferences. There are hundreds to choose from. If you don't have a favorite or aren't sure, here are a few recommended search engines you can try:

- **Google**   http://www.google.com

- **AltaVista**   http://www.altavista.com

- **Yahoo**   http://www.yahoo.com

- **search.com**   http://www.search.com

- **EasySearcher**   http://www.easysearcher.com

- **Ask Jeeves**   http://www.ask.com

- **Lycos**   http://www.lycos.com

- **MSN**   http://www.msn.com

 NOTE *Yahoo, search.com, and EasySearcher can search the indexes of other search engines, making them a great way of using multiple search engines simultaneously.*

Once you've chosen a search engine, you need to learn how to use it effectively so that you can narrow down the billions of pages on the Internet to the few that hold the information you are seeking.

Search engines are simply websites that create a list of web pages likely to contain information based on the search criteria you enter. A search engine consists of three components:

- A *spider* (also known as a *bot* or *crawler*) that visits every page on every website that wants to be searched or listed, and reads it. It also uses hypertext links on each page to discover and read other pages on the site.

- An indexer that creates a huge index (or "catalog") from the pages that have been read.

- A program that takes your search request and sifts through the entries in the index, and returns results to you.

The part that we are concerned with here is the part that takes your search criteria and searches the index looking for this. This is the part of the search engine that you want to learn how to make full use of.

Search Engine Power-User Tips

Here are a set of tips that should help you narrow down your searches and get access to the pages you want. Remember that you are searching through indexes containing billions of pages, so being as precise as possible is always to your advantage.

■ Be specific: if you are searching for Windows XP problems, search specifically for Windows XP, or Windows XP bugs, or Windows XP crash, not just Windows, or XP, or bugs. This kind of search will find pages containing any or all of the words you use as search criteria.

■ Be even more specific: if you want to find a page containing all of the words you enter as search criteria, you have to use the + sign. So, to find pages on the Net that contain the words *Windows*, *XP*, and *bugs*, you'd type **+Windows +XP +bugs**. Again, combine this with being specific.

If you received an error message, enter the error message, making full use of the + sign. For example, if faced with an error message such as a Windows XP stop error like "Stop 0x0000000A Error," search specifically—for example, **+Stop +0x0000000A +Error**.

■ Eliminate unwanted pages: sometimes when you search for, say, Windows XP, you also get pages referring to other versions of Windows, such as Windows 3.1, 95, 98, ME, NT, or 2000. You can filter these out using the - sign. So, again using the stop error example, if you don't want to see pages that relate to Windows NT or 2000, use the following search: **+Stop +0x0000000A +Error -2000 -NT**.

■ Search for strings of words: searching for pages that contain *Windows* and *XP* and *bugs* somewhere in the page is handy, but sometimes it's even better to be able to search for the three words appearing in a row. This is easily done using quotation marks: **"Windows XP bugs"**.

■ Use combinations: using combinations can make your searches even more specific. Here is an example: **"Stop 0x0000000A Error" +XP -2000 -NT**.

Using these techniques can help you narrow down websites containing information that is of use and interest to you. But it's not just websites that can be gold mines of information.

Internet Forums

One of the most common ways that online communities come together on the Internet is via web forums. Web forums are set up so that members can post messages on the forum topics on the website. Usually, you do not have to be a member in order to read messages, but membership is generally required in order to participate (by posting messages) or use built-in search facilities.

There are many different types of forums, ranging from official support forums set up by manufacturers and vendors to privately run communities. The quality of information varies wildly, and as with any unofficial resource, there are no guarantees. Nonetheless, they can be a great information repository, allowing you to see the kinds of problems people have, the solutions offered, and whether the solution helped or didn't.

Most forums are mini-communities, so remember to be polite, and also introduce yourself first if possible. Entering a forum can be a bit like entering a conversation already in progress, so be polite, be clear, and be patient. Nothing annoys the participants in a forum more than someone posting a question on a topic that's already been covered. So, do yourself a favor and do a search before you make a post. With this in mind, here are a few tips on how you can get the most from forums:

■   Do a search first. As with anything to do with the Web, a search is the quickest and best way to get the information you are looking for. You could go through each page and post on a forum manually, which can be educational and informative, but laborious. Much better to do a search!

■   If you find a possible solution or advice, see if anyone posted to say whether it worked for them or not. No point trying a solution that other people said didn't work.

 NOTE *Not everyone posts to say whether the solution worked, so don't take the absence of a follow-up post as confirmation that it didn't work.*

■   Once you find a potential solution, do a search with an Internet search engine to see if you can find references to that solution elsewhere. This might not be easy and could test your searching skills, but it is worth trying.

■ Use common sense when following any advice. Does it seem clear? Are instructions easy to follow? Do there seem to be any gray areas to the instructions or solutions?

■ Look for other posts made by the people who posted solutions you find. You're looking for information on how knowledgeable they are, whether they seem to have helped others, how many posts they have made, how long they have been members, for example.

Newsgroups

Another resource available for searching is newsgroups. Newsgroups are discussions that revolve around a particular subject. Messages are written to a central Internet site and redistributed through Usenet, a worldwide network of news discussion groups.

Newsgroups are organized into subject hierarchies, with the first few letters of the newsgroup name indicating the major subject category and subcategories represented by a subtopic name (although many subjects have multiple levels of subtopics).

Some of the major subject categories are

■ news

■ rec (recreation)

■ soc (society)

■ sci (science)

■ comp (computers)

The ones likely to be of greatest interest to you in tracking down a solution to a computer problem are the comp groups.

Users can post to existing newsgroups, respond to previous posts, and create new newsgroups. To participate in a newsgroup, you will need a newsgroup reader (built into many email programs, such as Outlook Express), or you can choose a stand-alone application to do the job (free or paid for). This allows you to download the list of available newsgroups and subscribe to the ones you are interested in. You will also need access to a news server, which is usually provided by your ISP. Failing that, you will need a separate subscription service.

 NOTE *There are many thousands of newsgroups, with a few containing content that some might find offensive or unsuitable for children. Use discretion.*

If you don't want to participate, there are search engines (such as Google) that allow you to search through most of the newsgroup postings. This means that you can do a thorough search through all the posts and find potential solutions to your problem without needing a newsgroup reader or subscription. A good place to start might be http://groups.google.com.

Whatever you choose, you will find that newsgroups hold a vast amount of information related to computer problems.

When to Call in the Pros

Nobody should be better at supporting a product than those who made it! There are times when, despite having the best PC DIY skills, you will have to call in the experts. Under some circumstances, you might be right and justified in not spending your time and efforts tracking down and solving problems yourself. For example:

- You encounter a major hardware problem and your system is under warranty.

- You encounter software problems and you are still in the free technical support period.

- You install a new piece of hardware or software and you can't get it to work.

 FIX-IT-YOURSELF HOME REMEDY *One thing you do need to know before calling tech support is what piece of hardware or software is actually causing the problem. Generally with software, you should call the people who made or published the software that crashed, although even software problems might have a root cause in some hardware you have installed. Be especially careful to call the right people if you have to pay for the support.*

Be careful and check your rights before calling tech support! Support periods on hardware normally expire a year after purchase (although many hard drive manufacturers have longer warranty periods).

Software is very different, and what you get can vary wildly. Some software makers/vendors/publishers give you unlimited tech support. (This is usually only the case for shareware that you download from the Internet because their overhead is low.) Others might give you a year. Some give you a limited number of "support incidents." Some companies allow you to choose how you want to contact them for your support (Internet, phone, and so on), while others offer Internet support only and charge for telephone tech support.

Be cautious, and if you are not sure of your entitlement to free support, ask. Technical support can be very expensive if you are calling outside of your free entitlement.

FIX-IT-YOURSELF HOME REMEDY *If you have old software that you would like support on and the free entitlement period has expired, a cheaper option might be to upgrade your software and see if that upgrade fixes your problem. If it doesn't, you have free support again!*

Online Tech Support

Usually the most common option nowadays for technical support is online, because the companies involved need fewer people to provide it. You notice how long it takes to answer a phone call but not usually an email. An added advantage is 24-hour availability.

Online support is great if you can still use your computer or Internet connection. Typing out an email or completing an online form is a lot faster and a lot less hassle than phone calls. You also have written instructions to follow if needed—a huge advantage over notes you scribble down during a phone call.

Be wary of companies who offer *only* Internet support. If your computer cannot access the Internet for whatever reason, it could mean trouble for you!

Telephone Support

The traditional tech support method is not necessarily the best. The main complaints about telephone support include

- Lengthy wait time: some people have stayed on the phone all day for support.

- Expensive call cost: some tech support lines use premium rate toll lines that can cost you significantly.

- Inconsistent support: you are told one thing by one technician and something else by another.

- Hard-to-follow, complex, or incomplete instructions

- Office hours support only: home users find it hard to get support at times when they are actually at home.

However, telephone support can be invaluable if you cannot actually use your computer to access the Internet (or you don't have a second computer handy).

On-Site Warranty

The computer that you purchased might come with on-site warranty, whereby instead of packing up your PC and shipping it back to the manufacturer, the manufacturer sends an engineer to your home or workplace to fix your problems.

On-site warranty is excellent because you are free from troubles and can get someone else to fix them for you. The downside is that this kind of warranty is expensive and not often offered on home PCs.

Return to Base

Three words that no PC owner wants to hear: *return to base* (RTB) means the manufacturer or retailer can't help you fix your own system, and it has to be returned to the factory. No matter how good the company you are dealing with or how fast they solve your problems, a system that has to be returned to base for repair is going to mean hassles for you.

The hassles you may face with an RTB are huge:

- Having to dismantle and pack the system. This is where you'll be glad that you kept the original packaging!

 NOTE *Some manufacturers won't accept any responsibility for damage to a system returned to them if it's not packed in the original boxes and packing material.*

- Arranging pickup (hopefully not at your expense, but don't be surprised if some don't try it)

- Being without a system for an indeterminate length of time

- Being without your valuable data in the meantime

- Possibly never seeing your data again (if they replace parts or give you a new/different system)

- Waiting for redelivery

- Unpacking and setting up the system again

- Checking the system to see if the problem remains. (It's not unheard of to get a system back suffering from the same, or a completely new, problem.)

- Reloading your applications and data if all is OK

RTB Tips

Here are some tips that will help make an RTB as painless as possible:

- Do you have a backup of your data? If not, inform the company and see if they will help.

- Repack the system carefully and sort out who pays for shipment. Sometimes manufacturers want the whole system back, while others will only want certain parts (such as the main system unit). Keep a note of everything that you send back just in case things go missing.

- Try to get an idea of when the system will be looked at initially.

- Once the system has been examined, the manufacturer/maker/retailer should be able to tell you when you can expect the system back. Make sure you arrange for a date when you can take delivery. The longer your computer remains with a carrier, the more likely it is to sustain damage.

 NOTE *If the system sustains any damage in transit, inform the sender immediately of the problem and keep all paperwork and packaging as proof.*

- Find out what was wrong and what was replaced or fixed. If the problems persist after return to you, this will be valuable information.

- When you get the system back, check it thoroughly. Make sure you get back everything you sent. Then check that the problem has actually been fixed (although it might take some time for you to be sure). Run the system for a while (a day is sensible) to make sure it works right before loading your applications and data back on (of course, you will need the operating system loaded on for the test).

- If there are any problems (either new or old), get in touch with the company immediately. Don't delay!

Tech Support Tips

There's a knack to getting the best out of tech support, no matter what type you use. Here are my tips for getting the most from technical support technicians. Before you call or email:

1. If your problem is with a PC, make a note of the make, model, and serial numbers. The last thing you want to be doing midcall is messing around the back of a system looking for serial numbers. If you need help with software, make sure you have the name and version numbers handy, along with details about your system (processor type and speed, memory, how much free disk space).

NOTE *Having all this information at hand reduces the length of your call as well as allowing you to get down to the problem quickly.*

2. Make notes about the problem, when the problem occurs, any error messages, or anything else you think tech support might find useful.

3. Make sure you know the right number or the right email address for tech support. Getting it wrong can waste time and lead to delays in getting the problem fixed.

When making the call or sending the email message:

1. Take down the name of the support technician. If you need to call back or your call is disconnected, this will help you get back to the right person.

2. Describe the problem carefully and clearly. The more details you can give, the better placed the support technician is to help.

3. During a phone support call, make sure you have a pen and paper close at hand so you can take notes. You might need to follow instructions after you're off the phone. With email support, always print out any instructions just in case the system crashes.

4. If any step or procedure seems at all unclear, ask for clarification. Don't be pressured into doing anything that you are uncomfortable with or unsure about.

5. Along with taking notes about procedures, make detailed notes about any changes you make and whether they are successful or not. If they are unsuccessful, you are better off undoing the changes before making any new changes.

Be careful if you are advised to use the "recovery CD" that came with your system. These reformat the entire PC and reload all the programs back onto it, taking it to the state it was when you first took it out of the box. All your data, new applications, updates, and settings will be gone. Don't do this lightly! This is a drastic measure. If the system is usable, take time to back up your data first.

If You Have to Pay for Tech Support

What if you aren't entitled to free support? What do you do now? Well, if you really are stuck and need help, you might have to pay—but is it worth it?

You need to get a few questions answered before you hand over your credit card details. For example, how much will the support cost? Is it charged by the minute or by the incident? Either way, make sure that the cost is clear to you from the start. Also find out if a fix is guaranteed, and if you don't get a fix, do you still have to pay for the help?

Consider these alternatives to having to part with cash for support:

- If your software is outside the support period, sometimes buying an update is cheaper than paying for support (especially nowadays with good deals and other incentives).

- If your PC is outside the free support period, the individual parts may not be. Hard drive, memory, processors, and graphics card might have a support period longer than one year. It is most definitely worth checking with the manufacturer just in case.

Finally, if you have to pay for support, you might as well shop around. You might find a cheaper option elsewhere. Get the best deal that you can for your cash. But remember that cost isn't the only issue; it's getting the problem solved!

Hidden Costs of Replacements

Being offered a replacement computer for a faulty one might seem like an excellent solution. But, as with most things in life, there are downsides you must consider:

- A new PC means having to spend time setting it up again. This is not a big problem if the other one developed problems early on, but if it is a few months old, it might be a different story.

- Remember that you will lose any data that's on your PC. OK, you might have backups of all your stuff, but are you happy with your data falling into other hands?

 FIX-IT-YOURSELF HOME REMEDY *You can get software that will do a thorough job of wiping your hard drive, if the system still works (see Chapter 4). If it doesn't, you could always move the hard drive to a working system for wiping.*

- Know whether you are actually getting a new system or a reconditioned/ repaired system.

■ Remember that you have to remove any additional hardware you have installed on the system. A new modem or network card in the system might be easy to overlook. Also, if you've added more RAM or a bigger hard drive, remove it. The same is true for cables.

 NOTE *Keep all the parts that you replace. They could tide you over if you have a problem with the new component that forces you to replace the old parts.*

■ Do you get the replacement before they pick up the old one, or will the old one be picked up first? If you are going to be without your PC, how long will that be? Get a firm timeline!

■ Will the new system come with a new warranty, or will the warranty pick up from where the old one left off?

■ What about the software that comes with the system? What will you be getting? Make sure you get this clear in advance.

■ If you use newer software (such as Windows XP or Office XP or 2003), it might use product activation as an antipiracy system. This means that your license is bound to the hardware setup of your system. A replacement system may cause you problems in this area when you come to reinstalling. You might need to approach those companies for advice if you run into problems.

Subscription Services

Many big software publishers offer professionals a subscription service whereby they can get the latest details on the software, plus free copies of *beta*, or prerelease, software and the entire knowledge base of bugs, problems, and fixes—the same stuff that tech support professionals use!

The better known ones are probably the two from Microsoft:

■ **Technet**   Knowledge base of bugs, problems, and fixes

■ **MSDN (Microsoft Developer Network)**   A subscription service aimed at programmers

Technet is the definitive knowledge base for bugs and issues for nearly every piece of software from Microsoft. It is a subscription service aimed at support professionals and comes on CD-ROM or DVD discs with monthly updates for as long as you keep the subscription going. The depth and quality of the information really needs to be seen to be believed, but there is a catch—the price tag. At several hundred dollars a year, this isn't for everyone. If you are supporting a large number of PCs in a business environment, this is certainly for you (especially if you can get your boss to pay for it). If you make a living from fixing other people's PCs, this kind of information will be invaluable.

However, if you are a home user and have only one PC to look after, this kind of subscription service is probably overkill. Think of it as you would when buying a dictionary. For most people (myself included), the abridged or concise dictionary is good enough and contains all the words you'll ever need to look up. These kinds of dictionaries are cheap and easy to find. However, if you are a language professor or historian, you would certainly need to have one that is more detailed, which is where the unabridged or complete version comes in. These are far more specialized and cost an awful lot more!

Are Subscription Services Worth the Cost?

This is the $64 million question! And the answer is "it depends." Much of the information that you find in, say, Technet is freely available on the Internet, and all you have to do is look for it. However, it's not in the same handy format and not as easy or quick to search. You can carry the CDs around with you and access the information in places where you might not have an Internet connection. Again, this is very handy. It could also be said that because you get so much (dozens of CDs with monthly updates), it's hard to know where to look. After all, there's no better place to hide information than in more information! You do need to make sure that you keep track of the updates and take care not to lose any of the discs too, especially if you are moving a lot from one place to another.

The main downside is still cost. If you don't have enough problems so that the service pays for itself, it's probably not for you. You would be better off using web searches and probably making a few support calls (even paid-for support) each year.

 NOTE *Working your way through parts of a subscription service database can be very educational indeed, which might in itself be enough to justify the cost.*

Giving Something Back

You've already seen that the Internet is a great research tool when it comes to computer problems. With billions of pages, there's a lot of information out there to sift through. But remember that a lot of this information is there because people have put it there. If you come across a problem and figure out a solution, consider doing the same. A simple web page or a newsgroup or forum post will do. By giving something back, you are helping others like yourself. What could be better than that!

Doctor's Notes

Which option you choose when you need help with a problem is, of course, entirely up to you. Nonetheless, I'd always recommend exhausting the free and low-cost options such as Internet searches before moving on to more costly methods. (Remember that for those who use dial-up and perhaps pay a per-minute charge for the call, the Internet is not a free option.)

Also, not knowing the solution to a problem doesn't mean you can't get a clear idea of what the problem is before trying to fix it. If you don't know what the problems are, you can't really go about fixing them! This is one place where doing a bit of research on the Net can come in handy.

Remember, if you have a problem, chances are, someone else has had it too!

Help Yourself Checklist

☑ Understand the warranty that came with your PC or peripheral and have a good idea of what your support options are.

☑ Know the difference between return to base and on-site warranty, and know which you have.

☑ Be aware of the downsides of sending your system back to the manufacturer.

☑ If possible, try to isolate the issue. It will save you time!

☑ When using a search engine, use specific search criteria.

☑ Evaluate whether a subscription service is worthwhile for you.

Chapter 6

What You Need to Fix-It-Yourself—and Stay Safe

There's no escaping the fact that a modern PC is an electrical device. And an electrical device plugs into the outlet sockets. As such, it demands a certain level of respect if you are to stay safe while working on it and remove the risk of electric shock. And it's not just you that can get damaged either; your computer can also suffer damage.

In this chapter we're going to take a look at the simple rules and precautions you need to follow so that everything goes according to plan and you (and your PC) stay safe.

Staying Safe Checklist

Just because your computer is an electrical device doesn't mean that it is unsafe to work on. All you need to do is to follow a few simple rules:

- Golden rule of PC repair: if in any doubt, don't! Don't take risks or do something you are uncertain about. Not only can you damage yourself (even permanently!) but you can also damage your PC.
  Stop. Think. Research a bit more, and then come back to it later once you're ready.

- Never take chances!

- Always disconnect your system before beginning work. This includes disconnecting it from a UPS (uninterrupted power supply) device (or other battery backup system that you may have installed) that takes over in the event of a power cut or power dip. These systems deliver house current electricity and can kill!

- Never dismantle monitors (more on this in a moment).

- Work in a clear area, away from children and pets.

- Keep liquids (coffee, cola, cleaning fluids, and so on) well away from the work area. In fact, it's always better to keep liquids away from your PC at all times.

 PC DOCTOR'S ORDER! *Don't go about deliberately creating steam though, as condensation is harmful.*

■ Be organized. Get the tools you need and put them within easy reach (more on tools in a moment). Get little containers for screws ready to prevent loss (more on this too!). Get a pencil or a pen as well as paper to make notes on (connector locations, orientations, and so on). (A note about pens: plastic is better in case you drop it into the system. Metal pens, because of their weight and the fact that they conduct electricity, can cause a lot of damage to a system.) Small sticky labels are also useful to have handy.

■ Don't wear loose clothing, as it can catch on components and cables and cause damage.

■ If you have long hair, tie it back and keep it out of the way.

■ If possible, take off rings and jewelry such as necklaces or earrings that might fall into a PC. If you can't (or don't want to) take off your rings, cover them completely with a strip of insulating tape.

■ Keep small items away from the PC. A small screw or a paperclip left in the system can cause massive, expensive damage the instant the system is switched on.

 FIX-IT-YOURSELF HOME REMEDY *A good way to keep track of small items is to stick them into a blob of modeling clay or plasticine.*

Figure 6-1 shows an example of a workspace before reading PC Doctor; Figure 6-2 shows it after.

Leave the Monitors to Experts

There aren't many areas of a PC where I'll tell you not to investigate, but the monitor is one you must leave alone.

If you have any problems with your computer monitor, I suggest you unplug it and take it to a reputable professional who knows how to protect against the risks. The next section describes the reasons why.

 WARNING *Only a trained professional using the right equipment should ever attempt to work inside a computer monitor.*

FIGURE 6-1   Work area "before" the PC Doctor treatment

FIGURE 6-2   Work area "after" the PC Doctor treatment

Monitor Dangers

Here are some of the reasons why you should not consider opening the case on a monitor to attempt any repair or even to take a look inside at what it contains:

- Monitors are very dangerous. Even monitors that are unplugged can still hold lethal levels of electrical charge. Worse still, they can hold these lethal charges for days after being unplugged. Specialist knowledge and equipment is needed to deal with this charge safely.

- When inside a monitor there is an ever-present risk of breaking the glass CRT (cathode ray tube). The glass that makes up the CRT is very thick at the front end (the bit you look at), but the other end is thin, delicate, and easily damaged. Since the tube contains a partial vacuum, breaking the tube will result in a violent implosion of the tube, which presents a significant risk of injury from flying glass.

- Breaking the tube poses a risk of injury not only from the glass, but also from the chemicals that it contains. A CRT contains large amounts of lead and other toxic chemicals that, while the tube is sealed, pose no health risks. However, this changes when the tube is broken.

- A monitor doesn't contain any user-serviceable parts anyway, so you might as well leave it alone!

 PC DOCTOR'S ORDER! *Dispose of old, broken, or unwanted monitors responsibly. If you have an old monitor that still works but you want to get rid of it, ask around in case someone else wants it before you dispose of it. Also, if you have the space, consider keeping it. You never know when you might need a spare!*

Handling Devices Safely

Working on a computer doesn't just pose a risk to you; you also pose a significant risk to the computer's well-being. This risk comes from the invisible, normally harmless, electrical charge that we can carry about with us. This is a risk from static electricity.

What Is Static Electricity?

Static electricity is a type of electric charge. It is generated by one material rubbing against something else.

At its grandest scale, static electricity gives rise to enormous lightning storms. Before a lightning storm, static charge is generated by air molecules brushing against other air molecules. The static charge builds up until it gets so big that the spark jumps from the clouds to the ground, where it is discharged (or *grounded*), releasing millions of volts.

 NOTE *A single lightning bolt has enough electrical power to run a 100-watt electric bulb for more than three months.*

The human body also generates static, albeit not on the same grand scale as that of a lightning storm. Just walking across a room with synthetic carpeting can generate a static charge in excess of 25,000 volts. You will carry this charge around on your body until you are grounded and the charge is dissipated. Normally, this charge is harmlessly lost to the environment, quietly and without your ever knowing it, although there are times when you might feel it as a small spark. This is known as an electro-static discharge, or ESD, and this type of discharge occurs harmlessly all the time around us. However, damage can be caused if this electrical charge is discharged into an electrical component.

ESD (Electro-Static Discharge)

ESD is a fast, silent, invisible killer of PC components. Most people don't give this threat much thought as they carry out upgrades and repairs to their systems—not because they like taking chances, but because they don't understand ESD and what causes it. ESD is real, and you need to take it very seriously each and every time you open a PC case.

ESD is just like lightning, only on a very small scale. An ESD is caused by a buildup of static electricity on one object discharging to ground through another object. Without a buildup of static electricity, the discharge itself cannot occur.

The ESDs we are concerned with differ from lightning in two ways. First, the power in a bolt of lightning is much greater than that in an ESD. Also, instead of a spark traveling between the ground and the clouds, the spark travels between you and components within the PC. These discharges might be on a very small scale— so small that you probably won't feel them—but these high-voltage sparks can easily damage delicate electronic devices.

There are two ways that static charge can build up to the point where an ESD becomes a danger:

■ Anything that moves or rubs against anything else has the potential to generate static electricity, which could result in ESD. The list of things around us that generate static is endless, including common household appliances such as motors and brushes in vacuum cleaners or the pumps and motors of refrigerators, as well as your own feet moving on the floor.

■ A spark resulting from a poor electrical connection or an unshielded or damaged cable is also a form of ESD.

When an object charged with static electricity (for example, a person) comes close to a grounded object (the PC), this massive charge can be discharged through it to ground. There are many routes that this surge can take. The most common, and fortunately safe, route to ground is via the metal chassis or case of the PC. The charge difference between the person and the PC is equalized and the danger removed. However, internal components can provide just as good, albeit destructive, routes to ground. This surge of power is what is damaging to electrical equipment.

You don't need a large amount of movement to generate enough static to cause a destructive ESD. Something as simple as sliding components over a surface, especially plastics and Styrofoam, can be enough to damage them.

Weather also plays a major part. An ESD is most likely to occur in cold, dry air because the conditions best insulate you from gradually dissipating the charge before it builds up to high levels. When air humidity is greater than 50 percent, an ESD is unlikely to occur.

Symptoms of ESD Damage

Because ESD damage occurs silently and without warning, the symptoms of such a discharge are the only indication you could have that one has occurred.

Here are some of the most common symptoms:

■ A new component/replacement doesn't work.

■ You've just carried out an upgrade/repair and a previously working component is no longer working.

■ A new component (or components) fails within one to two years of installation.

Why Is ESD Damaging?

To show you why ESD is bad for computer components, compare the voltages involved:

- The typical PC component runs on between 3 and 12 volts.

- Zap a component with as little as 30 volts of ESD, and there's a very good chance that it has sustained damage that will dramatically shorten its life.

- You can easily generate over 1000 volts just by walking on carpeting.

- You won't feel the tingle of an ESD unless the charge is greater than 2500 to 3000 volts. At this level the chance of permanent damage to electronic components is very high.

- To see an ESD spark (of the type that you see when shaking nylon clothing from the dryer), the charge needs to be 20,000 volts or greater. ESDs on this scale can be very damaging and cause instant component failure.

Is ESD Dangerous to You?

The short and simple answer is no, you are not in danger from ESD. Why then are 25,000 volts contained in a monitor lethal, whereas 25,000 volts of ESD are not? It's not the volts that are dangerous to us, but the amps. A monitor can deliver several amps of current, whereas the strongest ESD spark will be less than a thousandth of an amp. Put another way, 1 amp from house current (120V AC) can be lethal, but the microamps of current from a 25,000V DC ESD are not.

Preventing ESD

By knowing how the buildup of static electricity happens and why an ESD occurs, you can begin to take precautions against damage from it. The easiest way to protect your equipment from ESD is to wear an antistatic wrist strap whenever you are working inside a PC (see Figure 6-3). You wear one end of the strap around your wrist and the other end attached to a good grounding point.

Good grounding points for wrist straps include

- The metal chassis of the PC (near the power supply, well away from the motherboard).

- A water pipe or radiator. Make sure it is bare metal. Paint, grease, and corrosion act as insulators, preventing the discharge from grounding.

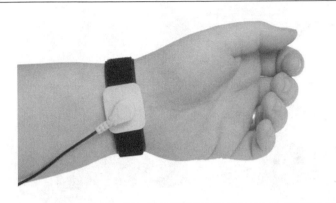

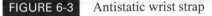

FIGURE 6-3   Antistatic wrist strap

Wearing a wrist strap has two advantages: it safely discharges any static charge you have accumulated, while preventing you from accumulating further buildup. Wrist straps are the cheapest and most effective solution to ESD.

Minimizing ESD Dangers

In addition to wearing a wrist strap, there are other steps you can take to reduce the dangers of ESD:

■ Eliminate the risk of causing a spark from a short by removing all rings, bracelets, and dangling necklaces. If you have a ring that you can't or don't want to remove (such as a wedding ring), cover it well with insulating tape.

■ Handle components as little as possible. Don't touch components unnecessarily. Never handle components by their contacts or any components attached to their circuit boards. Figure 6-4 shows an example of how to handle a circuit board.

■ If you want to clean components, never wipe them, brush them, or point vacuum cleaners near them, as these can induce ESD. The best and safest way to clean components is to use canned compressed air.

 PC DOCTOR'S ORDER! *Avoid air from compressors. This air is usually contaminated with oil and fine metallic particles and can be so powerful that it will break components.*

FIGURE 6-4   Proper circuit board handling

■ Because an ESD is much more likely to occur when the humidity is below 50 percent, one way to reduce the risk if you live in a dry air region is to invest in a humidifier. Keeping the humidity at or above 50 percent almost completely eliminates the risks of ESD.

 FIX-IT-YOURSELF HOME REMEDY *Keeping the humidity of the room you work in at 50 percent is perfectly safe for your PC. Don't, however, push the humidity too high to the point that you get condensation forming on surfaces, as this can cause electrical equipment to short out.*

■ Dust is another factor that affects ESDs. Buildup of dust on components allows static charges to accumulate faster and to greater levels of charge. Therefore, keeping PCs clean and the dust down to a minimum will not only improve air circulation and therefore cooling, but also reduce the potential for ESDs.

■ If you do a lot of PC repair and upgrading, you might consider investing in an antistatic work mat. For total static protection, you could get an antistatic workstation, ensuring complete protection from ESD. These stations make working on a PC much easier and offer you a good grounding point for your wrist strap too. This kind of ESD prevention doesn't come cheap, but if you do a lot of repairs, it might be a worthwhile investment.

Keep in mind that you are not the only one who can damage things with ESD. Electronic equipment is sensitive to ESD throughout its life, all the way from the factory floor to the point it is installed in your system. Most new components sold are protected by antistatic bags, sometimes called ESD-proof bags or Faraday bags (after the scientist Michael Faraday). These bags are made from a special foil, and some have a crisscross grid of black lines on the outside. They work by giving any ESD an alternative, easy path to flow. Instead of the charge surging into the sensitive device, it flows harmlessly along the outside of the bag, shielding the contents from the effects. Figure 6-5 shows a hard drive protected inside an antistatic bag. For best protection, keep the end of the bag folded over while stored. If you are sold RAM, CPUs, expansion cards, or hard drives that aren't properly protected, refuse them, as they might have suffered invisible damage from ESD that has rendered them useless or, worse still, reduced their operational life span (so they might outlive their warranty, but not much more).

FIGURE 6-5   Hard drive in antistatic bag

WARNING *Never power up a device—for example, a motherboard or hard drive—while it is on or near an antistatic bag. The surfaces of these bags are conductive, and doing this can electrically overload a device instantly, damaging components which either instantly disable the device in question or contribute to shortening of its life.*

ESD Myths

Many myths surround ESD and the ways to protect from its damaging effects. Let's examine a few of the most common myths you may have heard or read elsewhere.

Myth 1   If you handle components by the edges and avoid contact with pins and electrical contacts, there is no risk from ESD.

FALSE: ESD sparks don't only jump from your fingertips; your whole body is charged. Brushing an arm near the motherboard can cause a spark to jump. ESD can damage components you don't think you have touched!

Myth 2   Touching the PC case discharges all the static buildup you have collected and eliminates any further risk of ESD.

FALSE: This certainly reduces the risk initially, but remember that as you move around, your clothes and carpeting could be building up more static charge, ready for another discharge.

NOTE *Although some people find that touching the PC case is effective, I cannot recommend this as a way to prevent ESD. It is not foolproof, and when you compare the low cost of an antistatic wrist strap (a few dollars) to the cost of damage that ESD could cause (several hundred dollars if you lose a motherboard or video card), it's just not worth the risk.*

Myth 3   Antistatic carpet treatments can help eliminate the risk from ESD.

FALSE: If you work on PCs often, it's a good idea to treat the carpet in your work area with an antistatic carpet spray. It won't offer complete protection, but it may help, especially if you live in a dry climate. Using fabric softener on your clothes also helps because it is designed to reduce static cling. But don't fool yourself into thinking that either of these solutions will come even close to the effectiveness of wearing an antistatic wrist strap.

Myth 4   Placing components on top of ESD bags is as good as keeping them inside the bag.

FALSE: By placing components on top of an ESD bag, you are actually placing them in greater danger than if the bag wasn't there at all! ESD bags work by diverting any ESD "spark" along the outside of the bag, protecting the space inside the bag, and any components it contains. For the best defense against ESD damage, keep all components inside the ESD bag until you need them.

 FIX-IT-YOURSELF HOME REMEDY *Keep any bags you come across for future use; then you can reuse them for storage of components that are no longer in use, or during troubleshooting.*

Myth 5   Having more than one component inside an antistatic bag renders it useless.

FALSE: As long as the end of the bag can be folded over, the bag will protect any components inside from ESD. However, by having more than one component in a bag, you still run the risk of one component damaging the other by impact.

Checklist for Preventing ESD

1. Buy and always wear an antistatic wrist strap. Make sure it is connected to a good grounding point, such as the chassis of the PC.

2. Keep components inside antistatic bags until you need them.

3. Never handle components unnecessarily. When you do have to handle anything, do so carefully, avoiding electrical contacts and delicate components. Never drag or slide components over any surface.

4. Keep static-causing surfaces such as plastics and Styrofoam away from the work area.

5. If possible, keep the air warm and the humidity above 50 percent.

6. If there is a risk of ESD, avoid wearing synthetic clothing if possible.

7. Keep dust to a minimum.

8. Only use clean, canned compressed air and a soft bristle brush to clean inside the PC case.

9. Make sure that all contacts and connections are done up firmly before switching the system on.

The final message is this: never take chances when it comes to ESD. Prevention is not only simpler, but also much cheaper than curing the damage that ESD can cause.

Tools of the Trade

Having the right tools makes any job easier, and PC upgrading and repair is no different. Using the right tools is not only quicker and easier, but also safer for both yourself and your PC.

You don't need a whole workshop full of tools in order to work on your PC; in fact, you only really need a handful. Here is a list of the basic tools you need to have before you begin work:

- Screwdrivers—both straight edged and crosspoint (also known as a Phillips). It is best if they are nonmagnetic to eliminate the risk of damage (not just from the magnet, which is a minimal risk, but the greater, more real risk of impact damage to components caused by objects being magnetically attracted to the head of the screwdriver.
  The sizes that you'll probably need are as follows:
  Crosspoint: No1 and No2
  Straight edged: 2.5, 5, and 6
  For convenience, you might prefer to get a multibit screwdriver that contains a set of bits with all the head sizes.

- Antistatic wrist strap.

- Small pliers—needle nosed are best.

- Tweezers for picking up dropped screws and other bits. Shown in Figure 6-6 is a small "grabber" for small items (the plastic item that looks like a syringe). These are handy for retrieving dropped bits from awkward places.

- Container for little screws. Plastic film canisters are good for this, but you can buy small clear plastic boxes with snap-lids specifically for this purpose. They are shown in the sample toolkit in Figure 6-6.

Along with these basics, here is a list of a few other useful items for your toolkit:

- Wire cutters/stripper. You won't be doing much wire cutting and stripping, but this may come in handy for tasks such as putting in place network cable or rewiring electric plugs.

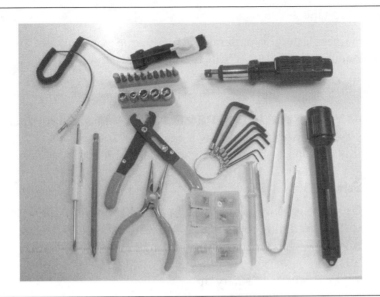

FIGURE 6-6   A toolkit with the necessities—and a few extras

- Torx bits/screwdrivers. Some of the things on/inside your PC might be held on with Torx head screws. Torx head screwdrivers have a six-pointed star shaped head and come in a variety of sizes.
  The most common sizes for PC users are T-6, T-8, T-10, T-15, T-20, and T-25 (from smallest to largest).

- Small socket set. Small nuts and bolts are common on some PC cases. Handy sizes to have are 1/4, 5/16, 11/32, and 3/8.
  These sockets can either fit on the end of a screwdriver or a small ratchet from a socket set.

- A set of small Allen keys. Allen keys are like Torx bits but hexagonal. Good sizes are 3/32, 7/64, 1/8, 9/64, 5/32, 3/16, 7/32, and 1/4.

- A multimeter for measuring resistance and voltages. A digital or analog multimeter will do.

- Electrical outlet testing screwdriver, so you can test to make sure the power is off!

- Plastic ties. These are very handy for tying back loose cables and keeping the inside of the PC tidy.

- Insulating tape.

- A container flashlight (preferably a plastic one as metal ones are heavy and can conduct electricity—a bad combination around PCs).

- Soft cloth.

 FIX-IT-YOURSELF HOME REMEDY *Never throw away a screw, nut, or bolt. You never know when you might need a spare.*

Workshop Safety

OK, you might not be working on your PC in a workshop (it might be the kitchen counter, office desk, or dining room table), and working on a PC is not exactly car repair, which carries with it some significant dangers, but PC repair isn't without dangers to the DIYer!

Here is a quick rundown of safety tips:

- **Eyes** Medical science is a wonderful thing, but repairing broken eyes is neither easy nor guaranteed and quite definitely not pain free. Even though you are not grinding or cutting things, there is still a significant risk of eye damage from flying springs or accidentally hitting your eye against a sharp corner or burred edge.
PCs also have a lot of dust in them that is easily made airborne; so rather than risk a foreign object in the eye, it's better to protect your eyes with a decent pair of safety goggles.

- **Lungs** Again, hard to repair if you damage them. Computers can be very dusty, and this will affect some people more than others.
If you have allergies such as asthma, rhinitis, or hay fever, you might want to consider wearing a dust mask—the kind designed to protect while sanding, for sale in most hardware stores.

- **Skin** Great stuff—soft, supple, and semipermeable. It is also strong until it reaches a breaking point, whereupon it leaks.
Sharp edges and corners of a PC case can easily cut. Small bits of wire can puncture the skin and be very painful. Care is what is needed here, as well as checking the case for sharp edges in advance.
There are no parts of the human body that are resistant to heat. Take care when working on a PC that was turned on for some time prior to

working on it. Better to give the system 10 minutes to cool down before beginning work.

The dust that a PC picks up is also an irritant and can affect some people more than others. If you are affected by this, consider thin rubber gloves or barrier cream.

Loose clothing and long hair can and will snag. Usually it snags on the most expensive component or fastest moving fan possible. Keep loose hair and clothes well out of the way.

Doctor's Notes

In this chapter we've looked at the tools you need to work on your PC and how to work on it safely. Having the proper tools makes any job you have to do a lot easier and reduces the risk of damaging screws, bolts, and other fasteners.

Nothing is worth risking life and limb over, which is why this chapter has a heavy emphasis on safety—safety for you and safety for your PC.

Bear in mind the golden rule:

"If in doubt—Don't!"

Stay Safe Checklist

☑ Disconnect a PC from the power supply before starting work on it

☑ Double check that it is disconnected—remember that there may be a battery backup device that delivers power to the PC in the event of a power failure.

☑ Never take chances—EVER!

☑ Never work on monitors—EVER!

☑ Get a good quality toolkit.

☑ Keep your work area tidy.

☑ Take steps to protect the system from damage resulting from ESD. As a minimum always wear an antistatic wrist strap.

☑ Keep all components inside the antistatic bags they come in until they are needed.

☑ Never touch any of the electronic components on devices—always handle them by edges.

Part II

The Details: Hardware

Chapter 7

The PC Case and the
Power Supply

Apart from the monitor, the case will be the part of the PC that you look at the most (well, that and the keyboard, if you happen to be a bad typist!). It's also the bit you are going to have to get inside of before you can carry out any work on your system.

Besides housing the main components of the PC, the case also contains the power supply unit (PSU). Usually cases come complete with a PSU installed, which is why I cover the case and the PSU in a single chapter.

Function of a PC Case

The case might seem like an insignificant part of the system—almost cosmetic you might think—but it plays several vital roles:

- The first and most obvious is that the case keeps all the components together, making a PC one box rather than a collection of parts—obvious but vital.

- Second, the case serves to protect the components from dirt, dust, and damage from impact and static discharge.

- The case is also a vital part of the PC cooling system. A well-designed case will provide adequate air intakes as well as airflow around the components. To help this, it might come with fans that draw in cold air and exhaust the warm air out of the system.

If you already have a PC, you'll have little choice over the case, but that doesn't stop you from replacing the case with a better one if you feel your PC might benefit from it, or if you have run out of space for additional drives or hardware.

Case Types

Cases come in a staggering variety of sizes and styles. Beginning at the basics, you have three common types of case:

- **The desktop**   This is the horizontal case that stands flat on the desk. These cases take up a lot of desk space and aren't as common nowadays as they were a few years back.

- **The minitower** This case stands on end vertically to save on the amount of desk real estate that the computer needs. The minitower, shown in Figure 7-1, is now the most common case configuration for a PC.

- **The tower** This is the same as the minitower, only taller and capable of holding more drives. Because it is bigger, the tower is easier to work on than the minitower.

If you are fortunate enough to be in the position of choosing a case, you will benefit greatly from choosing the best case that your budget allows for. What follows is a look at some of the important features of PC cases and how to get the best.

Case style isn't the only thing you can choose. There are literally hundreds of colors and styles to choose from. But color and style are cosmetic. If you are choosing a new case for your system, here are a few things to look out for:

- Is the case big enough for your needs? Will it hold all your drives as well as have room for future upgrades (such as more drives).

FIGURE 7-1   Minitower with outer metal skin removed

PC DOCTOR'S ORDER! *Remember that the bigger the case, the easier it will be to work inside the PC, especially if you have big hands.*

■ What types of drive bays are available? How many have front access for CD and DVD drives, and how many are internal for hard drives?

■ If at all possible, take a look inside the case and check for any sharp edges or, worse still, metal burrs left over from the manufacturing process. If you see these, don't buy the case! Not only are the kind of cuts that you'll get from them nasty, but blood inside the system won't do the electrical components any good either. Figure 7-2 shows an example of a well finished case.

 PC DOCTOR'S ORDER! *Don't think that wanting a well-finished case is being soft or that you can tough out the sharp edges. Cutting yourself on the case could well mean that you damage expensive components with blood, or you might knock your hands against something delicate while pulling away quickly. A poorly finished case is a false economy.*

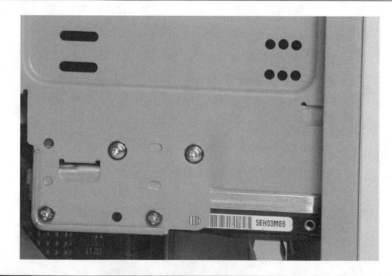

FIGURE 7-2   This case has nice rolled metal edges for safety.

- Take a close look at the inside of the case. Does the layout of the case allow good access to items such as RAM and the power connections? This is a hard thing to judge if you don't have the motherboard installed, but try to visualize the layout.

- Are you getting a full set of spares and fixings with your new case? A good-quality case will come with screws for drives and the motherboards as well as spare screws and a few spare slot covers. You'll need these at some point, so make sure you have them!

- PCs are noisy things—lots of moving parts and fans going. Because more and more people have their PC in their living room but they dislike the noise from them, there is a big market in sound-reducing cases for PCs. These have sound insulation built into the sides and also low-noise fans. Don't expect miracles though. Your PC will be a lot quieter after you've changed the case for a sound-reducing case, but it's not going to make it completely silent.

 FIX-IT-YOURSELF HOME REMEDY *If you want the quietest PC possible, you will need to replace a lot more than the case. Other sources of noise are the case and CPU fans as well as the PSU fan. Also, the hard drives are a significant source of noise, and these can be made quieter by using sound-insulated drive covers (although these do run the risk of causing your drive to overheat and usually come with temperature-sensitive paper for you to keep an eye out for problems). No matter what lengths you go to, your PC is unlikely to become totally silent, but it will be noticeably quieter.*

Removing the Case

Sometimes the hardest part of carrying out an upgrade can be taking the case apart so that you can get inside to work. Sometimes it's easy, and sometimes it's a major headache, and there is no "right way" to get it done. However, if you look closely enough at the case, you should be able to figure it out.

 PC DOCTOR'S ORDER! *The following applies only to desktops, minitowers and towers and not notebooks or laptops.*

Here's what to look for:

- First off, safety! Make the PC safe by unplugging it from the power.

- Next, check the manual. This may seem obvious, but many people overlook it. Most manuals should tell you how to open the case.

- Check out the top and sides of the case. Is it made of one piece of sheet metal, or is it several plastic bits?

- If it's a one-piece metal sheet, look at the back for several screws that hold the sides of the case onto the main metal chassis of the PC, as shown in Figure 7-3. Loosen these screws and see if the sides/top of the case will begin to slide backwards. (Place your hand on the top of the case and push back, as shown in Figure 7-4). There should be no need for levering to get the exterior off, but you might find it useful to use a flat-headed screwdriver to lever at the joints gently.

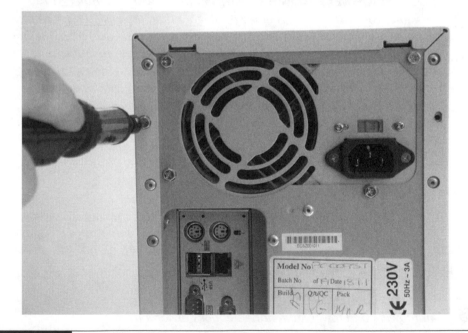

FIGURE 7-3   This case has the screws holding the outer metal skin in place on the rear.

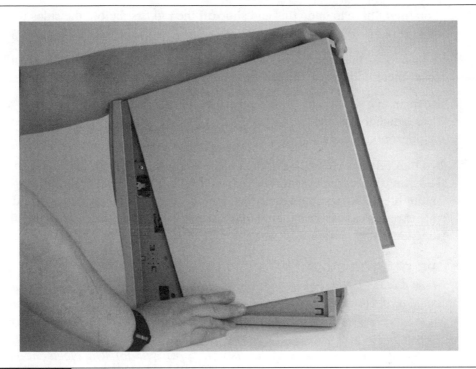

FIGURE 7-4 Outer case skin slides back to expose the interior

PC DOCTOR'S ORDER! *Be careful to undo screws that go through the metal of the side sheet. There may be other screws on the back that hold the power supply and other parts in place, and if you undo the wrong ones, you might damage the interior. If you are unsure, undo the screws only slightly and test to see if it is having the desired effect. Use gentle levering to loosen the case—hammering and excessive prying can be very bad for the system!*

■ If the case is plastic or you cannot find screws at the back of the case that hold it together, you will have to look elsewhere. Underneath is one possibility. You might find two or three screws underneath the case that hold the sides on, and if you undo these, you'll be able to lift the sides off.

■ Sometimes you'll find one screw on the back of the case that is used to hold the top piece of the case on that acts as a strengthener for the sides.

You might have to undo this and slide off the top first before the sides will slide off.

■ Take a look for any thumbscrews on the case. On many of the high-quality cases there will just be the one holding it together.

■ Keep an eye out for any Torx screws too. Some manufacturers use these to discourage the owners from opening the cases! To tackle these you'll need an appropriate screwdriver or bit.

■ No luck? Take a close look at the plastic front of the case. See if you can slip your fingers underneath the plastic front and pull it off. Be gentle, as it might break; but on some cases you pull the front fascia off the case, and this exposes case screws that hold the top/side on. Undo these and slide the top/side off by pulling it forward.

 PC DOCTOR'S ORDER! *Take care when working with plastic parts, as they can be easily broken or screw threads stripped. If you do accidentally strip a plastic thread, a good repair might be fashioned using epoxy resin adhesive. Apply liberally to the stripped screw thread and then gently screw in the screw after giving it a quick spray with a lubricant (any automotive water displacing/lubricating spray will do). The lubricant on the thread prevents the epoxy from binding too tightly to the screw threads.*

■ If you're still not sure, take another look at the case as a whole. Look at how it is put together and try to figure out what each of the screws does. Try to look at the case logically and with the idea that no matter how difficult it is to undo, it does in fact come apart! Check all the visible screws and also tug on the plastic panels to see if they move. Use a flashlight to help you see better.

■ If you are totally stuck, contact your system manufacturer for advice, although I doubt that you'll need to do this.

Spring Cleaning the Inside of the Case

Once you get inside the case, the first thing you'll notice (if you haven't already been in there) is just how dusty and dirty the interior of a PC can get. Don't be alarmed if you find quite literally a carpet of dust covering the bottom of the case and also all the components inside. This needs cleaning, as it can cause overheating of components and increase the risk of electro-static discharge.

Cleaning the System

If you've had the system for some time and you are opening it for the first time, you are likely to discover a layer of dust—much more than you would normally expect to find in a home. (Your TV and stereo will also collect similar levels of dust around them, but more than likely you'll be cleaning that away on a regular basis.)

WARNING *Treat this carpet of dust with respect. If you have allergies, this type of dust is likely to aggravate them, so wear a dust mask (the kind sold in DIY stores for woodworking) and rubber gloves. (The thin "surgeon" style ones are the best because they offer excellent protection along with greater sensitivity in your fingers and a high level of manual dexterity.) Even if you aren't allergic to dust, reduce your exposure to it because it can cause skin irritation and sensitivity in many people. Avoid direct inhalation too because this can cause respiratory irritation. Make sure you wash exposed skin thoroughly after finishing or before eating or drinking.*

Cleaning—the Tools

Before you can start cleaning your system, you need the right tools. Here's what I recommend:

- Tools to get the case open

- ESD protection (wrist strap will suffice)

- Clean, lint-free cloths. Cotton is by far the best. Avoid synthetics as they increase the chances of ESD.

- Vacuum cleaner. Find the crevice tool; it will be useful.

- Can of compressed air. These are sold by office suppliers and in computer shops.

PC DOCTOR'S ORDER! *Don't use air from a compressor. Not only will it be far too powerful and you run the risk of damaging the system, but it is also likely to be contaminated with oil and metal particles, exactly the wrong thing to add to a working system.*

- Dust sheet to lay over the work area to make cleanup easier.

Cleaning—the Steps

Here are the steps for clearing your system of accumulated dust. These steps might seem long, involved, and complicated, but by doing the job this way, you do it right and keep the mess down to a minimum. The more often you clean your PC, the cleaner it will be and the less mess there will be.

1. Get everything you need for the job. Check that you have air in the compressed air can.

2. Protect your skin with rubber gloves (or barrier cream), and wear a dust mask if you need to.

3. Cover the work area with a dust sheet. Doing this now will save you a lot of effort cleaning up later.

4. Disconnect the system and open the case (taking all the necessary ESD precautions).

5. Wipe the bare metal surfaces with your cloths to pick up as much of the dust as you can. Remember to do the inside of the case lid too!

6. Now carefully use the vacuum cleaner, and with the crevice tool, get into all the nooks and crannies in the system. Keep yourself wired to a good ground using your antistatic wrist strap throughout, as this will dissipate any static charge buildup in the vacuum cleaner itself.

7. Clean the CPU fan (and any other small fans in the system) by giving them a short blast with the compressed air. Figure 7-5 shows a typical fan.

 PC DOCTOR'S ORDER! *Don't handle any of the small fans in the system (CPU fan, chipset fan, fans on graphics card), as they can be easily damaged. This doesn't include case fans, which, if you handle carefully, you can easily clean.*

8. If the system has fans in the case, it is likely that they and the air intakes/ exhausts are filthy. Remove the fans (either by squeezing the plastic body of the fans to detach them or unscrewing them from the case). Carefully give the fan blades a good wipe and clean the air holes in the case.

9. Now, using your compressed air, clean off the motherboard and other circuit boards. If the expansion cards are badly covered, remove them for

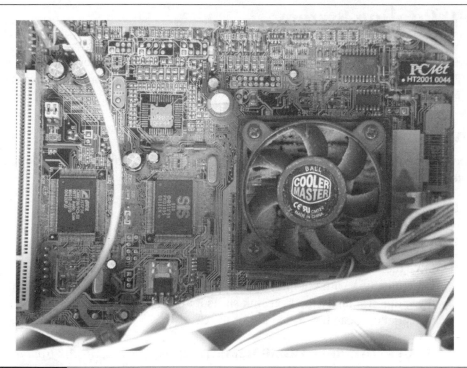

FIGURE 7-5   Small fans collect a lot of dust, as well as spread it about the interior of the case.

cleaning with the compressed air. Use the vacuum cleaner (again, sporting the crevice tool) to catch the dust as it is being blown away.

10. Once you are happy with the job you've done (don't expect to be able to remove 100 percent of the dust on your first attempt), give the metal surfaces a final wipe down to pick up any escaped dust.

PC DOCTOR'S ORDER! *Never touch electronic parts while cleaning, and don't wipe expansion cards or the motherboard with a cloth to get the dust off, as this can trigger ESD.*

11. Reassemble the case.

12. Wrap up the dust sheet and clean up any escaped dust.

13. Wash your hands well.

The PC Cooling System

Cooling is vital to a PC. Run one without adequate airflow over the critical components and you will dramatically reduce its life span, possibly even destroying it. Making sure that your system has adequate flow of fresh air through the case is important to the good health of your system.

Giving the Cooling System the Once-Over

Next time you have the case open on your PC system, check out the PC's cooling system. Here's the right way to do this:

1. Clean all the fans (as detailed earlier).

2. Make sure that all the air inlets are clear of dirt, dust, and paper.

3. Give the CPU heat sink (the metal block that sits on top of the CPU) a good cleaning with compressed air. The CPU generates a lot of heat, and the more efficiently the heat sink shifts it away from the CPU into the air, the quicker it can be carried out of the case.

 FIX-IT-YOURSELF HOME REMEDY *Removing a heat sink from a processor without good cause (such as replacing it) is not generally recommended, as there can be a layer of special thermal paste or thermal grease between the CPU and the heat sink. If you need to remove the heat sink or are replacing it, make sure that you replace the thermal jointing compound; otherwise overheating can occur, causing serious damage to the CPU.*

4. Check that all the fans appear to be rotating; dust on them is a good sign. However, you can't trust this. The only way to check that fans are working is visually. With the case open, carefully plug the PC back into the outlet, switch it on, and look at the fans, (Use a flashlight, and make sure that you keep long hair, jewelry, and clothing well out of the way.)

5. Don't put your PC down on a carpeted floor, as this can increase the dust pulled into the system. Also, hair can enter the system and clog the fans by wrapping around the spindles.

6. When you've finished, place the case back in an area where it will have ample airflow around it. Give it 6–8 inches (15–20 cms) at the back and 12–18 inches (30–45 cms) at the sides.

7. Make sure that the air intakes and exhausts are kept free from papers and books.

Signs of Trouble with the Cooling System

If you have trouble with your PC's cooling system, don't ignore it. It is a serious problem that needs immediate attention. There are many signs of impending cooling trouble. Not all the following signs are unique to cooling trouble, but the cooling of the system should always be checked to make sure that it is functioning properly.

■ The PC is crashing or locking up after prolonged use. This is not unique to a cooling problem by far, but it warrants your checking the cooling.

■ Burning smells emanate from the system.

■ The case feels hot to the touch, or the air coming out of the system feels unusually hot.

■ Fans sound louder or quieter than usual. Check them for dirt, and clean if necessary. If they are noisy, the bearing may be worn out and the whole fan will need replacing.

■ Fans are not working (check visually when the case is open).

PC DOCTOR'S ORDER! *Never run a personal computer if the CPU fan or any other fan on the motherboard or graphics card is not working. Heat buildup can happen very quickly and cause permanent (and expensive) damage to the system.*

■ Excessive dust is visible around air intakes. Clean the case.

The system BIOS might, depending on type, give you information on the case temperature, CPU temperature, and motherboard temperature (see Chapter 8 for more details). Software (such as SpeedFan, shown in Figure 7-6) is also available that can give you a quick visual on system temperatures, but you need the right hardware to support it.

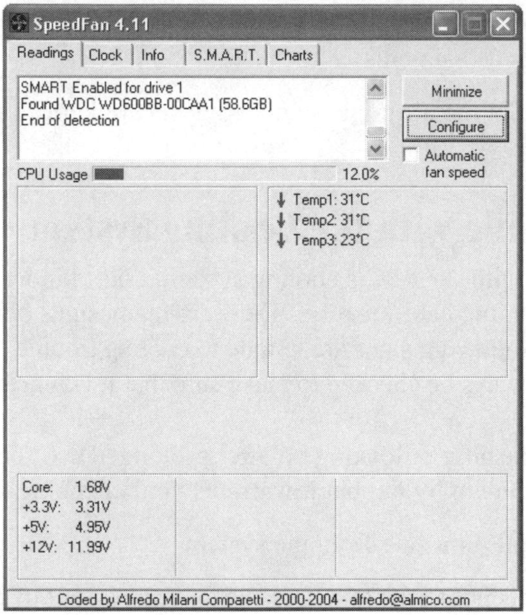

FIGURE 7-6   Software such as SpeedFan (http://www.almico.com/speedfan.php) can be useful to get a quick visual on system temperatures.

The system BIOS might also show you the speed of any fans running. However, if your motherboard doesn't have all the fans it can support installed, then some will show a speed of 0 RPM simply because of their absence.

Taking the System's Temperature

OK, how do you know that the system is overheating? Well, by taking its temperature! There are two main ways you can do this:

■ Use the system BIOS (as mentioned previously) to access the temperature sensors that are built onto the motherboard. This will give you temperature values for the CPU and, usually, the motherboard temperature and the internal case temperature.

■ Use a thermometer. Place a thermometer in the case (well out of the way of any moving parts or circuit boards). If you are worried that it is going to move about, tape it in place. Close the case and run the system normally for about 30 minutes to an hour. Then shut the system down, open the case quickly, and read the temperature. For safety, make sure that the thermometer you use goes high enough not to be damaged (100° C, 212° F). This will give you a general idea of the case temperature. If you can, splurge on an electronic thermometer with a sensor that you can place in the case and keep the display outside. Many of the high-end multimeters have this feature.

PC DOCTOR'S ORDER! *Take care great when using glass thermometers inside a PC. Make sure that they have a high enough temperature range to prevent damage to them, and handle them with care. Some thermometers contain the liquid metal mercury, which is both poisonous and electrically conductive. This means spills can be bad for both you and your PC.*

Case temperatures in excess of 50° C (122° F) are worthy of further investigation, while CPU temperatures in the region of 70–90° C (158–195° F), depending on the processor, should be investigated with an eye to reducing them.

FIX-IT-YOURSELF HOME REMEDY *Information on the appropriate temperature for your processor can be found on the relevant manufacturer's website (www.intel.com, www.amd.com). Take a look in their "datasheets" section under their products, and all the thermal specifications will be listed. However, if you stay in the regions specified above, you won't go wrong.*

Bear in mind that system temperature can vary based on the ambient air temperature as well as the amount of airflow into the room that the PC works in. Also, if the PC is in a sunny window, the summer temperatures will be higher still.

Improving the Cooling System

If your system is running too hot, don't panic! Just like pretty much anything else on your system, the cooling system can be upgraded.

1. First check that the case is complete and that there are no gaps or slot covers missing. Any gaps between case panels or missing slot covers can seriously disrupt the airflow inside a case. Remedy these issues and check the temperature again.

2. Give the system a good cleanup of the accumulated dust.

3. While you are cleaning the system, check that all the fans appear to be working. Replace any that appear to be defective.

If the problems persist, you'll need to take more direct action to cool the system and add new cooling hardware. There are a number of possible solutions, depending on the problem you are experiencing:

■ If the CPU is running hot, but the internal case temperature is low, you need to change the CPU cooling fan and possibly the heat sink for a more efficient one. There are many to choose from (both mail order and from computer stores). Make sure you get the right type for your CPU! After you have done this, check the temperature again. You should see a dramatic drop in CPU temperature. (If not, check that the new fan is working and that you remembered to apply the thermal jointing compound.)

 FIX-IT-YOURSELF HOME REMEDY *Improving the efficiency of the CPU cooling system might mean that you see an increase in the temperature inside the case.*

■ If you have a problem with a higher than acceptable case temperature and you've cleaned out all the air inlets/exhausts, you need to get more air flowing into and out of the case. You can upgrade the fans built into the case. (If there aren't any, you need a case that has them or at least has a housing for them.) You can also add an air exhaust card in the expansion slot. It will force hot air out of the system.

■ System drives also produce a lot of heat, and they can create hotspots inside the system case. This is usually only a problem in a system where you have more than one drive. (If you have two hard drives and two optical drives in a minitower, they are likely to be close together.) Adding a drive cooler (an aluminum chassis for the drive that acts as a massive heat sink, usually with fans at the front to draw in air over the drive) can help carry this heat away and dissipate the hotspot.

 PC DOCTOR'S ORDER! *Never drill holes in a system case to try and get better airflow. You are unlikely to achieve it, and it will allow more dirt to enter the system and possibly damage your case.*

Power Supply Unit (PSU)

Without a functioning power supply unit, your PC would just be an inert hunk of metal and plastic. The PSU gives the stuff of life to a PC—electrical power. The power supply converts the alternating current (AC) line from your home to the direct current (DC) needed by the personal computer.

The power supply unit is usually housed in a metal box in a corner of the case. It is visible from the back of many systems because it contains the power-cord socket at the back and the cooling fan. On the back of many PSUs is a small, red switch near the power-cord connector. This is used to change line voltages (115 volts and 230 volts) in various countries.

 PC DOCTOR'S ORDER! *Take care not to change the voltage selection switch. If you have small children around your PC, you might want to cover this switch with tape to discourage them from playing with it. An incorrect setting can damage the PSU or the PC itself.*

PSU Outputs

Power supply units, also sometimes called "switching power supplies," use switcher technology to transform the AC input to lower DC voltages. The typical output voltages supplied are

- 3.3 volts
- 5 volts
- 12 volts

The 3.3 volt and 5 volt supplies are normally used to power the digital circuits inside the PC, while the 12 volt power is used to run larger devices such as hard drives, floppy drives, and fans. The main specification of a power supply unit is measured in watts.

FIX-IT-YOURSELF HOME REMEDY *You can work out the power in watts by multiplying the voltage (measured in volts) and the current (measured in amperes, or amps).*

If you've had PCs for many years, you probably remember that in the early days, PCs had a large (usually red) switch on the back that you used to turn the system on and off. When you turned the PC on or off, you knew you were doing it. These switches actually controlled the flow of power to the power supply. When off, the power to the PSU was physically cut.

Today, you switch your PC on using a little push button, and you normally turn off the computer with a menu option in the operating system. The operating system can send a signal to the power supply to tell it to turn off. To turn it on, the push button switch sends a 5 volt power signal to the power supply to tell it when to turn on completely and start feeding power to the rest of the system. Interestingly, PSUs also contain a circuit that is always live (unless the system is disconnected or the power is turned off) that supplies 5 volts even when the system otherwise appears to be switched off, so that the on/off button or switch can work. This is called VSB, or standby voltage.

PC DOCTOR'S ORDER! *Shorting this standby voltage can cause significant damage to components inside your PC.*

Power Supply Connectors

The cables that come from a power supply unit nowadays all use standardized, keyed connectors at the ends of the output cables. This means that it is difficult, if not impossible, to connect the wrong cable to the wrong device. The presence of color-coded wires and industry-standard connectors means that it is possible for the consumer to have the widest possible choice when it comes to devices inside the PC as well as replacement power supplies.

Fan manufacturers often use the same connectors as the power cables for hard drives, allowing additional fans to be placed in the case, drawing the necessary 12 volts they need from either a spare hard drive cable or from a tap placed on an existing connection.

The output connectors on a PSU consist of:

- Motherboard power cables

- Hard drive power cables

- Floppy drive power cables

Advanced Power Management (APM) and Advanced Configuration and Power Interface (ACPI)

When you hear about power and power supply units in modern computers, you might also come across the terms Advanced Power Management (APM) and Advanced Configuration and Power Interface (ACPI). APM is a technology that was developed by Microsoft and Intel to make PCs use less power and make them both more economically and more environmentally friendly. APM, however, isn't just a feature of the PSU; the operating system, basic input/output system (BIOS), motherboard, and attached devices all need to be APM compliant to be able to use this feature. ACPI differs from APM because it is controlled by the operating system and not the BIOS. This has advantages in that the operating system can take control of the system, freeing that responsibility from the BIOS, and the settings and options are more available to the end user.

Power management offers a set of five different states that your system can be in:

- **Ready**   The system is fully powered up and ready to use.

- **Standby**   A state that the PC enters after a preset period of inactivity of the CPU or devices (such as hard drive or peripherals). However, moving the mouse or using the keyboard reawakens the system. While the system is in standby, all data and settings are preserved. If you have a program open containing, say, an unsaved word processor document, when the PC comes out of standby, the document will still be onscreen in the same state it was before the system entered standby.

- **Suspended**   A PC in a suspended state is in the lowest level of power consumption available that still preserves operational data and parameters. The suspended state can be initiated by either the system BIOS or software. The system BIOS may place your computer into the suspended state without notification if it detects a situation that requires an immediate response, such as the battery entering a critically low power state (in the case of a laptop).

■ **Hibernation**   Hibernation saves the complete state of the computer to a file on the hard drive and turns off the power. The computer appears to be completely switched off. Hibernation is the lowest-power sleeping state available, and the system and the data are secure from power outages. When you switch the system back on, it comes back to the exact state that it was in when you turned it off. This kind of start-up can take longer and needs extra hard drive space to store the hibernation files on it.

■ **Off**   When in the off state, your computer is powered down and inactive. The data and settings may or may not be preserved in the off state, depending on whether they were saved or not.

A Question of Power

The only real measure of a PSU (apart from the form factor or type, which refers to the kind of motherboard it supports) is the power output of it, measured in watts. The greater the watts, the more internal devices it can power. However, a bigger PSU (in terms of watts) does not mean a waste of power. A 400 watt switching power supply will not necessarily use more power than a 250 watt supply.

You might find yourself needing a larger PSU if you use every available slot on the motherboard or every available drive bay in the personal computer case. Also, never push a PSU to the limit. It is not advisable to have a 250 watt PSU if you have 250 watts total in devices, since the supply should not be loaded to 100 percent of its capacity.

But how do you know how many watts you need? Well, the following table gives you a quick way to find out. Just look at what you have and total up the watts.

PC Component	Watts
Motherboard (without CPU or RAM)	30
CPU	30
RAM	10 per 128MB
Hard drive	15
AGP card	30
PCI card	5
Network card	5
Floppy disk drive	5
CD-ROM drive	25

Add up what you have in your PC, and make a note of the current power usage of your PC.

My PC needs approximately   watts.

Troubleshooting PSUs

The PSU in a PC is one of the items most prone to failure. This is because it suffers from the effects of heating and cooling each time it is used (which in turn cause expansion and contraction of the electrical circuitry and components), and it is on the receiving end of the AC current when the PC is switched on.

Usually, the main cause of death for a PSU is a stalled or jammed cooling fan inside the unit. Without this fan, components quickly overheat, and permanent damage can occur within minutes. Because all devices inside a PC receive their DC power via the PSU, once it dies, the whole PC stops working.

Symptoms of a Dying PSU

Fortunately, PSUs usually give some warning before they die:

- You smell a burning smell that is worse at the back of the PC near the PSU.

- Rattling, grating, or an otherwise irregular noise is coming from the PSU fan.

- You experience intermittent rebooting or crashes of the operating system or applications.

- Devices attached to the system won't work. Basically, the PSU cannot supply enough watts. Overloading the PSU like this is bad for it and can permanently damage it.

For any problems you suspect to be the fault of the power supply, you will need to replace it with one of the same form factor and same or greater wattage.

 PC DOCTOR'S ORDER! *Never attempt to repair a PSU. Unless you are a qualified repair technician, there is nothing in there you can fix. Just unplug it and get expert help.*

Replacing a power supply isn't difficult at all, and because of the keyed connectors, there is little or no scope for getting the connections wrong. However, you do need to make sure that you get the right replacement PSU. Fortunately, most places that sell PSUs know what they are doing and will be able to advise you on the right purchase.

1. Disconnect the PC from the power outlet.

2. Open the case.

3. Disconnect all the cables going from the PSU, including the motherboard, hard drive, and floppy drive.

4. Locate the screws holding the PSU to the case (usually four screws on the back of the case, as shown in Figure 7-7). Carefully undo them, taking care that the PSU doesn't slip and break something.

5. Once the screws are undone, carefully remove the PSU from the case chassis.

6. Reverse these steps to install a new PSU.

7. After replacing the PSU, check the voltage setting on it to make sure that it corresponds to your local voltage.

FIGURE 7-7   Screws holding PSU to system case

Doctor's Notes

There isn't much that can go wrong with a system case, but a good case can make all the difference when it comes to upgrading and working on your system. If you are building a system for yourself, make sure to use a high-quality case. Also, make sure that your case is adequate not only for your current needs, but also for your future needs. Planning at the early stages can save you money and hassle later.

Power supply units are a different matter altogether. They work the whole time that your PC is switched on (and the modern ones even work the whole time that your system is plugged in). As such, they can suffer from wear and tear caused by high voltages and the heating and cooling of the components. Accumulated dust can accelerate this damage, as well as damage to the cooling fan inside, so regular cleaning is vital.

PC Case and PSU Checklist

☑   If you are buying a case, get the best one you can afford.

☑   Make sure that any case you get offers plenty of scope for future upgrades such as hard drives and CD drives.

☑   Check the case for sharp edges and that it offers easy access to components on the motherboard.

☑   Make sure that the PSU you are using has enough power to do the job.

☑   Clean the case and the PSU regularly, paying special attention to fans.

☑   Never dismantle a PSU or attempt a repair. Replace faulty PSUs.

☑   If you are adding a new PSU, make sure that the voltage switch on the back is set correctly for your region.

Chapter 8

Motherboard, RAM, CPU, and BIOS

In this chapter we will look at the parts that make up the core of a PC:

- The motherboard

- Random access memory (RAM)

- Central processing unit (CPU)

- Basic input/output system (BIOS)

Without these four components, your PC is nothing but a box. You might have CD drives, hard drives, PCI and AGP cards, and peripherals, but without the motherboard you have no way to connect them so that you can make use of them. Add a motherboard without a CPU, and the system won't work. Also, without RAM or BIOS—nothing! That's not to say that there aren't other core components (such as a monitor), but these four make a PC into a working PC.

The Motherboard

Take a look inside any PC, and usually the motherboard is the main component you'll see—a big, flat circuit board covering the whole of the base (or side) of the case, like the one shown in Figure 8-1.

FIGURE 8-1   A motherboard inside a PC

NOTE *You might come across the motherboard referred to as a "mainboard." This is not a different style of motherboard, just another word for it.*

The motherboard is a single physical item in your PC—a circuit board with components and connectors attached to the surface of it. There is not just one manufacturer of motherboards, however. Like hard drives, processors, memory, and expansion cards, motherboards are made by a variety of manufacturers, and as ever, differences exist between the brands—quality of the parts generally being the key factor. As with most PC components, there are high-quality parts and there are budget parts. I've said this before, and I'll probably say it again: cheaper budget parts are probably not what you want to be buying if you are looking for performance and stability! Buying cheap frequently turns out to be false economy, and so I generally do not recommend it.

Layout, or Form Factor

If you look at motherboards from different PCs or from different times, you will notice significant variations between them. I don't mean having different components or being laid out differently, but rather I'm talking about differences in the position of the expansion slots, power inputs, and connectors. These are not just cosmetic or manufacturing differences, but are in fact so significant that one kind of motherboard might not even fit into a case designed for another.

The layout of the board is referred to as the *form factor*. The most common form factor around today is the ATX form factor. These boards are approximately 12 x 9.6 inches (30.5 x 24.5 cm). The ATX form factor is a redevelopment of an earlier form factor called the AT form factor, which was common on older Pentium and Pentium II processor PCs.

Another common motherboard is the microATX board. The layout is similar to that of an ATX board, with the main difference being that this form factor is smaller. It is approximately 9.6 x 9.6 inches (24.4 x 24.4 cm). A smaller board means a cheaper board and this is the single strongest point of the microATX—if space isn't an issue I'd always recommend that you go for the ATX because it offers greater scope for upgrade. A smaller board also means it needs less power, so a PC using a microATX board would need a smaller power supply unit than a similar PC using an ATX board. This again helps pull down the price of systems incorporating a microATX board.

The motherboard is crucial to a PC because it determines the configurations and type of all the following hardware:

■ CPU

■ Coprocessors (optional)

- RAM

- BIOS

- Expansion slots

- Interconnecting circuitry

- Input and output ports

If you want to add more stuff onto your PC, you can do it easily. Additional components can be added to a motherboard through its expansion slots. You buy a card with the features you want, open the PC case, slot in the card, power up the PC, load any necessary drivers, and you're done! This flexibility and scope for end users to build and expand upon what they bought is one of the features that has made the PC so popular.

NOTE *The electronic interface between the motherboard and the smaller boards or cards in the expansion slots is called the* bus.

Motherboard Connections

There are numerous connections on a motherboard that you should be familiar with. Unfortunately, the types and positions of the connectors vary depending on form factor and type of CPU/RAM the motherboard is built to take. The best way to recognize these connectors is when the PC is assembled and with all the connections in place. This takes away all the guesswork!

The following sections give you a rundown of the connections on the board.

Input/Output Connectors

The input/output connectors are usually on the back of the motherboard and stick out of a specially designed cutout in the case. They typically look like Figure 8-2. In the old days, these connectors all needed wiring in and connecting to sockets on the motherboard. Now, they are built directly onto the board and so are hassle free. These connectors usually consist of the following:

- Keyboard

- Mouse

- Serial port

- Printer parallel port

■   USB

■   Network adapter port (some motherboards only)

Connectors for Power, On/Off Buttons, and Indicator Lights

I'm not talking here of the power cable connecting into the power supply unit (PSU) but instead the power cables running from the PSU to the motherboard. The easiest way to find this is to follow the wires from the PSU to the motherboard. You'll come to a connector block attached to the motherboard. This is the power supply to your motherboard.

This connector is keyed so the plug cannot be inserted into the socket incorrectly and usually has a plastic snap-lock retainer. To release, squeeze the plastic lever on the face of the plug and pull gently.

FIGURE 8-2   Connectors on the back of a PC. These are directly off the motherboard.

Hard Drive and Floppy Drive Interface

Follow the data cables from the hard drive(s) to the motherboard—easy to find! These are keyed so that the plug cannot be put into the socket the wrong way, and are simply push-fit connectors.

Another easy one to find is the floppy drive connection. Just follow the data ribbon running from the floppy drive to the motherboard. Again, these are keyed so you can't put the plug into the socket the wrong way, and are also push-fit connectors.

CPU Socket

The CPU connection is easy to spot because it's under the CPU chip on the board. There are several different kinds of CPU sockets, depending on the type of CPU supported by the motherboard. The most common type of socket is called a ZIF socket. ZIF stands for zero insertion force. A ZIF socket is the physical way that most CPUs connect to the computer motherboard. As the name suggests, the ZIF socket is designed to make manufacture of PCs easier and enable the average computer owner to upgrade the CPU simply and easily. At the heart of a ZIF socket is a lever that opens and closes, securing the CPU in place. Because a CPU has so many small pins at its base, a push-fit connector would more than likely damage the CPU, making upgrading your CPU a risky prospect.

 NOTE *If you have an older PC, it might be running a CPU called the Pentium II CPU. For this processor, Intel changed how the CPU was connected to the motherboard. Instead of a CPU with pins that fitted into a ZIF socket, the Pentium II processors packaged the CPU into a cartridge that fitted onto a 242-contact or 330-contact slot on the motherboard.*

RAM Slots

Just as with CPU sockets, RAM slots have undergone change based on rapidly changing RAM technology. There are three different kinds you are likely to see: SIMM, DIMM, and SODIMM.

SIMM (Single, Inline Memory Module)   This type of memory is usually found on older servers and desktop PCs. These are distinguished by having small metal retaining clips at each end of the slot.

To remove SIMM-type RAM already installed, follow these steps:

1. Pull both of the clips to the side, and the RAM module will flip forward to about 45°.

2. Now remove the module by gently sliding it out of the slot, still maintaining the 45° angle.

To install SIMM-type RAM:

1. Align the notches in the row of metal pins at the bottom of your module with the keys in the SIMM slot on your motherboard. If the notches don't line up properly, flip your module over and try it the other way. It doesn't matter which side of your module has the black chips or the stickers on it. The thing you want to get right is the alignment of the notches.

2. Holding the module at an angle of 45° to the slot, slide the module into place. The module will now be in the slot but at the 45° angle.

3. Rotate the module so that it stands upright in the slot and the two retaining clips on either side of the slot can snap into place.

DIMM (Dual, Inline Memory Module)   This type of memory is found on newer servers and desktop PCs. These are distinguished by having small plastic retaining/ejector clips at either end of the slot (see Figure 8-3).

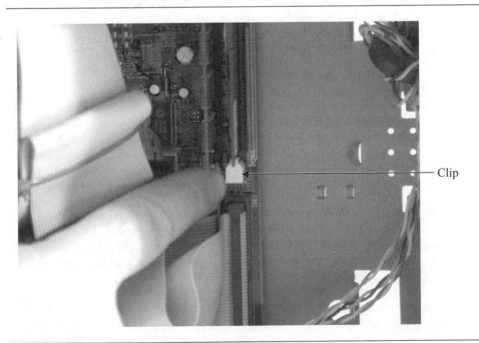

Clip

FIGURE 8-3   The retaining clip on a DIMM slot

To remove DIMM-type RAM already installed, press down on the ejector clips at each end of the module and lift the free module away from the slot.

To install DIMM-type RAM:

1. Press the ejector clips on either end of the free slot down.

2. Line up the notches in the row of gold pins at the bottom of your module with the keys in the DIMM slot on your motherboard. If the notches don't line up right away, flip your module over and try it the other way. It makes no difference which side of your module has the black chips or the stickers on it. The important thing is to line up those notches.

3. Once you have the notches lined up, use your thumbs to press the module into the slot. You will need to press quite hard, as it takes about 20 pounds of pressure to get the module properly inserted into the slot.

If you have a tower PC, you may find it easier to place the tower on its side for this. When you hear a "click" and both side ejector clips snap up around the module, the module will be installed correctly.

SODIMM (Small Outline Dual Inline Memory Module)   The SODIMM type of memory is found in notebook and laptop computers. Locating an access point for the RAM on a notebook can be tricky, and since all are built differently, you might have to consult the manual for precise details. Common ways to access RAM are either to lift the keyboard off the chassis, or open an access panel on the underside of the notebook. Check the instruction booklet that came with your notebook before trying to rip off the keyboard!

To remove SODIMM-type RAM already installed, press down on the retaining clips on either side of the slot. The module will spring up to an angle of about 45°. Slide the module out of the slot.

To install SODIMM-type RAM:

1. Line up the notches in the row of gold pins at the bottom of your module with the keys in the SODIMM slot on your motherboard. If the notches don't line up right away, flip your module over and try it the other way. It makes no difference which side of your module has the black chips or the stickers on it. The important thing is to line up the notches.

2. Hold the module at a 45° angle to the slot and slide it firmly into place. When the module is properly seated, no more than 1/16 inch (less than a millimeter) of the gold contacts should be showing.

3. Finally, press the top of the module down until it is lying flat against the motherboard. When properly seated, you will hear it snap into place.

PC DOCTOR'S ORDER! *Remember when handling RAM to take all necessary ESD precautions and not to handle the modules by the chips or connectors.*

Miscellaneous Connections

There are several more connectors present on a PC motherboard:

- CPU cooling fan connector: this is the power output for the main CPU fan and is normally just a simple two-pin connector. These connectors are keyed to prevent the plug being fitted incorrectly.

- Case fan connectors: case fans also require power, and this comes from a connector similar to that of the CPU fan.

- Case speaker connector: this small connector is how the case speaker connects to the motherboard. However, don't expect anything more than beeps from this speaker!

Backup Battery

Take a closer look at the motherboard. Can you see a shiny-looking component on there? Yes. Take a closer look, and you should see that it's a small button battery of the kind that you find in digital watches. This battery is used to store the parameters of the system BIOS even when the system is switched off (more on this shortly).

Because this is a battery, inevitably a battery will run down and exhaust. When this happens, you'll see errors such as the "CMOS Checksum Error." When this happens, or you get other symptoms, such as the clock resetting to a much earlier date (usually in the 1970s), it's time to replace the battery.

Replacing the Battery

Usually, replacing the battery is easy. However, before you do anything, you should make a record of what your computer is supposed to know. If your battery is already dead, there's no way you can do this, but if your configuration is still held in the BIOS, save yourself some time and record it. Go into the BIOS (more info coming up on this) and write down the info. After you remove the old battery, your computer will forget everything held in there.

FIX-IT-YOURSELF HOME REMEDY *An easier, if more wasteful method of saving your system configuration is to go to those screens that are important and just press the* PRINT SCREEN *button on your keyboard. The settings will be printed out.*

Here's the procedure for replacing the battery:

1. Turn the computer off, unplug it, and remove the case.

2. Remove the old battery. Take care to note which end faces which direction. Each end has either + or - on it. The old battery should just snap out. Study it, and you'll figure out how to get it out. You might find it helpful to carefully make use of a jeweler's screwdriver as a pry bar. Don't force it, though, as it may be soldered in. If it's a new-style motherboard, you may only need to move a prong that covers a small corner of the battery to take it out.

 FIX-IT-YOURSELF HOME REMEDY *If the battery is soldered in (and some manufacturers actually do this!), then how you proceed depends on your skill. If you are skilled with a soldering iron, you should be able to remove the battery yourself. However, if you aren't skilled with a soldering iron, take the PC in for repair.*

3. Get a replacement battery. Take note of the battery type or take the old one to the store and match them up. It should be pretty easy to come by. If you have trouble, try jewelers, as they stock many of the watch battery styles.

4. Put the new battery into the holder, making sure the + and - face the same way as they originally did.

5. Put the case back on, and plug it in. When you turn it on, expect some type of error message. Don't worry. This will happen. You just need to go into the BIOS and plug in all the info you recorded before you started. If you didn't record the information, you'll need to find the manuals and locate the info the hard way.

Common Motherboard Problems

Motherboard problems are, thankfully, rare. This is because electronic devices are very robust and long-lived and because the motherboard itself doesn't have any moving parts. That doesn't mean that you can't get problems!

Here, I'll cover some of the most common problems, along with possible solutions to them.

Dead PC

The worst-case scenario is a dead PC because there are a handful of things it can be, some relating to the motherboard, some not. Check the following on the motherboard:

- Check for signs of damage or corrosion on the motherboard. Corrosion can occur for a variety of reasons, from poor manufacturing to a sweat drip landing on the board from you or someone else working on the system. Check for cracks and burn marks too, as these might indicate damage from a careless upgrade or overvoltage from the power line or a lightning strike.

- If there are no signs of damage, corrosion, or burn marks, take a look for any loose connections onto the board. Over time, usually because of a small amount of corrosion or the continual expansion/contraction of the connections from heating and cooling, a *cold joint* (bad electrical connection) can occur, causing all kinds of problems. The remedy is to undo and redo the connections and test again.

- If the system still doesn't work, shift your attention to the power connections from the power supply unit to the board. Check that all the cards, CPU, and RAM are properly seated onto the motherboard. Check for any signs of activity on the motherboard. This includes fans moving or lights illuminating. If there is nothing, the next item to suspect (if you know that the electricity supply is OK) is the PSU.

Unstable PC

If your PC is unstable, there are many possible reasons for this. Generally, it's a software issue that you have to resolve, but if you find that your PC is unstable and you can't pinpoint the instability to a particular piece of software or connected hardware, then it could be a good idea to open the case and check that everything is OK. Look for:

- Loose wires or connectors: check all of them for soundness. Undo and redo the connection if in doubt.

- Loose or incorrectly fitted expansion cards: remove modules if in doubt. Check contacts carefully for corrosion. Carefully remove any visible corrosion with a pencil eraser.

- Loose or improperly fitted RAM module: remove modules if in doubt. Check contacts carefully for corrosion. Carefully remove any visible corrosion with a pencil eraser. Carefully reattach.

PC Reboots Periodically for No Reason

A system that reboots of its own accord is extremely irritating because the reboot usually hit without any warning. There are a few things to check if your PC reboots for no reason:

- Check the connections, especially any fan connections (especially the CPU cooler fan).

- Check for loose connections from the power supply unit.

- Check that the PSU has the right power capacity for all the devices you have installed.

Keep the Inside of the Case Tidy

Because there are so many wires and cables inside a PC case, it is sometimes tempting to leave all of them hanging loose inside; after all, if you tidy them up and you need to remove or replace one later, you'll just have to undo all your tidy work, won't you?

This is sloppy thinking that will just lead to problems! Leaving cables hanging is one way to encourage them to work their way loose under the stresses of being heated and cooled because gravity gives them that additional helping hand. So here are some pointers on keeping things neat:

- Wrap cables up and keep them tidy with plastic cable ties.

- Don't go overboard—keep the loops of cable quite big and don't overtighten the cable ties. As a guide, you should be able to get your little finger inside the cable tie too. This ensures you don't damage the cable and that you can safely cut the tie off, should the need arise.

- The thinner the cables you are tying up, the wider the cable tie you need to use to prevent damage to the cable.

- Don't stress the connectors when tying up cables. Leave some slack in the cable.

- Tie away all loose hard drive power cables to eliminate the risk of shorting out.

- Clip off the unused plastic tie ends, taking care, however, not to cut the cable itself by accident, and be careful of any sharp edges left on the cable ties.

 PC DOCTOR'S ORDER! *Don't underestimate the risk of cutting the cable when cutting a plastic tie. Take care, and use scissors or wire cutters to do the job right. Avoid using pocket knives.*

RAM

Your PC's short-term memory—random access memory—is located on the motherboard of your PC. This memory comes in the form of modules, such as the one shown in Figure 8-4, that are inserted into slots on the motherboard.

Generally, RAM doesn't cause much of a problem at all. Modules have no moving parts, and they are robust and require little maintenance beyond blowing the dust off of them with some compressed air. Still, there are a few times when RAM can give you problems, but fortunately these are generally restricted to a handful of circumstances.

 A DIMM RAM module

Troubleshooting RAM Errors

Other than through a thorough troubleshooting of system instabilities, RAM problems are usually diagnosed at system start-up, when the system BIOS returns error messages relating to memory. The type and wording of the error message depends on the system and the fault, but some of the most common errors are

- "Memory size has changed"
- "Memory access failures"
- Any other error message containing the word "RAM" or "memory"

You may see these messages after you've carried out work on your PC or after you've added, removed, or replaced RAM.

Let's say you've had the case open to carry out some work unrelated to the RAM modules, and when you restart the PC, you get RAM-related errors. There are several possible reasons why this might happen:

- You might have knocked a module loose. Check that the modules are securely in the slots.
- ESD damage might be a possibility if you didn't take adequate steps to prevent it (such as wearing an ESD wrist strap).

Let's say you've added, removed, or replaced RAM in the PC:

- There is a very good chance that you haven't fitted the module into the slot correctly. Remove the modules one by one and replace.
- There is a chance that the module you added is faulty, either because of ESD damage (unlikely if you took proper ESD precautions), or it was damaged in transit or even before shipping.

Testing RAM

Testing RAM is easy, and you need no other tools than your own PC. You do, however, need to have more than one module in the PC (if it takes DIMM or SIMM modules singly) and two banks of two, if it takes SIMMs in pairs.

PC DOCTOR'S ORDER! *Take great care during these tests to protect the system from further damage from ESD. Wear a properly fitted antistatic strap, and handle the modules with care. Keep any modules not in use in proper antistatic bags to protect them.*

Here's how you test systems that take RAM modules in pairs:

1. Clean around the RAM modules before removing any of them.

2. Remove all the RAM modules.

3. Take two modules and insert them in the system.

4. Reboot the system.

5. Continue to swap modules and reboot the system until you get a problem.

6. Once you come across the pair that gives you problems, you know that one of the two is defective. So, take one module and store it away safely and replace it with a known good one.

7. Reboot the system. If the system works, it is the module you removed that is defective. If the system doesn't work, it is the module that you kept in the system that has the problem.

If your system takes modules singly, the job is a lot easier and all you need to do is remove all the modules and install them one at a time into the system until it no longer works—time consuming, but easy!

FIX-IT-YOURSELF HOME REMEDY *Testing RAM modules isn't an exact science. You may go through the tests only to find that all the modules pass the test. You might have to extend the tests by adding modules and running the operating system for a while before replacing them. This way, the modules get a more thorough testing.*

CPU

The central processing unit is the computer within your computer. This is the component that does the actual work within the system. It is commonly called the "brains" of the PC, but its job is more than just the brains; it is also the commander-in-chief of the system, directing how most of it is run.

A CPU isn't much to look at—a little black or gray square of plastic-looking material with stuff etched on the outside of it. Rather than plastic, it's usually a ceramic because this helps to dissipate heat better than most other materials. And if there is one thing CPUs make a lot of, it's heat! On the reverse of the CPU will be a myriad of gold (or gold-coated) pins that are used to connect the CPU to the motherboard using the ZIF socket. Inside the ceramic is the actual silicon heart of the CPU. Unless you take an old, unwanted CPU and bust it open (not easy), this is the part that you'll never see.

I could write whole chapters on CPU development and progression over the years and how it has been possible to squeeze more and more power out of the silicon heart of the CPU, but that would be unnecessarily academic and irrelevant here. Suffice it to say that a CPU is a mind-bendingly complicated device built to the highest tolerances and specifications possible. It is amazingly complex and beautiful in design, and we can expect that not only this complexity but also the power and speed available from CPUs will continue to increase at an amazing pace.

CPU Speed

The speed of a CPU—commonly called *clock speed*—is measured in millions of cycles per second, or megahertz (MHz), or billions of cycles per second, or gigahertz (GHz). This number designates how fast a CPU can process information. If you see an advertisement for a computer with a Pentium 4/1.4, it means the CPU operates at 1.4 GHz.

CPUs work in cycles. Depending on the power and internal circuitry of the chip, a CPU can do a variety of tasks within each given cycle. A CPU's clock speed dictates its performance. Generally, the more cycles per second the CPU can do, the faster it will be at doing a task.

CPU and Socket/Slot Types

Upgrading a CPU isn't as straightforward as upgrading, say, a graphics adapter or a hard drive. This is because there are several different kinds of ZIF sockets. Which kind you have on your motherboard depends on the kind of CPU it is designed to take. You may not have a socket at all; you may have a slot that a cartridge-type CPU plugs into. Slots are rarer than sockets, though, and not now widely used. Table 8-1 lists some of the most common types of slots and sockets and the compatible CPUs.

Socket Type	Compatible With
Socket 7	Original Pentium processors, Cyrix 686, Cyrix MII, AMD K6, AMD K6-2, AMD K6-III
Socket 370	Intel PII, Intel PIII (not the cartridge type), Cyrix III
Slot 1	Intel PII, Intel PIII (cartridge type only)
Slot A	AMD Athlon (cartridge type only)
Socket A	AMD Athlon Thunderbird (not the cartridge type), AMD Duron, AMD Duron XP
Socket 423	Intel P4
Socket 478	Intel P4 (second generation)
754-Pin Socket	Athlon 64
940-Pin Socket	Athlon 64fx

TABLE 8-1   CPU and Sockets Types

The socket (or slot) used is a limiting factor in upgrading. Each range of CPU fits into a specific socket on your motherboard, and motherboards are designed with one socket type and cannot take another. For example, if you have a motherboard designed for the early Pentium 4 CPUs that use socket 423 (because the CPU has 423 pins to connect to the motherboard), you cannot upgrade the CPU to a second-generation CPU that has 478 pins without changing the motherboard.

Upgrading a CPU

Let's look at how to upgrade a CPU assuming that the motherboard you have will take the new CPU you want to use. If in doubt, check Table 8-1, or check the manual that came with your system for detailed specifications of your system.

Because there are so many different kinds of CPUs, and I don't want to burden you with instructions for every kind of CPU out there, what follows are generic instructions for socket-mounted CPUs and slot-mounted CPUs.

PC DOCTOR'S ORDER! *Sockets on a motherboard are not removable. They are permanently attached to the board, and any attempt to remove them not only invalidates any warranty you have on the board, but also carries a high risk of damaging your motherboard.*

Upgrading a Socket-Mounted CPU

If you have a socket-mounted CPU, follow these steps to remove the old one and replace it with a new CPU.

1. Switch off the system and unplug from the power supply.

2. Take the case off.

3. Locate the CPU on the motherboard.

4. Clean around the CPU to remove all traces of dirt and dust using compressed air.

5. The CPU is likely to have a heat sink on it and also a fan. The heat sink is usually a metal block (aluminum or copper) that sits on top of the CPU and carries the heat away from the CPU. If it has a fan, undo the power connector for the fan.

6. If you want to remove the heat sink, do this now before removing the CPU from the socket. This will usually be held in place by a spring clip.

7. With a ZIF socket, you'll notice a metal lever next to the socket. To put the lever into the open position, gently bend it outward while lifting away from the motherboard. Once the lever is upright, the CPU is free to be removed.

8. Lift the CPU up and away from the socket. Be careful not to put the CPU down on the pins, as they are very easily bent or broken. Always place the CPU on a flat surface with the pins upward! Take great care not to drop the CPU, and do not put it where something could be placed on top of it.

9. Now you are ready to replace the CPU. First of all, make sure you align the CPU with the socket properly. This is normally done by aligning the notch or dot at one corner of the CPU with a similar notch or dot on the ZIF socket.

10. Give the socket another clean with air to make sure no dust will be forced into the socket by the pins, as this could damage the socket, and once it's in there, the dust is very hard to get out of the socket.

11. Drop the CPU straight into the socket. Don't drop it at an angle or force it in; it should go in without any effort at all. (Remember what ZIF stands for: zero insertion force.)

PC DOCTOR'S ORDER! *If the CPU won't slide into the socket easily, check to see that you have the alignment right. If you still have problems, double-check that you have the right CPU. Also, check the pins on the CPU to make sure they are not bent. If one is bent, you can use small tweezers to straighten it. But be very careful! If many pins are bent, take it back to the store and get a replacement.*

12. Now with the CPU in the socket, you need to lock it down. Push the handle all the way down and secure it under its plastic retainer.

13. Fit the heat sink. (Follow the instructions carefully if using a new one. If you are using the old heat sink, be sure to first clean all the surfaces with alcohol—isopropyl, not beer or wine.) Apply a thin smear of thermal grease between the CPU and the heat sink. This will properly conduct the heat away. Failure to do this will cause the CPU to overheat and sustain damage.

PC DOCTOR'S ORDER! *Do not use your finger to smear the grease, as oils from hands can reduce the effectiveness of the grease. Many come with a spreader but failing that I usually make myself a plastic spatula from a clean plastic spoon.*

14. Hook the heat sink fan back into the power connector.

15. Make sure everything is tidily put away, nothing is left undone, and no tools are left in the PC case.

16. Close the case.

17. Test the PC. The new CPU should be detected automatically by the system. (If you have an older system, check the manual for information.)

Upgrading a Slot-Mounted CPU

If you have a slot-mounted CPU, here are the steps for replacing:

1. Follow the first four steps of the preceding instructions for socket-mounted CPUs.

2. A slot-mounted CPU might have two mountings because of the weight. Look for screws holding the CPU to the motherboard. Carefully undo these.

3. On the cartridge, there will be a retaining clip at each end. Squeeze these clips and lift the cartridge up and away from the slot.

4. Replacement of the new cartridge is the opposite of the removal.

5. Check the manual for the motherboard as to any changes you need to make for the system to recognize the CPU.

6. Test your system.

Overclocking

You might hear or read about *overclocking* with relation to CPUs. This term is generally used to describe running a CPU at a faster speed than intended (graphics adapters can also be overclocked). This is possible because CPUs are manufactured to such a high specification that overclocking may not damage them.

Should You Overclock?

Overclocking is not simple, and if you have to ask the question, then you aren't ready to do it. There are several factors that stand between you and overclocking your system:

- It may not be possible to overclock your system. Some systems cannot be overclocked, and laptops in particular should not be overclocked, because they cannot cope with the additional heat generated.

- The cooling system of your PC may need upgrading. An overclocked PC generates a lot more heat than a normally running CPU.

- The quality of your other components might not be up to overclocking. Because overclocking stresses the PC more than normal, other components are pushed to their limits. If they are of poorer quality, the overclocked system might prove too unstable.

The Enemy—Heat

If you overclock your system, you will need to make absolutely certain the CPU is adequately cooled. Fortunately for you, most motherboards and CPUs contain sensors that enable you to read the running temperature from the BIOS screen (alternatively, you could download free software to do it). Either way, you need to keep an eye on the temperature!

An ideal temperature to aim for is something in the region of 40° C. The higher the temperature, the more unstable and prone to crashing your system will be; the cooler it runs, the fewer crashes you will experience (up to a point anyway).

 FIX-IT-YOURSELF HOME REMEDY *Heat causes a system to crash because a CPU is made up of millions of transistors. When a transistor gets hot, it tends to leak current. If that current leak becomes too great, it can result in calculation errors, and too many errors will cause a crash. So keep the system cool!*

If you are having trouble keeping the temperature at around 40° C, here are some tips that might be of help to you:

■ Remove the heat sink and fan, and make sure there is a thin film of heat sink compound between it and the CPU. This is easily found at PC outlets and electronics stores. Sometimes you will see thermal pads being sold alongside the thermal grease; these may seem more convenient but are not as good as thermal grease.

■ Make sure the heat sink fits the CPU properly. Some brands fit certain CPUs better than others. Check for tilting of the heat sink or obstruction by other components on the board.

■ Make sure the case is well ventilated. There is no point having a good heat sink and fan if there is nowhere for the heat to go. Ideally, you should have at least two fans in your case through-putting air, one blowing inward (normally in the front of the case) and one blowing out.

■ Get yourself a better heat sink and fan assembly. There are many specially designed for use in overclocked systems that are far superior to the heat sink and fan assemblies that come with most PCs.

■ Keep heat sinks clean and dust free. Clean them regularly with compressed air.

■ Make sure the PC case is in a well-ventilated area (not too confined by books or shelves) and that it's not positioned in a hot place (like near a heater or stove).

An inexpensive way to find out if more system cooling will help your system is to go to an electrical store and ask for a can of "freeze down" component cooling spray (designed to keep delicate components cool during soldering). A 14-ounce can should be ample to keep a CPU running at well below $0°$ C for over five minutes. Use this to cool your CPU down so you can find out if the system stability improves before you buy expensive cooling gear.

Signs of Trouble with the CPU

Spotting CPU problems isn't generally easy. You might get error messages relating to the CPU, or you might get beep codes that indicate problems with the motherboard/CPU. (I'll cover these start-up beeps in the BIOS section that follows.) Fortunately, CPU problems aren't common, and if they do happen, there are usually other signs and symptoms you can pick up on.

If you perform regular maintenance on your system, take this opportunity to check the CPU and the heat sink/fan assembly. Are there signs that the fan is working? If you're unsure, briefly (but *carefully*) switch the system on to see if it rotates. If there is a problem with the fan, do not use the system, as even if damage hasn't already occurred, it eventually will. Replace the fan or the heat sink and fan assembly immediately.

Also, clean the heat sink and fan of accumulated dirt and dust with compressed air, and check the heat sink to ensure it is securely attached to the CPU and the fan is securely attached to it. Check for signs of overheating, for example, color changes such as browning and blackening of plastics or cracking and peeling, and components that look like they are damaged (especially the big capacitors that look like small cans on the board, because heat can cause these to swell up and burst).

Make sure that you also clean out all the dust around the CPU, as this can act as an insulator for heat, causing localized overheating and damage over the long term. Again, carefully use compressed air to do the cleaning.

Double-check that the cooling fan power cable is properly connected and that the cables aren't fouling the fan.

While you are carrying out your checks, make sure the lever on the ZIF socket is properly locked in the closed position.

BIOS

The basic input/output system is the instruction program that every PC uses to get going when you switch it on. When you fire up your system, the CPU springs into life and accesses the instructions contained in the BIOS. As the name suggests, the BIOS also manages data flow (input and output) between the operating system installed on the PC and devices attached to the system, such as hard drives, video adapters, printers, and even mice and keyboards.

NOTE *Although the BIOS theoretically always acts as a go-between for the CPU and other input/output devices and controls information and data flow, it is possible in some cases for the BIOS to allow for data to flow directly to memory from devices (such as video cards) that require faster data flow in order to be effective.*

The BIOS is a program, but not like other programs installed on your system. With most programs, you can pick and choose what's on your system (what operating system to have, what word processor to use, and what other applications and games you have installed). With the program stored in the BIOS, you don't get an option because it is part of and specific to the motherboard installed in your system.

The BIOS and the EEPROM

Typically, the BIOS information is stored on a special chip on the motherboard called an EEPROM (which stands for Electrically Erasable Programmable Read Only Memory). Figure 8-5 shows the EEPROM, as well as other parts of the motherboard.

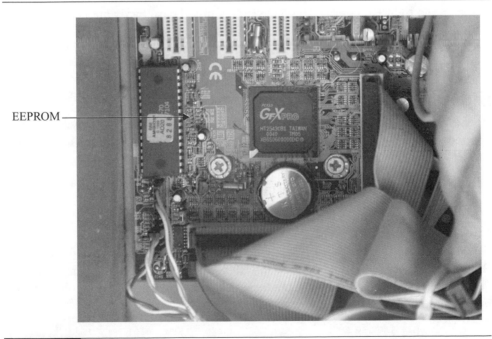

EEPROM

FIGURE 8-5   The EEPROM on a motherboard

When you switch on your computer, the CPU passes control to the program stored in the BIOS, and the remainder of the start-up sequence is carried out. The CPU can find the program stored in the BIOS because it is always located at the same place (or to be technical, the same data address) on the EEPROM chip.

What Does the BIOS Do?

The BIOS is a pretty complex program, and it varies significantly from one motherboard to another. However, in general, when the BIOS boots up your computer, its first job is to establish whether all of the devices attached to your system are still in place and operational. Additions or absence of devices can cause errors or a message to be displayed on the screen, depending on the device in question. Once it has finished doing this, the BIOS loads key parts of the operating system from your computer's hard drive (or a disk containing the necessary files in the floppy disk drive) into your computer's RAM.

You might be wondering why you need a BIOS at all; after all, operating systems and drivers seem perfectly capable of controlling most hardware, why not the motherboard? The reason is that the motherboard, being the hub that all the other hardware connects to, is very complex. This is a specialized task, and the program controlling it needs to be specialized to handle the job. The best way to match the right BIOS program to the right motherboard hardware is to load it directly onto a chip on the motherboard, which is what usually happens. The BIOS also provides software support for all the hardware in the system before the operating system kicks in.

Not All BIOSs Are the Same

Bear in mind that not all BIOSs are the same. In fact, the programs they contain are generally specific to a motherboard type or range. There are three major BIOS vendors for motherboards:

- AMI (American Megatrends Incorporated)
- Phoenix
- Award

These three vendors make most of the BIOSs you will encounter. Other vendors make specific BIOS applications, but these aren't as widespread as the ones made by the three major vendors. Other vendors include

- Quadtel
- Toshiba

- Microid Research (MR BIOS)

- SystemSoft

- IBM

- Intel

- ASUS

- Acer

To find out which BIOS you have, you can do one of three things:

1. Download a utility that will ID your BIOS for you, such as BIOS Wizard from http://www.esupport.com/ (see Figure 8-6).

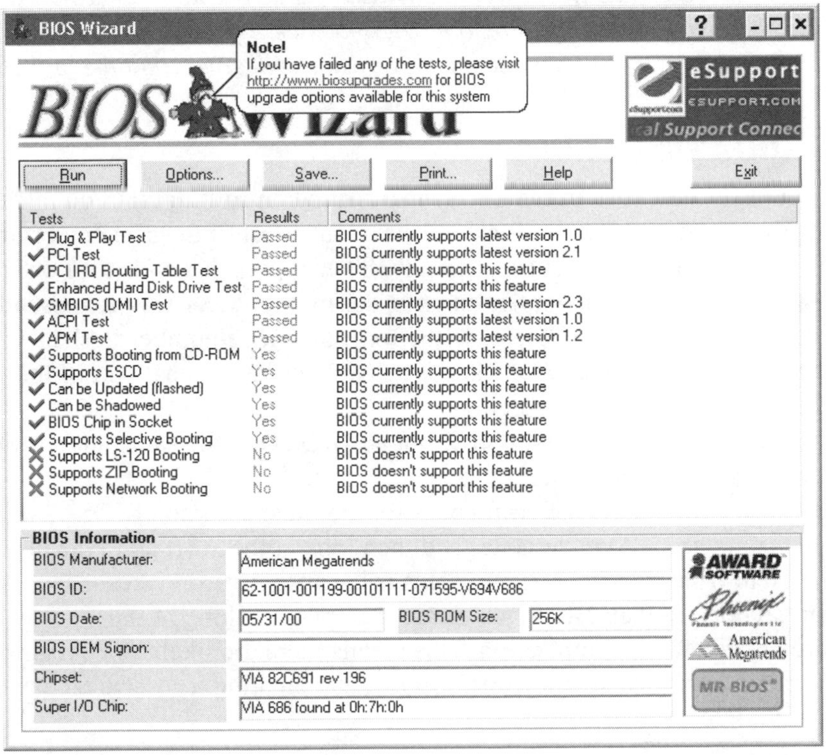

FIGURE 8-6   BIOS Wizard in action

2. Take a look at the text displayed on your monitor as soon as you switch on the PC. A good trick here to give you time to read what it says is to detach your keyboard while the system is switched off and restart it or hold a key down and restart it, both of which will cause an error and give you time to read the screen! On the lower-left side of your screen, a long string of numbers will be shown. This will be the BIOS ID of your motherboard.

3. Open the case and look for the BIOS chip on the motherboard. This will have an information sticker on it giving you basic information about your BIOS.

Number 1 is the easiest option, but because it relies on running an application, you must have a working system. Number 2 is handy, but again it relies on a working system (or at least a partially working system). Number 3 is great for a dead system or on systems where the screen is dead.

FIX-IT-YOURSELF HOME REMEDY *Make a note of the BIOS your system uses, and write it on a label, and stick it to the case somewhere. If you do this before the system goes down, it will save you time and effort.*

BIOS and POST Codes

One of the main functions of the BIOS, apart from controlling input/output and allowing the system to start up, is also to carry out a test of the system at start-up to look for problems. This test is called a POST test (which stands for Power-On Self Test). If the system encounters an error during the POST test, it is usually indicated either by an audio beep or in the form of a code number flashed across the screen. With this *beep code* in hand, you can determine what part of the system is having problems and find a solution.

There is a problem though: because not all BIOSs are the same, all error codes and beeps will not be the same.

What follows are tables of error codes for the most common BIOSs. We'll look at the standard IBM error codes and then look at the AMI and Phoenix codes. Absent from this list is Award. This is because Award makes many different versions of their BIOS, which are then passed along to third-party hardware vendors for customization. This means there are likely to be many vendor-specific error codes for Award BIOSs, and creating a compact, convenient list isn't possible.

PC DOCTOR'S ORDER! *For issues relating to an Award BIOS, or issues that you cannot identify using the following tables, contact your hardware vendor or supplier. Award and Phoenix have merged. Information relating to Award can now be found at http://www.award-bios.com/.*

Standard IBM POST Error Codes

We'll start with the IBM POST beep codes:

IBM Beep Code	Description
1 short beep	Normal POST—system is OK. However, if the system is showing nothing on the screen, check that the monitor is correctly plugged in and working. If this doesn't help, check the RAM for faults (refer to the earlier section "Troubleshooting RAM Errors"). If the system continues not to work, then suspect a dead motherboard.
2 short beeps	POST error—the error code will be shown onscreen.
No beep	Power supply or system board problem
Continuous beep	Power supply, system board, or keyboard problem
Repeating short beeps	Power supply unit or system board problem
1 long beep followed by 1 short beep	System board problem
1 long beep followed by 2 short beeps	Display adapter problem
1 long beep followed by 3 short beeps	Enhanced graphics adapter problem—check that the card is seated.

IBM POST Code Descriptions

Here is what the code numbers mean:

Number	Description
100—199	System board problem
200—299	Memory problem
300—399	Keyboard problem
400—499	Monochrome display problem
500—599	Color display problem
600—699	Floppy disk drive or adapter error

Number	Description
700—799	Math coprocessor error
900—999	Parallel port error
1000—1099	Alternate printer adapter error
1100—1299	Communication device, port, or adapter error (asynchronous)
1300—1399	Game port problem
1400—1499	Color printer problem
1500—1599	Communication device, port, or adapter error (synchronous)
1700—1799	Hard drive or adapter error
1800—1899	Expansion unit problem
2000—2199	Communication device, port, or adapter error (bisynchronous)
2400—2599	EGA system board error
3000—3199	LAN adapter error
4800—4999	Internal modem error
7000—7099	Phoenix BIOS chip error
7300—7399	3½-inch floppy drive error
8900—8999	MIDI adapter error
11200—11299	SCSI adapter error
21000—21099	SCSI fixed disk or adapter error
21500—21599	SCSI CD-ROM error

AMI BIOS Beep Codes

Here are the AMI beep codes:

AMI Beep Code	Description
1 short beep	System is OK. However, if the system is showing nothing on the screen, check that the monitor is correctly plugged in and working. If this doesn't help, check the RAM for faults (refer to the section "Troubleshooting RAM Errors"). If the system continues not to work, then suspect a dead motherboard.

AMI Beep Code	Description
2 short beeps	Memory problem—the first thing to check is the monitor. If the display is working, chances are you'll see an error message displayed. If not, manually check the memory. Reseat the modules and reboot. If this doesn't help, refer to the section "Troubleshooting RAM Errors" for advice. If all your memory tests OK, you probably need a new motherboard.
3 short beeps	Similar to 2 beeps—follow the diagnosis above.
4 short beeps	Similar to 2 beeps—follow the diagnosis above.
5 short beeps	Motherboard problem—however, before you replace the board, check the memory modules and reseat them.
6 short beeps	Keyboard problems—first try another keyboard. If that doesn't help, look for loose chips on the board and reseat. If this doesn't help, it's new motherboard time.
7 short beeps	CPU problem—troubleshoot the CPU.
8 short beeps	Video adapter problems—the best way to check the card for problems is to install it on another system.
9 short beeps	BIOS issue—check the chip in case it has worked loose. If this doesn't help, you'll either have to replace the BIOS or the motherboard as a whole.
10 short beeps	Motherboard problem with the CMOS (complementary metal-oxide semiconductor) memory (the chip that stores the BIOS parameters)—this indicates a problem inside the BIOS chip, and the chip or the motherboard will need replacing.
11 short beeps	Cache memory chip problem—check for loose components on the board and reseat.
1 long beep, 3 short beeps	Memory problem—usually this error occurs after adding memory to the motherboard. Generally this is caused by a memory chip that is not seated properly. Reseat the memory chips.
1 long beep, 8 short beeps	Display problem—reseating the graphics adapter usually fixes this error.

Phoenix BIOS Beep Codes

These audio codes are a little more detailed than the AMI codes. This type of BIOS emits three sets of beeps. For example, 1 -pause- 1 -pause- 3 -pause. This is a 1-1-3 combo, and each set of beeps is separated by a brief pause. Where there is an *x* in the table, it stands for any number of beeps.

FIX-IT-YOURSELF HOME REMEDY *Listen carefully to this sequence of beeps and count them. If necessary, reboot and count again.*

Phoenix Beep Code	Description
1-1-2	Motherboard problem—replace.
1-1-3	Your computer can't read the configuration info stored in the CMOS. Replace the motherboard.
1-1-4	The BIOS needs replacing.
1-2-1	Bad timer chip on the motherboard—replace the motherboard.
1-2-2	Defective motherboard—check and possibly replace.
1-2-3	Defective motherboard—check and possibly replace.
1-3-1	Defective motherboard—check and possibly replace.
1-3-3	Defective motherboard—check and possibly replace.
1-3-4	Defective motherboard—check and possibly replace.
1-4-1	Defective motherboard—check and possibly replace.
1-4-2	Defective memory—refer to the section "Troubleshooting RAM Errors" for advice.
2-x-x	Memory problem—refer to the section "Troubleshooting RAM Errors" for advice.
3-1-x	Motherboard problems—this is usually caused by a damaged chip.
3-2-4	Motherboard problems—this is usually caused by a damaged chip.
3-3-4	Video adapter problem—troubleshoot the video adapter.
3-4-x	Video adapter problem—troubleshoot the video adapter.
4-2-1	Motherboard problems—this is usually caused by a damaged chip.
4-2-2	Check the keyboard. If the keyboard is connected and working, suspect the motherboard.

Phoenix Beep Code	Description
4-2-3	Check the keyboard. If the keyboard is connected and working, suspect the motherboard.
4-2-4	Bad expansion card—remove them one by one to find the faulty card. Replace the defective card. If no card seems defective, replace the motherboard.
4-3-1	Motherboard problem—replace.
4-3-2	Motherboard problem—replace.
4-3-3	Motherboard problem—replace.
4-3-4	This is a system clock problem. The system battery may need replacing. If that doesn't work, the power supply may need replacing. If this still doesn't help, the motherboard may need replacing.
4-4-1	Serial port problems—if these are on the motherboard, you will either have to replace the motherboard or add ports. If you add ports, you will need to disable the onboard ports using the BIOS screen.
4-4-2	Parallel port problems—if these are on the motherboard, you will either have to replace the motherboard or add ports and disable the onboard ones using the BIOS screen.
4-4-3	Math coprocessor problem—replace.

Accessing the BIOS

The BIOS settings are accessible by the user; it's just that most users never notice the prompt!

When Does the BIOS Prompt Appear?

Start up your system and watch the screen. Keep a close eye on it and try not to blink. Keep watching!

What you are looking for is a prompt, but because there are many different BIOS vendors, there is no single description of what this prompt might look like. However, the clues are there if you look for them. Generally, a prompt will say something along the lines of:

```
Press <F2> to enter BIOS setup
Press <DEL> to enter BIOS setup
```

The trick is to press the right key when prompted. You're not going to have a lot of time, so it might take you a couple of tries before you get in. In fact, to make things easier, most new BIOS vendors have standardized on five possible keys for entering the BIOS:

- F1
- F2
- F10
- ESC
- DEL

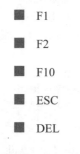 **FIX-IT-YOURSELF HOME REMEDY** *If you are unsure of what key to press to access the BIOS when the computer is booting, try pressing and holding any key on the keyboard. This will trigger a stuck key error, which may allow you to enter the BIOS setup.*

Older systems may have a more involved set of keystrokes that you need to enter in order to get into the BIOS. Here are some of the most common:

- CTRL-ALT-ENTER
- CTRL-ALT-S
- CTRL-ALT-ESC
- CTRL-ALT-INS
- PAGE UP
- PAGE DOWN

Navigating the BIOS

Once you're into the BIOS, you can begin to find your way around. Usually you will find a variety of menu options, generally arranged in a two-column format. At the top of the screen will be a title telling you that you are in the setup utility. It will also tell you the brand of BIOS you have. At the bottom of the screen will be the key legend that tells you how to navigate around your BIOS with your keyboard. Now this may seem old-fashioned to you, but most BIOS editions do not let you use the mouse (although there are some that do), and you have to navigate with your keyboard only. But don't worry, it's not too tricky.

Here is a typical mapping of keys and their functions:

Keystroke	Description
F1	Brings up a list of options available for each item
F5	Restores the values that were in place at the time the user entered the BIOS, which is useful if you made an accidental change or can't remember what you changed. However, it is only valid if you have not yet rebooted.
F6	Loads all the options with the basic preset values that should allow the system to start
F7	Loads all the options with optimized preset values that should allow the system to start and perform better
F10	Saves changes and reboots the system
ESC	Returns from any subscreen to the main menu screen
ENTER	Enters a subscreen
+/- PAGE UP/PAGE DOWN	Toggles up and down the available options for a particular item

The main problem with navigating the BIOS screens is that there can be a great deal of variation between the layout and items contained in each. However, some things are similar between all the BIOS user interfaces. There will be a setting screen for entering details on the hard drive; boot options (such as whether the system should boot up from the hard drive or a floppy drive and which order it checks each for boot information); power options (power-saving options, etc.); and security, which includes a boot-up password and system settings password to prevent changes to the system without the password (handy to prevent unauthorized fiddling).

The BIOS also gives you information on the system: CPU type and speed, RAM, and BIOS version. The BIOS might also give you other details such as the temperature of the CPU and the system, and the speed of the fans and whether they are working properly. This can be useful when troubleshooting overheating problems, the only disadvantage being that the system has to be rebooted before the BIOS is accessed and the information read.

Upgrading the BIOS

As with most things to do with a PC, you can upgrade the BIOS. And, as with most things on your PC, there is more than one way to do anything. With BIOS upgrades, there are two ways to upgrade, depending on the age of the system and the type of BIOS:

- Replace the chip
- Flash the BIOS

Chip Replacement

On older systems, replacing the chip is usually the only way to upgrade the BIOS. It involves buying a new chip (from your motherboard vendor) and replacing the chip already on the board with the new one. To do this you have to lift the old chip out of the socket and insert the new one—no mean feat sometimes because the socket can be tight, and it's easy to damage a chip. Life is made easier if you use a special chip puller (available from most PC outlets), which is used to grasp the ends of the chip so that you can pull it out of the socket.

Aside from the cost and trouble of replacing the chip, the other issue is the length of time the upgrade takes and the availability of new chips. Usually, unless you have a serious problem that warrants replacement, it is better not to bother.

Flash Upgrade

A flash upgrade, also known as *flashing* the BIOS, involves loading new software onto the BIOS chip. This is much quicker, cheaper, and a lot less hassle than messing around with replacement chips. All you do is get the right software update and either run it directly or allow it to create a bootable disk (you will need a spare floppy disk for this) that you can use to restart the system and do the flashing. Easy, or so it seems. There are possible downsides, but as long as you take care, you will be safe.

- Only carry out the upgrade if it is worthwhile. Don't carry out a BIOS upgrade just to have the latest version. Sometimes upgrades are merely cosmetic, adding a new translation into another language or offering a feature that is of no use to you. Also, a lot of fixes are released that might not be relevant to your needs. Either way, don't risk your BIOS unless you have to.

■ Get the right update! Never take chances with flashing the BIOS. Make sure that you are using exactly the right kind. If you flash the BIOS with the wrong software, the system may fail to boot up. As for recovery after this kind of foul-up, well, you may be lucky enough to be able to reload the correct software over the top of the wrong software and things might come back to normal. But failing that, you might need to send the system back to the manufacturer so that the BIOS can be revitalized. So save yourself time, effort, and trouble by making sure you use the right BIOS software the first time around. Remember the golden rule: "If in doubt - Don't!"

■ Save a note of the current settings of your PC BIOS just in case you need them.

■ Follow all instructions to the letter. Don't take shortcuts or make guesses Again, if in any doubt, don't carry out the upgrade.

■ If possible, try to have your system hooked into a UPS battery backup for the upgrade. If the power goes off mid-upgrade, it can corrupt the BIOS, which can mean your PC will need a trip back to the manufacturer.

Doctor's Notes

In this chapter we've taken a close look at the motherboard and the associated devices and hardware. The core hardware of the PC consists of:

■ Motherboard

■ CPU

■ RAM

■ BIOS

We've looked in detail at the types of problems you could have with these devices and the troubleshooting steps that you go through in the event of problems occurring. The motherboard is a big circuit board and controls a lot of the functions of a PC. Because of this, there is a lot of scope for a lot to go wrong (which, fortunately, doesn't happen very often). However, armed with knowledge and information, you can begin to deal with even catastrophic hardware disasters.

General Checklist

☑ The main potential trouble area, especially after upgrading, is loose or improperly fitted devices or connectors. Check and then double-check that every connector and component is firmly and properly attached before closing the case.

☑ If you have added or upgraded a component in your system and subsequently your system no longer works, suspect the latest item you added, and remove it and see if the system works without it.

☑ Keep a note of the positions of all cables and attachments. Draw a simple diagram if you think it will help.

☑ Never make guesses; always make sure you know exactly what you are doing at all times.

Chapter 9

Hard Drives and Floppy Drives

E very PC sold has one hard drive installed for data storage. More and more storage capacity is needed to cope with all the huge applications such as games and application suites (many games now routinely require over a gigabyte of storage space) as well as the massive volumes of data accumulated by a home user through digital cameras, camcorders, and the Internet. It is unlikely that the desire for more and more storage will ease off in years to come; so hard drives in the future will hold far more data than their current counterparts.

The flip side of this is the floppy drive. The floppy drive used to be the de facto way of installing, storing, and sharing information. Nowadays however, even when most machines still come with a floppy drive installed, fewer and fewer people are making use of it. Instead we use networks and the Internet to share information, and CDs and DVDs for installation of new software and for backups.

Let's take a look at hard drives and floppy drives and the most common issues that arise in their use.

The Hard Drive

The capacity of a modern hard drive is quite staggering. In a little over 10 years, we've seen hard drive capacity grow from hundreds of megabytes, through low-gigabyte levels, and now into the hundreds of gigabytes. It's amazing when you look back at a drive that has less capacity than a CD (and it still works). All this has been done with little change to the actual design and layout of the drive. Data is still written to and read from a metallic disk, or *platters*, inside the drive, using little magnet heads. (Each side of every platter will have a read/write head especially for it.) The platters are stacked into layers and are driven around using a motor. The heads are moved about the platters using another motor. The whirring sound you hear from a hard drive is the platters turning, while the fast rapping is from the moving heads.

The other amazing thing is that in order to achieve this awesome increase in capacity, the drives themselves have not changed in size at all, and they can still fit into a 3½-inch drive bay. What's changed is the capacity of the data stored on the platters inside.

Hard Drive Upgrades

After memory, upgrading a hard drive is the second simplest and best upgrade you can carry out on a system. You see instant results: you have more space for data!

Here are my pointers on how to make a hard drive upgrade go smoothly. You need to choose the right drive, based on your system, and prepare your system for installing it.

Choosing the Right Drive

You will have a choice of IDE (Integrated Device Electronics) or SCSI (Small Computer System Interface). Unless you have added a controller for SCSI or your system came installed with one (unlikely with a desktop), you will want an IDE drive. IDE has now been superseded by EIDE (Enhanced IDE), but there are no differences you need to worry about. Figure 9-1 shows a typical IDE hard drive.

 FIX-IT-YOURSELF HOME REMEDY *Never buy drives that are not packaged in an antistatic bag and stored in a box. Drives are delicate and can suffer damage easily from the abuses of poor handling. Don't take the risk—get one that's properly packaged. If you encounter a problem with the drive during the warranty period, you'll need this packaging to return it to the manufacturer.*

Choosing a drive can seem complex in itself because there are so many options. Let me demystify a few of them.

- ■ **Speed**   Look on any drive label, and you'll see several references to speed listed. Well, they're not really speed; there will be an RPM (revolutions per minute) listed (something like 7200 RPM) and a time (something like 12

FIGURE 9-1   Modern IDE drive

milliseconds). The RPM refers to how fast the platters holding the data rotate, while the time refers to the *seek time*. This is the average time it takes the drive to "seek" the data it is looking for on the disk. Generally, the higher the RPM and the lower the seek time, the faster the hard drive. The flip side is that the faster the drive, the costlier it will be! Another factor that determines the speed of a hard drive is how much cache memory it holds. Most hard drives have a few megabytes of onboard memory that is used to store data before it is written to the hard drive. This reduces the data transfer bottleneck from the motherboard to the hard drive. The larger the cache memory, the better. But again, you pay for this.

- ■ **Capacity**   Once you've chosen the type of drive, consider how much space you need. In monetary terms, the difference between a 40GB drive and a 60GB drive is not likely to be much, but in terms of storage space, the difference is huge. It is fair to say that as far as most users are concerned, you cannot have too much space.

Preparing for Installation

Decide where the drive is going to go. Is it a replacement, or are you adding a second drive? There are other considerations depending on your system.

- ■ Do you need a new adapter card? If your system already has four drives, for example, you will need to add a new adapter card to take the drive. Ideally, this should match the standards supported by your built-in hard drive controller. (At the very least, if your system currently uses IDE, get an adapter that supports this.)

- ■ Check for power. If you are replacing a drive, you'll be using the data and power cables currently in use by the drive that will be replaced, but if you are adding a drive, make sure it can be powered. If you don't have a spare power cable, you'll need a Y-splitter cable to split an existing cable into two.

- ■ Get the right kit for you. You can buy drives in two ways: a bare-bones drive that contains nothing other than the drive (and perhaps an instructional leaflet) or a full installation kit that comes complete with all the screws, drive rails (for fitting a 3½-inch drive into a 5¼-inch drive bay), cables, software, instructions (oh yes, and a hard drive!). These kits are a pleasure to use, but there is one drawback: they are really expensive when compared to just buying the drive in a plain brown box. However, if you think that it will make your life easier, it is worth the extra cost.

■ Do you have the right tools? Check the screwdrivers you are using to see if they are the right fit and that the tips are not damaged in any way. Take care that you keep track of all the screws and fittings (especially if you are using new ones). The last thing you want rattling around inside the system is free-roaming screws that might short-circuit the delicate electronics. Count them as you remove them, and be careful not to lose any in the upgrade process. Use plasticine to hold screws on the tip of the screwdriver:

As always, make sure that all cables and fittings are properly done up, especially the power cable. If you don't fasten it properly, it can short-circuit and cause damage. If you are uncertain, pull the plug out and reseat it.

Hard Drive Problems—and Solutions

Hard drives have a lot of moving parts and generate a lot of heat as they work. This makes them susceptible to malfunction. Let's take a look at some of the most common drive faults and causes of problems, and see what can be done about them.

Dead Drive

Nothing is scarier for the PC owner than to switch on a system and get an error message related to the hard drive. The number and wording of the different errors that can be presented are too numerous to list here, but they usually contain one or more of the following words from these phrases:

```
Primary hard disk/drive fail
Master hard disk/drive fail
Cannot find operating system
Boot device fail
```

Many combinations and variations are possible. Make a note of any error message you get, as this might be useful later.

The best thing to do at this point is to try rebooting, which sometimes remedies the problem when the cause of the problem is that the drive hasn't got up to working speed quick enough for the motherboard, resulting in the system returning the error message. This is more of a problem when you've put an older hard drive in a new system (but this shouldn't happen if the hard drive is less than two to three years old).

The next place to look is the system BIOS (basic input/output system). Reboot the PC, and watch for the prompt to press a key (usually either F2 or DEL) to enter the system BIOS at the early stages of the boot-up process. Once in the BIOS, navigate to the section that covers the hard drive. (Look for "IDE HDD Auto Detect," or "IDE HDD," or similar, in the list of options.) Check that the drive or drives you have installed are being detected. If not, run the "auto detect" process (if present). This will reload the settings if the drive parameters in the BIOS have been deleted or corrupted. (Variations in power voltage or a drained motherboard battery can cause this problem, as can random glitches.) Test the system again.

If that doesn't help, switch off the PC, unplug it, open the case (taking all the necessary ESD precautions), and check all the connections. Remove both the data cable ribbon and the power cable, and reseat them firmly. In Figure 9-2, I'm removing the hard drive power cable. (Remember to take steps to ensure your safety before working on your PC.)

 PC DOCTOR'S ORDER! *Never use tools or pliers for removing cables, as you can damage the cables, connector, or the plug on the device. Also, always pull by the plug and not by the cables or ribbons.*

If you still have a problem, chances are that you are looking at either a faulty drive or motherboard or power issues. The simplest way to determine whether the drive is working is to take it and install it in another system. If it works, you are looking at a different PC problem, and you will need to investigate further. If the drive doesn't work in another system, it is likely to be a drive issue and the unit needs replacing (check your warranty). The manufacturer may offer software that will help to diagnose the problem, so check their website, or telephone technical support. The warranty on your drive might far outlast the warranty on your PC!

Intermittent Drive Problems

Thankfully, intermittent problems are more common than a drive simply dying, and they give you the chance to get some, if not all, of your data off the drive before replacing it or before it fails altogether.

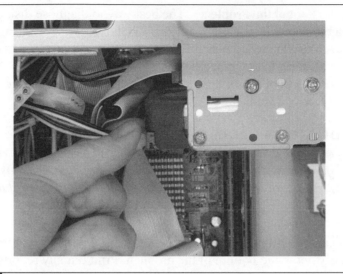

FIGURE 9-2   Removing a connector by hand the right way

There are many signs of a drive with an intermittent fault:

■ Consistently not being able to gain access to a file or files

■ Crashes, lockups, or rebooting while accessing data on the drive

■ Drive intermittently not available at system boot-up

■ New, unusual noises coming from the drive. Scraping, grinding, or rattling are the usual signs of a worn-out drive.

■ Error messages from the operating system concerning the drive

If you experience any of the above, stop what you are doing immediately and try to make a safe, off-the-PC copy of any data saved since the last full backup.

 FIX-IT-YOURSELF HOME REMEDY *This is a bad time to have to put the drive under the stress of a full system backup if it isn't needed, although if you have to, you will have no choice. So it's better to back up regularly—*before *you have a problem!*

Try to Get to the Root of the Problem   The best way to diagnose disk problems is to use the diagnostic tools offered by the manufacturer. These tools, along with details of how to use them and what they do, are available from the manufacturer's website. You will need to download the tools (either from your PC or another PC) and usually create a floppy disk to hold the files. Print out any instructions from the website so that you are clear on what to do.

PC DOCTOR'S ORDER!   *Some of the tests that can be carried out may wipe out your data as a result! Be very careful to choose the right test (and if you have two hard drives installed, be certain to choose the faulty drive). And, if at all possible, make sure you have an up-to-date backup first.*

The tests can take a long time. Don't rush them. They are very comprehensive and will usually get to the bottom of the problem. Print out any reports that you get (unless they say nothing is wrong).

PC DOCTOR'S ORDER!   *See Appendix B in the reference section at the end of this book for website addresses of the major hard drive manufacturers.*

Keep the Drives Cool

Heat is a major killer. Nothing wears out electronics and moving parts like heat. Continual heating and cooling causes the components to constantly expand and contract, and that is bad for everything! Despite being a complicated device with lots of moving parts designed to work at close tolerances, drives are extremely reliable. Keeping them cool is one way to prolong their life. Here are some ways to do this:

- Ensure that the PC has adequate airflow. Don't cover or block air holes, and be sure to clean them regularly. Replace any defective case fans.

- If possible, make sure there is a free drive slot above or below your drive. Heat from other drives (especially optical drives) can cause as many problems as the heat from the drive itself.

- Placing hard drives in 5¼-inch drive bays is better than 3½-inch as far as heat is concerned.

- Keep cables tidy, as they can obstruct airflow.

- Clean the dust from your system regularly, paying special attention to the carpet of dust that seems to cover hard drives.

- If you live or work in a hot environment, you might want to consider investing in special drive coolers. These are aluminum cases that contain fans to help carry away the heat.

 FIX-IT-YOURSELF HOME REMEDY   *One drawback of drive fans is that they can be very noisy and as such may not be suitable for all PCs.*

Be S.M.A.R.T.

S.M.A.R.T. (Self-Monitoring, Analysis, and Reporting Technology) is implemented in almost all modern hard drives. S.M.A.R.T. is an interface between a computer's start-up program or BIOS and the computer's hard drive. It is a feature of the EIDE technology that controls access to the hard drive.

If S.M.A.R.T is enabled when a computer is set up, the BIOS can receive analytical information from the hard drive and determine whether to send the user a warning message about possible future failure of the hard drive. A special program inside the disk constantly tracks the condition of a range of the vital parameters: driver, disk heads, surface state, electronics, and so on. At the present time, S.M.A.R.T. predicts up to 70 percent of all hard disk problems.

Don't ignore any messages you get about disk health. There may not be any obvious problems initially, but these problems never go away by themselves and usually get worse quickly. Take immediate action to ensure the safety and integrity of your data.

A good way to make use of S.M.A.R.T. is to use software that continually monitors the health of the hard drives in your system, looking for the first signs of trouble. There are many tools available (some free and some paid for). A search (using your favorite search engine) for the following keywords (or variations on them) will yield many good hits:

```
smart hard drive monitoring
```

If you monitor the information provided by S.M.A.R.T. on a regular basis, you can watch out for changes in values such as error rate counts and spin-up times (how long the drive takes to spin to a working speed).

FIX-IT-YOURSELF HOME REMEDY *If you have a hard drive failure, there are companies that can probably recover the data from your drive even if you cannot access it. This is handy reassurance for those times when you've lost something important. But do remember that this type of data recovery can cost hundreds of dollars. Also remember that recovery, while possible under most conditions, isn't guaranteed.*

Master/Slave Layout of Drives

If you have more than one hard drive installed in your PC, you might want to make sure that they are installed in such a way as to give you the best possible throughput.

With two drives, the best configuration is to have each of them on a separate IDE channel. Physically what this means is that you attach each to a separate cable. In this way you get the best data transfer rates, both between the two hard drives and between your hard drives and any optical drive (CD or DVD drive) installed. The best, least-fuss layout is to have both hard drives as masters, the main drive containing the operating system being primary master and the other being secondary master.

With three hard drives, you have less scope, and the third drive can go on either the primary or secondary channel.

Floppy Drives

While hard drive capacities have grown dramatically in recent years, the humble floppy drive has remained pretty much unchanged. The floppy drive that you have in your PC fits into a 3½-inch drive bay at the front of your PC and will take disks known as "High Density" (with "HD" stamped on the disks) 3½-inch floppy disks. These disks hold 1.44MB of information. Figure 9-3 shows a floppy drive and a disk.

The humble floppy drive used to be the main way to transfer data to and from a PC. Software was installed from them, and users backed up their files onto them for safekeeping. It wasn't until the widespread introduction of CD drives that the reign of the floppy drive came to an end. However, the legacy lives on, and most PCs sold today still come equipped with a floppy drive.

Today the most common use for a floppy drive and disk is to recover from a system problem by the use of a system boot disk. You can make one of these yourself through the operating system, or you might have been supplied with one

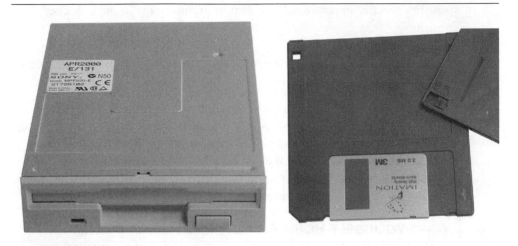

FIGURE 9-3   A floppy drive and disk

when you bought the PC. A system boot disk contains all the files necessary to start a PC and allow access to the file system. It is now possible to boot up using a bootable CD (as long as your drive supports the "bootable CD" standard or the "El Torito" standard), and these standards are rapidly making bootable floppy disks a thing of the past.

 PC DOCTOR'S ORDER! *Test your CD drive to see if it is actually bootable. If you are using Windows XP, you can use that disc to see if the drive detects it during boot-up.*

If you have a floppy drive in your system, you may as well have a working one. Let's take a tour of some common floppy drive issues that you might encounter.

Floppy Drive Problems

Floppy drive issues can be a result of a problem with the drive itself or with the disks you are using. If you find that you are having problems, here's a checklist for you to work through.

■ The first thing to do is try another disk, as it could be the disk that is faulty. Check the lock on the floppy disk. Is it in the fully unlocked or fully locked position and not in between? The disk in Figure 9-4 is in the unlocked position.

- If that doesn't work, try a different brand of disk. Not all brands are created equal.

- If that fails to work, check to see if the light on the front of the drive is illuminating when you try to read the disk. If the light does not illuminate, it's time to check the data and power connections to the drive. Undo and redo the connections and try the drive again. If this does not help and all the connectors look sound, consider the drive to be defective and replace it. The floppy drive connectors are shown in Figures 9-5.

FIX-IT-YOURSELF HOME REMEDY *Don't despair if you have to replace a floppy drive. They are quite cheap and easy to replace.*

- If the light does illuminate, but the disk is not being read, the next action you could try is cleaning the drive with a disk cleaner. This is a special cleaning disk that looks like an ordinary floppy disk, but instead of containing magnetic media, it contains a special surface specifically designed to clean the read/write heads in the drive.

FIGURE 9-4   Floppy disk lock in the unlocked position

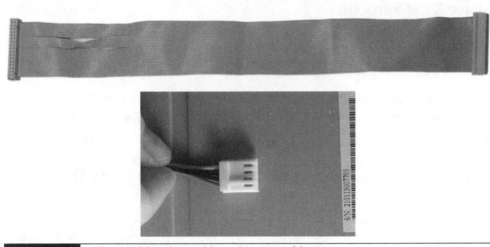

FIGURE 9-5   Floppy drive data cable and power cable

> **PC DOCTOR'S ORDER!**   *Follow any instructions in the drive cleaning kit to the letter because incorrect use or overuse could lead to permanent damage to the magnetic heads of the drive.*

Change of Disk Not Recognized

Another problem I've seen is that the drive correctly reads one disk, but on changing it to a different floppy disk, the drive still appears to be reading the old, removed disk. The usual cause here is that the data cable has become partially detached, and the system doesn't recognize the new disk. Firmly reattaching the data cable usually fixes this problem (check the power cable at the same time).

Another common cause is that the data cable is reversed. One or both ends of the ribbon cables are not connected in the right way—Pin 1 should be aligned with Pin 1 on the drive. Find the side that is incorrect and flip it around.

The final thing to check for when the drive is not reading the disk is that you have the drive attached to the nearest connector to the twist. All floppy drive cables have two connectors (one for the drive and the other for the motherboard) with a twist in between. The purpose of the twist is simply to reverse the voltages, but if you get this the wrong way around, the floppy drive won't work. Undo the case, detach the cable at both ends, and reverse the connectors.

Drive Light Stays On

When the data ribbon cable is attached the wrong way, the drive light will stay on. Check the Pin 1 configurations and make sure the Pin 1s are aligned on both sides. If that does not solve the problem, the floppy drive is most likely defective.

 PC DOCTOR'S ORDER! *Normally, Pin 1 is always closest to the floppy power connector. This means that the red stripe on the floppy cable should be facing the power connector on the back of the floppy drive.*

The Computer Tries to Access the Floppy Drive Every Time You Boot Up

The PC is simply looking for a system disk. It is not a fault and is normal. However, if you do not like it, disable "floppy drive seek" in your BIOS. Or you can flip the boot order to C:, A:, which will make the PC skip the A drive as long as there is a hard drive present.

Replacing a Floppy Drive

Sometimes replacement is the only option to a problem. Replacing a defective floppy drive is quite easy and straightforward.

■ Unplug the system and open the case (refer to Chapter 7 for details on how to disassemble cases). Take all possible steps to avoid damage to the system from ESD.

■ Carefully unplug the power cable and data cable from the back of the drive. (Do this before undoing the screws holding the drive in the bay.)

■ Once the cables are undone, take out the screws holding the drive in place. (There are usually two on either side, although you might only have one.) Take care not to damage the screw heads.

■ Once the screws are out, you can remove the drive. Pull it forward and out of the case.

■ Refitting the new drive is the reverse of the steps in removal of the old.

■ Take care not to trap or damage any cables when pushing the new drive into the bay.

Floppy Disk Care

Floppy disks need greater care than CDs and DVDs. Here is a rundown of the dos and don'ts of floppy disk care:

- Keep your disks in a box to keep them free from dirt, dust, and animal hair. Be aware that any dirt on the disks will find its way into your drive.

- Keep disks away from magnets and magnetic fields.

- Keep disks in a cool place away from direct sunlight and heat. Store them in a cool, dry place.

- Never open the metal flap of a disk and touch the media inside, as this will damage it.

- Write on disk labels carefully. Don't press too hard, as this will cause damage to the delicate media inside. Use a felt-tipped pen (instead of pencils or ballpoint pens if at all possible), and write on the label before it is attached to the disk.

- Make sure that any labels you attach to a disk are firmly stuck on. Never use a disk with a loose label or with a sticky note attached, as they can come off and work their way into the drive, damaging it.

- Never use a damaged disk in a drive, as it may wreck the drive.

Doctor's Notes

Hard drives and floppy drives are the backbone of storage on most PCs—hard drives espccially so. Losing a hard drive usually means losing all the data that's stored on it. This is why it is vital to keep an up-to-date backup on a reliable medium. Learn to look (or more accurately, listen) for the signs of damage or wear, and pay close attention to any drive-related error messages. For added piece of mind, get into the habit of running S.M.A.R.T. tests on your drive.

While it's true that most people have, in part at least, abandoned the use of floppy drives, they nonetheless have their uses and could come in handy if you need emergency access to your system using a boot disk. Just because you don't use it often, don't underestimate its importance.

Your drives are important (as is your data). Give them the respect and attention they deserve.

Hard Drive/Floppy Drive—Troubleshooting Checklist

For floppy drives, check the following:

- ☑ If you cannot read or write to a disk, try an alternative disk.

- ☑ If another disk does not work, try a different brand.

- ☑ If this doesn't work, unplug the PC, take steps to protect against ESD, and open the case.

- ☑ Check that the cables are properly and correctly done up. Undo the connections and redo them to make sure, trying an alternative power supply cable if you want.

- ☑ Test the floppy drive again.

- ☑ If the drive still doesn't work, test it on a known working system (if possible).

- ☑ If the drive still doesn't work, consider it defective and replace it.

For hard drives, check the following:

- ☑ Make note of any error messages that are displayed.

- ☑ Have there been clues or pointers to a failing hard drive before the drive failure?

- ☑ In the event of sudden drive failure midoperation (which might be accompanied by error messages), reboot the system and see if it works.

- ☑ Check that the drive is being detected by the system BIOS. Run the auto detect process to see if that helps.

- ☑ If the hard drive is still nonfunctional, unplug the system and (after taking proper ESD precautions), check the drive connections.

- ☑ Change the power supply cable to the drive to a spare in the case (if available).

- ☑ Check the data ribbon both at the drive end and the motherboard end. (Undo the connections and redo them to be certain that they are properly seated.)

☑ If you get the hard drive working, back up any data you have on it.

☑ While the drive is working, I recommend that you visit the drive manufacturer's website and download diagnostic tools to check the integrity of the drive.

☑ Check the warranty status on any defective drive.

Chapter 10

Other Data Storage Devices

Go back 10 years and the only storage options available to the home PC user or small-office computer user were

- Hard drives
- Floppy drives (the newer 3½-inch hard-cased disks, shown here, and the older 5¼-inch soft disk)

Now, the choices are huge and the paltry capacity of the floppy disk (1.44MB is what you can get now, although it started off a lot less than that!) is dwarfed by media like CDs and DVDs.

Let's take a look at the choices for storage that are currently available to the computer owner who wants more choice, more control, and, ultimately, more storage capacity. We'll also take a look at some of the problems that you might come across.

CD/DVD/CD-R/CD-RW

CDs seemed the obvious choice for data storage for years before they were used for that purpose. The discs could hold a lot of information, and they seemed almost indestructible. Perhaps you remember the ads for compact discs that claimed the disc would still work if it had been covered in mud or jam. CDs are robust, but as you'll see shortly, they're not that robust!

Attaching an optical drive to a PC revolutionized computing for the masses. The technology not only made it possible for home and office users to play music on their systems (which spurred the introduction of high-quality sound cards and speakers) but also allowed software to become bigger and have more features. A CD could hold enough data to fill more than 450 floppy disks, and as a result, software vendors created applications and programs of a size and complexity previously unknown. The CD was the obvious answer to a problem that had been limiting the growth of PCs for a few years.

CDs have given way nowadays to drives capable of reading both CDs and DVDs, as well as to writable discs that you can use for data storage and archiving needs.

The Discs

A CD (pictured here) is a polycarbonate disc 1.2 mm thick, 12 cm in diameter.

During the manufacturing process, the polycarbonate is impressed with microscopic bumps arranged into a single, unbroken spiral track approximately 5 km long. On the top is a really thin layer of aluminum, and on top of that is an acrylic layer. Then any label is on top of that. The tracks on a CD are small, approximately 0.5 micron wide, with 1.6 microns separating each track (known as *track pitch*—the distance from the center of one track to the next).

 NOTE *One micron is 1/25,000 of an inch. Human hairs measure between 30 and 120 microns across.*

Those bumps in the polycarbonate are small too; the reflective bumps (called *lands*) and nonreflective pits that make up the track are each 0.5 micron wide, a minimum of 0.83 micron long, and 125 nanometers high. (A nanometer is a billionth of a meter.)

 NOTE *You sometimes read about "pits" on a CD instead of bumps. These pits are on the aluminum side, but on the side the laser reads from, they are bumps!*

A CD can hold between 650MB and 700MB of data, depending on the type of disc used.

DVDs are different. To begin with, they can hold far more data. A single-layer DVD disc holds 4.7GB of data, but a disc can be double-sided and have two layers on each side (allowing it to hold 9.4GB per side of the disc).

NOTE *Double-sided discs have to be turned over to read the other side. You notice the layers on a DVD disc when playing movies on your home DVD player. There is usually a slight pause while the transition is made between the layers.*

Just as with CDs, DVDs store data using microscopic grooves running in a spiral pattern around the disc. Like a CD, a DVD drive uses laser beams to scan these grooves and read the data.

DVD technology uses smaller pits on the recordable media than CD technology. Smaller pits mean that the drive's laser must produce a smaller spot. DVD technology achieves this by reducing the laser's wavelength from the 780nm infrared light used in standard CD drives to 625–650nm red light.

NOTE *The smaller the wavelength, the smaller the pits that it can read.*

Smaller data pits allow more pits per data track. The minimum pit length of a single-layer DVD-RAM is 0.4 micron, compared to 0.834 micron for a CD. In addition, DVD tracks are closer together, allowing more tracks per disc. Track pitch is smaller. On a 3.95GB DVD-R, track pitch is 0.8 micron (on a CD the track pitch is 1.6 microns); while on a 4.7GB DVD-R disc, an even smaller track pitch of 0.74 micron helps boost storage capacity.

These narrow tracks require special lasers for reading and writing, and they can't read CD-ROMs, CD-Rs, CD-RWs, or audio CDs. The way that drive makers solved this problem was by putting two lasers in their drives—one for DVDs, the other for CDs.

Another big difference between DVD recording and CD recording is the recording format used. DVD recording uses Universal Data Format (UDF). UDF makes it possible to store data, video, audio, or a mix of all three within a single physical file structure contained on the disc.

This file structure ensures that any file can be accessed by any drive, computer, or consumer video. UDF includes the CD-standard ISO 9660 compatibility, but CDs do not comply with UDF.

Common Optical Drive Issues

Optical drives and discs are pretty robust, but they aren't foolproof. Here are some problems that you are likely to encounter.

Dirty/Damaged CD or DVD

The most common problem you are likely to encounter is damaged or dirty discs. The more use CDs get, the more likely they are to get damaged during use.

Scratches and dirt on the disc are the most common reasons that a drive won't read a CD/DVD, or will stop reading (or installing) partway through. (This can result in a bewildering array of problems, from crashes and lockups to strange error messages. Only rarely will you see a clear error message such as "Cannot read from drive X.")

Cleaning the disc should be the first thing you try. The best option for cleaning is to use special commercial disc cleaners that consist of a solution and tissues. Failing that, you can use cleaners designed for glasses or camera lenses. Isopropyl alcohol or methylated spirits can also be used.

When cleaning a disc, make sure you aren't going to make things worse by scratching it!

- Carefully place the disc label side down on a smooth work surface. Place a sheet or two of paper towel underneath to protect the label side.

- Carefully wipe off any particles that might scratch the disc (sand, grit, dirt).

- Work slowly and methodically using gentle actions, wiping from the center outward. Never rush or be vigorous with the disk surface.

- After cleaning, allow the disc to dry, and try using it again.

Scratches are a different matter. Figures 10-1 and 10-2 show scratched discs. A CD can have three distinct types of scratches:

- **Scratch on the label side**   This is the worst of all and destroys the data on the scratch because the reflective film stores the data. Scratches here are bad news; the disc is only good as a coffee coaster.

- **Radial scratch**   Scratches from the middle out normally aren't a problem unless they are deep. A CD has error correction and can accommodate these quite easily (because the damage is restricted to a bit or two in every byte).

- **Spiral scratch**   These are worse than radial scratches because they damage many bits or bytes in a track.

Emergency CD Repair   This technique is only to be used as a last resort, as it may well damage the disc. If the data is important, you should use a professional data recovery company, but beware, it will be expensive!

FIGURE 10-1   CD scratches

This is a two-step process:

1. Clean the disc as described in the previous section. Check it before proceeding to step 2—cleaning might do the trick.

2. Get a small amount of toothpaste (a tiny amount, less than a quarter of the size of a pea is enough, but use less if you can). Using a soft wet cloth, gently clean the disc from the center outward (see Figure 10-3). Do it very gently and go around the disc slowly, working out any scratches. This might take some time, but don't rush. Do it slowly, carefully, and methodically. This gently softens and reduces some of the deeper scratches and can help the CD laser read the data from the disc.

FIGURE 10-2   Label-side CD scratch

Once you have finished, wash the disc in water, dry it, and test it again. If you're lucky, it will work. If not, you haven't lost anything!

Practice if you want on a freebie disc before you try it out for real. Just add some scratches and see if you can get the disc to work!

Dead Drive

Sudden drive death, where it simply stops working, isn't common. Electronics are relatively robust and long-lived. Sometimes, however, when you go to use a drive, you will find that it has simply stopped working and the tray won't even open. Try rebooting the system to see if that helps. Next, try these suggestions:

- First, check for signs of life. If the tray won't open, check for lights illuminated on the front.

- If the drive seems completely dead, open the PC case and check the data ribbon and the power cable. Reseat the ribbon connector and try again.

- If the first two suggestions don't solve the problem, check inside the case for an alternative power cable and swap this one for the power cable currently being used. (There are normally spare cables in the case.)

- If the drive still doesn't work, and everything else on the system seems to work properly, then consider the drive faulty.

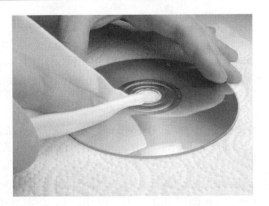

FIGURE 10-3   Disc cleaning in action

Releasing a Trapped CD/DVD

If you come across a completely dead drive, one of the problems you might face is a disc trapped inside the drive. It's automatic to think that you have to dismantle the drive to get it out, but fortunately there is usually a much easier way.

Look at the front of the drive, where (in most cases) you should see a small hole (about 1 mm in diameter). This is the emergency disc ejection port. Switch off the PC. Get a probe (some drives come with one, or you can easily fashion one from a paperclip), and push it slowly but firmly into the hole, as shown in Figure 10-4. You'll feel some resistance. Push against this, and slowly you'll see the drive tray open. Keep repeating this little by little until you have the tray open enough to get the disc out.

When you're done removing the trapped disc, close the tray slowly but firmly, taking care not to bend it.

FIX-IT-YOURSELF HOME REMEDY *Sometimes the probe releases the tray in one action (a common feature of drives like those found on laptops that are spring loaded as opposed to being powered by a motor), in which case you won't need to keep probing.*

Drive Won't Read/Play Some Discs

You have a disc that just won't read in some drives. It can be boiled down to two issues:

- The drive is somehow defective or incompatible with the disc or needs cleaning.

- The disc is faulty.

Some drives just won't read certain discs. Maybe the disc is of borderline quality and the laser in the drive cannot read it, or perhaps the disc uses some type of copy-protection system that is incompatible with the drive you have installed. Either way, there isn't usually much you can do beyond replacing the drive with one that is compatible with the disc.

FIX-IT-YOURSELF HOME REMEDY *Having two drives (say, one standard drive and one drive that can use recordable discs) comes in handy because it gives you two drives to try!*

The disc could also be faulty. Look for scratches or dirt on it and clean it if necessary.

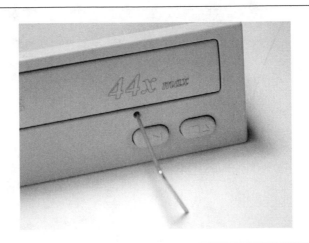

FIGURE 10-4   Ejection port

If possible, try the disc in another drive. If the disc won't work in two different drives, it is likely that the disc is faulty.

Cleaning a CD/DVD Drive   There are a lot of moving parts inside an optical drive that can get dirty, not to mention lasers and lenses used to read the data off the disc. Periodically these could do with a cleaning.

 PC DOCTOR'S ORDER! *Never dismantle a drive for cleaning. You will invalidate the warranty and could damage the drive.*

There are two ways to clean an optical drive:

- Use a proprietary cleaning disc as shown in Figure 10-5. These are special discs that have very fine brushes attached for wiping the lens clean of dirt and dust.

- Use compressed air from a can. This is good for generalized cleaning but not as good for getting dirt off the lens.

 NOTE *Only use compressed air from a can specifically designed for cleaning. Compressed air from a compressor can be contaminated with oil, dirt, and metal particles that will damage the drive.*

FIGURE 10-5   Cleaning disc

Poor DVD/CD Playback

You try to listen to an audio CD or watch a DVD and the playback is poor. Perhaps it stutters or the audio/video cuts out constantly.

There are a few possible causes for this common problem:

- Insufficient system resources available on the system to decode the data: close down unnecessary applications and try again. If this doesn't work, you will need to upgrade the system and add more RAM, a faster processor, or a faster drive.

- Dirty disc: clean and try again.

- Dirty lens in drive: clean the drive.

Recordable Drives Won't Burn CDs/DVDs

You try to burn a CD or DVD (maybe as a backup), go through the motions, and then try the disc, only to find that the disc can't be read or hasn't been written properly.

There are a few reasons that could be behind this:

- Poor discs: high-quality discs are worth the extra cost over cheaper, lower-quality discs. If you have problems with one kind of disc, try another kind.

- Try different recording software.

- The lens needs cleaning. Use a lens cleaner and try again.

■ The hard drive that you are copying from and the optical drive are on the same IDE channel. This dramatically reduces the data transfer rates and can cause what is known as *buffer underrun*, where the optical drive runs out of data and cannot write any more to the disc. If a pause in the data writing occurs, the disc is rendered useless. Modern drives have built-in features to protect against this.

■ Defective drive: if trying different discs, different recording software, and cleaning the lens don't work, consider the drive suspect and get a replacement.

Master or Slave?

When connecting a drive to an IDE channel, you can choose where it goes on the channel. You can have up to four devices on two separate IDE channels. These channels are

■ Primary master

■ Primary slave

■ Secondary master

■ Secondary slave

Both the primary and secondary channels consist of a cable with two connectors on it (three if you count the end that connects to the motherboard). This allows you to connect two drives to each channel. The question that many people ask is "How should the drives be connected?" If you have one hard drive and one optical drive, then for the best throughput and transfer rates, you should make the hard drive the primary master and the optical drive the secondary master. Overall, this gives you the best transfer rates to and from your optical drive to the hard drive.

But what if you have two optical drives? What's the best arrangement?

For maximum performance and throughput, it's better if they are on separate IDE channels. So, in a four-drive system (two hard drives, two optical drives), the best arrangement is to have the two hard drives as primary master and secondary master, and the two optical drives as primary slave and secondary slave. This arrangement of separating the two optical drives is especially beneficial if you have a recordable CD/DVD drive and you copy discs from one drive to the other.

Upgrading CD/DVD Drives

There comes a time when you simply want more out of your CD/DVD drive. Perhaps you want a recordable drive or you want to add DVD capabilities to your system. This is when you'll want to upgrade.

You will be faced with choices such as:

■ What kind of drive?

■ What capabilities?

Both of these should be easy to answer, as they form part of the reason why you want to upgrade in the first place. Chances are you'll either want to get a recordable drive, upgrade to a DVD drive, or get a faster drive so that playback is smoother. Whatever your choice, be clear about what you want and do some research.

If you currently have one optical drive and get another, then you might want to consider adding it as a second optical drive to your system, if you have a space for it. If you have up to two hard drives along with the existing optical drive, then this might be for you. Having two optical drives gives you greater flexibility with your system, but if you ever want to add another hard drive, you'll have to sacrifice the lower-specification optical drive.

When you get the drive, check it to see what kind of accessories you get. With some, you get a full complement of cables, screws, software discs, and fittings, while with others you get very little. If you aren't provided with any screws or fittings, check to be sure this isn't a mistake; if not, you will need to find some spares before adding the drive as a second one.

 FIX-IT-YOURSELF HOME REMEDY *Keep any spares that you end up with just in case you need them another time.*

Upgrading a CD Drive—The Steps

Upgrading or adding a CD drive is a straightforward process. Here are the steps that you need to follow:

1. Safety first! Disconnect the system from the outlet or UPS battery backup. Open the case.

2. If you are planning to add the drive as a second drive, check that you have a free drive bay in the case, spare power cables present, and space on the IDE cable. (Some manufacturers of cheaper computers supply ribbon cables with only two connectors, forcing you to buy a three-connector cable if you want to add another drive.)

3. Check the jumper on the drive that the new drive will share a cable with to see whether it is set as a master or slave. Use the jumper on the back of the new drive to select the opposite setting if you are adding the drive onto the data ribbon. Set it to the same setting if you are simply replacing the drive.

4. Choose the drive bay you will be using to house the drive, and remove the snap-off front panel and any metal blanking plate that might be beneath that. This plate is a sheet of metal that is part of the case that has been weakened so that it can be removed if need be. Generally it is removed by levering on it with a screwdriver but sometimes it might be quite tricky to remove, and you may have to use pliers and some force to break it off.

PC DOCTOR'S ORDER! *Take great care not to damage anything when removing the blanking plate. Also, take special care not to injure yourself on any sharp edges that might be present. If there are any sharp edges around the rim of the slot, protect yourself by covering them in tape. (Don't file them—the metal particles will be bad for the system.)*

5. If you are replacing the existing drive, disconnect the power cable and data ribbon from the back of the drive, as well as the audio cable that connects to the sound card from the CD drive (Figure 10-6), if it is present. (This cable is used to carry audio directly to the sound card instead of having to process it through the CPU, reducing CPU overhead needed to play music in the background.) Then undo the screws, taking care not to let them fall into the system.

6. Slot the drive into the bay and carefully attach it with the correct screws. Use two on each side, screwing them all partway first before tightening them up fully. Figure 10-7 shows the drive's attachment points.

PC DOCTOR'S ORDER! *Don't use too much pressure on the screws. Gentle hand-tightening is enough to keep them in place.*

7. Connect the data ribbon, power cable, and the audio cable (if present).

8. Double-check the connections and check to see that you haven't disturbed any of the other connections inside the case.

9. Close the case.

10. Plug the system back into the outlet or UPS battery backup.

FIGURE 10-6   Rear of drive showing connectors

11. Switch the system on and check that everything works. Depending on your system, you may need to enter the BIOS (usually by pressing the F2 key or DELETE key during bootup—there is usually an onscreen prompt for you to follow). Enter the hard drive section and choose the "auto detect" option if present.

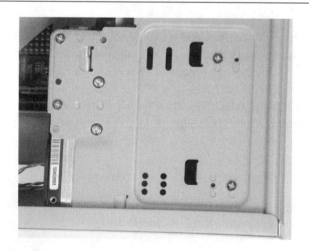

FIGURE 10-7   Drive attachment points

12. Install the supplied software (if required).

13. Test the drive fully by checking it with CDs and DVDs and recordable discs if appropriate.

External Storage

There are dozens of different kinds of external storage devices available to PC users who want convenience and flexibility from their storage. External storage has also become fashionable, with many devices now coming equipped with other features such as MP3 players or digital cameras. Forms of external storage range from external hard drives to micro flash memory drives that have no moving parts. What you go for depends on a number of factors:

- **Cost**   Some solutions are cheaper than others.

- **Capacity**   Generally, the more capacity you are looking for, the more you will have to pay. Remember too that hard drives (even external ones) are cheaper than any other method when you take cost per GB into account.

- **Speed**   If you will be storing a lot of data, go for speed. External hard drives are the fastest, while disk-based systems such as Zip are the slowest.

- **Fitting hassles**   Small USB systems are easier to use and install than, say, an external hard drive or tape streamer. With the advent of USB (and the faster USB 2.0), these devices are extremely popular because they are easy to connect.

- **Portability**   Small, pocket-sized micro storage devices that connect to the system using the USB port are very handy. You can carry anything from 1MB to 1GB in your pocket and transfer data easily between different PCs without the need to install drivers (on systems running Windows Me and above), plus, no wires or power supplies to run.

- **Robustness**   USB flash memory devices are quite robust when compared to external hard drives, and they can survive long-term pocket carry with ease.

- **Expandability**   If you won't need high capacity, but want to be able to create an effective archive, you might want to consider a system that stores data onto high-capacity disks, such as Iomega Zip.

■ **Regular backup or constant use**   Some systems (such as external hard drives) are ideal for regular use. For backup, it depends on the capacity you need and how robust you need the system to be. (A tape streamer is probably the easiest, most robust method to use for regular backups, but it is expensive and can be cumbersome at times.)

Make your choice based on how you respond to these factors. You might find that one solution won't answer all your needs; for example, a combination of flash USB memory and an external hard drive might suit you best.

NOTE *Buy a higher-capacity flash USB memory than you think you'll need. If you think you need 64MB, consider spending a little extra for 128MB. It won't cost much more, but I'm sure that you'll find you need it soon!*

While you are considering your needs, bear in mind the following points.

Transfer Speed

Think about how much speed you are going to need. Be honest! Otherwise you'll be looking to upgrade again too soon.

If you will be saving lots of data, you'll want speed. You may find variation among similar products. An external hard drive might use parallel port, USB, or USB 2.0, so choose which is best for you. USB 2.0 is the fastest of these three, and if you want high-speed data transfer, it might be worth upgrading your PC to have USB 2.0 capabilities (by adding an expansion card).

NOTE *USB allows transfer speeds of up to 12 Mbits/second, while USB 2.0 allows speeds of up to 480 Mbits/second with compatible devices.*

Physical Space

Consider too the issue of space—not storage capacity but physical desk space. How big a device do you want hooked up to your system? Again, be honest with yourself. Don't go for anything with power supplies and lots of wires if you don't think you'll be happy with that or don't want the capacity. Pocket-sized USB flash memory devices can hold many hundreds of megabytes of data and are easy to use, whereas an external hard drive can have capacities of many gigabytes. Balance what you need against size and convenience.

It's Not All About the Hardware

Remember that most hardware is only as good as the software that comes with it. External storage devices are usually used in conjunction with their own software. Good software can make a good piece of kit great, while bad software can mean that excellent hardware is rendered close to useless.

When you are checking out possible solutions, find out what software you get. Backup software comes with most devices, and this can range in quality and usefulness. If software is mentioned, check it out. Take a trip to the maker's website and see if they offer a free trial of the software. Also do a search to find out what other users think.

 FIX-IT-YOURSELF HOME REMEDY *Free software that comes with hardware, especially if provided by a third party, normally doesn't come with a license that allows you to upgrade to the latest version. If you change operating systems in the future, this could mean you will have to buy a new, possibly costly version. If possible, go with hardware that comes with software provided by the same company.*

Remember that more often than not, the software offered "for free" with the hardware is an older version; so before you buy, check that it will work with the operating system you are running. Windows 98 supports USB memory devices, but you need to install a driver in order to access them. (The driver needs to be installed on each machine that you plan to use the device on.) With operating systems later than Windows 98 (Windows Me, 2000, and XP), these devices are automatically supported, and no additional driver is required. Windows 95 does not support USB memory devices, so if you are still using that OS, you are out of luck. The same rule applies to memory such as Compact Flash cards, SmartMedia, and other types of removable memory generally associated with computer devices.

Other devices, such as Zip drives and external hard drives, will require you to install drivers and software in order to use the device on the PC. This means that what you gain in functionality you lose in the ability to easily move the device from one system to another.

FIX-IT-YOURSELF HOME REMEDY *Keep the software driver's disc handy with the device so that you always have it available if you want to use it on a different PC. If possible, tape the CD case to the device or the wall nearby!*

Is It External Storage That You Actually Need?

Finally, think about whether your needs might not be better met by adding another hard drive, or bigger hard drives. If you are thinking about external storage as a means to compensate for having little free drive space, be careful, as external storage might not be what you really want. If you have a lot of files on your system taking up a lot of space (such as digital photos or music), an external storage solution might help. But if you have loads of applications taking up space, more internal (hard disk) space is a better answer. External storage is no substitute for not having enough disk space!

 FIX-IT-YOURSELF HOME REMEDY *Don't use external storage just because you're afraid to open the case on the computer. Turn to external storage because you need a portable device, or to augment what you already have. External devices are not a substitute for a properly installed internal hard drive.*

Troubleshooting External Storage

External storage devices are very robust, especially the ones that rely on flash memory—they have no moving parts to wear out. Generally, issues fall into one of three categories:

- **Connections**   Somewhere, there is a bad connection. Check every connection in the chain, starting at the PC and working your way to the device. Check any power connection too, while you're at it. This is usually the problem when a device stops working suddenly.

- **A conflict or driver problem**   Maybe you've just attached it and can't get it to work, or you've changed something on the system (software or hardware) and that has affected the hardware/software associated with the device.

- **Device failure**   It does happen! This can either occur in the device or the power supply. Swap the power connector on the device (or, if it is a USB or FireWire device, try another port) and retry it. If this doesn't work, try it on another system.

Always check the connections first before investigating further. Connections (especially connections that aren't secured with screws) can work loose because of the heating/cooling of the PC. To properly check a connection, undo it, check the connectors for damage (bent pins, dirt, and so on), and redo. Work methodically from the PC end to the other, checking each in turn.

Doctor's Notes

The type and choice of external storage you choose is a very personal thing and it depends on your needs (speed, capacity, convenience, and so on). Think carefully about your current needs and your potential needs in the next 6 to 12 months. Buying the wrong device now could mean that you end up having to buy something else again soon to solve the same problems. Also, when it comes to optical drives you might find it convenient to have two: a CD or DVD writable drive and a playback drive for your CDs and DVDs. A two-drive system offers you greater flexibility and scope when it comes to drives, and if you ever need the space for an additional hard drve, just remove one of the optical drives.

Also, consider whether, instead of (or in addition to) an external storage solution, it might be time for a hard drive upgrade.

Other Storage—Troubleshooting Checklist

- ☑ If the device is newly installed, have you installed all the necessary drivers and software?

- ☑ Reinstall drivers and software.

- ☑ Check all the cables and connections between the PC and the device.

- ☑ Check that any external power supplies to the device are also plugged in and working.

- ☑ Try connecting the device to a different port on your PC.

- ☑ If possible, try the device on a different PC.

- ☑ If all else fails, contact tech support for the device.

Chapter 11

Monitors and Graphics Adapters

Some would argue that the monitor is perhaps the most important part of any PC. It is, after all, the part that allows you to see into the world of the PC, and it is the main output of any system. Once upon a time, a monitor was purely an output device, giving you access to raw data in much the same way as if it were on paper (with the added advantage that you could manipulate the data). Over the years, things have changed dramatically. The monitor nowadays is much more than a data output method, and computer graphics are far superior to what you could have expected five years ago because of the vast improvements made to the speed and power of a modern-day PC and the quality of the parts. Now the graphics output by the monitor are key to navigating around the digital environment that the operating system and applications create for us. It has made our work easier and allowed us to be transported to other worlds for play.

Powering the monitor is the graphics adapter. This is the part of the PC that controls what is sent to the monitor for display and how that information is displayed. The power and speed of this component determine the quality of the final output that appears on the monitor.

Let's take a look at these two key components—the monitor and the graphics adapter—and how they interact.

The Monitor

Let's get some terms clear before we move on. A *monitor* is the computer display and the related components packaged into a single physical unit that is usually (but not always) separate from other parts of the PC. The display is commonly a cathode ray tube (CRT) or liquid crystal display (LCD), but it can also be a light-emitting diode, gas plasma, or other type of projector. Figure 11-1 shows an example of a CRT monitor. The terms *monitor* and *display* (and in some circles, *screen*) can be used interchangeably. When I say monitor, I will mean all kinds of monitor.

NOTE *Notebook computers don't have monitors because all the display and related parts are integrated into the same physical unit with the rest of the computer. However, there is usually a port on most notebook PCs that allows you to connect the laptop to a full-sized monitor.*

Monitor Dangers

Under normal circumstances, a monitor presents little or no danger at all to the end user. However, if you undo the case in any way, you are exposing yourself to lethal amounts of electrical charge and voltages. The message is a simple one: **Don't do it!**

FIGURE 11-1   CRT monitor - iiyama LS502U G (Courtesy of iiyama)

There is nothing inside a monitor, no matter what type, that you can fix yourself. Or as the manufacturers put it, there are no "user serviceable parts."

 PC DOCTOR'S ORDER! *The biggest danger to a working monitor is a power surge from a lightning strike, which can cause the whole thing to explode. This is a thankfully rare, although real, danger, and the best protection comes from attaching a surge protector to your power supply (or a UPS that incorporates surge protection). Failing this, unplug the system during stormy weather.*

I don't often recommend that you pay experts, but for problems with monitors, you will probably need one. Leave any monitor repairs to the experts who have the safety equipment and the parts to carry out repairs. If paying someone for a repair is uneconomical, buy a new monitor. The only diagnostic procedure I recommend is swapping a monitor that is suspected to be faulty for a known good one and see if that works. That should tell you whether the problem is with the monitor or not.

 FIX-IT-YOURSELF HOME REMEDY *If you have a monitor problem, check your warranty. Many monitors come with warranties longer than the standard one year for a PC; so if you bought it separately from your system, you may still be covered. If you don't check, you'll never know!*

So, I'll say it again—never underestimate the dangers associated with monitors!

- Leave monitor repairs to the experts.

- Keep liquids away. A spill into a monitor can provide the electricity a route to you and deliver a lethal electric shock.

- Never open the case or attempt any repair to a defective monitor.

- If you suspect any problems, unplug the monitor immediately!

 WARNING *I don't mind repeating myself when it comes to safety: never open your monitor case, no matter what kind of monitor you have. If you suspect that your monitor has a problem, unplug it immediately and seek expert help.*

Monitor Care

There are three aspects of a monitor that you can take control over the care of:

- Keeping the screen clean

- Keeping the system dust free

- Keeping the power "clean"

Screen Cleaning

Dust and dirt on the screen can cause eyestrain as well as diminishing colors and screen brightness, both of which make using the PC a far less pleasant experience than it should be. Because of the huge electromagnetic fields that surround a monitor, combined with the heat produced, a monitor is capable of attracting a lot of dirt and dust to it. This dust clings to the system, but there's no worse place for it than on the screen.

There are many ways to clean the actual viewing screen on a PC, but there are also a lot of ways that it shouldn't be done. Never do any of the following:

- Never place liquids near a monitor, including detergent or water.

- Never spray liquids or mists near a monitor, as this can give the electricity a path to reach you! This includes window-cleaning solutions and spraying/ watering plants nearby. (Never keep plants or flower vases on top of your monitor.)

- Never use harsh chemicals to clean the monitor. These can damage the antiglare coatings on the surface of the screen.

- Although it's not going to result in a lethal electric shock or anything, never use anything abrasive to clean the screen. Scratches on the glass can distort the picture, which will seriously affect your view.

- Never use anything greasy to clean the monitor. You'll find it very hard to remove completely.

The best way to clean a monitor quickly and safely is by using a monitor cleaning kit. These usually consist of special tissues presoaked in isopropyl alcohol and a special absorbent tissue for drying the screen. These ensure both your safety and the safety of the screen.

Failing a proper kit, here are some alternatives, although they aren't as effective:

- A duster: simple and effective.

- Disposable static dust wipes: these are popular nowadays for general cleaning and quite effective at removing dust, although they do encourage it to reappear!

 FIX-IT-YOURSELF HOME REMEDY *When using a duster or cloth for cleaning, make sure you are actually using it to catch the dust and not just throwing dust into the air so that it can settle back in the same place again. This is why disposable wipes are better.*

Clean the screen methodically, working across the whole screen from side to side and then from top to bottom. Pay particular attention to the corners and make sure that you work to remove any streaks from the screen if using the wet-style wipes.

Dust-Free Monitors

If the screen attracts dust, then it's sensible to assume that the rest of the monitor does too. And indeed it does—lots of dust, in fact. Normally, dust isn't much of a problem, but when it builds up into a "carpet," it can prevent the monitor from having enough air to cool it. Even a thin carpet (less than 1 mm) can cause overheating and premature component failure.

The best tool is a vacuum cleaner. It's efficient and effective, and by simply running the nozzle over all the air vents a few times a year, you can keep the dust to a minimum and ensure adequate air flow.

Be careful when cleaning a monitor.

- Always unplug it before cleaning it.

- Be careful when moving it. CRT monitors are very front-heavy and can topple forward if tipped too far.

- Be careful not to put any strain on the video cable connecting it to your PC. This can easily result in damage to the monitor and/or the graphics adapter.

- Be equally careful about resting the monitor on its front, which might damage any switches, buttons or knobs.

Keeping the Power Clean

Poor power is bad for your monitor—worse than it is for the PC itself. The extremes of highs and lows play havoc with the delicately balanced electronics that it contains. Power dips and brownouts (when the voltage dips to a lower level) are just as bad as spikes (sudden increases). Both take the voltage being supplied to the system outside of the acceptable range, and prolonged consumption of "bad" power will take its toll on a system.

The easiest and best way to ensure that your system is kept safe from power fluctuations is to invest in a UPS (uninterrupted power supply) system (see Figure 11-2). This is basically a device that allows your computer to keep running for a short period of time after the main power supply is lost. All good UPS systems also provide protection from power surges.

FIGURE 11-2   UPS device

A UPS contains a battery that kicks in when the device senses that power has been lost or has dropped to a low enough level to cause damage. This allows it to fully protect your system from both the highs and lows that the power supply can go through. Having a UPS installed not only means that you can keep on working uninterrupted during brownouts and spikes, but also that in the event of a power cut, you get time to shut down the system gracefully, saving any work that's open first.

Graphics Adapters

A graphics adapter is also called a video adapter, display adapter, video card, video board, or other combinations of the words. Whatever the term, it is an integrated circuit board, such as the one shown in Figure 11-3, that is usually fitted inside a computer (or, in some cases, inside the monitor itself or integrated onto the motherboard itself). It handles digital-to-analog conversion, data storage in video RAM, and has a video controller so that data can be processed and passed on to the computer's display.

FIGURE 11-3   AGP graphics adapter

Today, almost all graphics adapters for displays adhere to a common-denominator, de facto standard known as Video Graphics Array (VGA). This standard describes how the data (essentially, color streams consisting of red, green, and blue data streams) is passed between the computer and the monitor. In addition to VGA, most displays today adhere to one or more standards set by the Video Electronics Standards Association (VESA).

One job of the graphics adapter is to control the frame refresh rates of the image. This determines how fast the image displayed on the monitor is changed. The faster the image updates, the smoother and better it is.

 NOTE *Screen refresh rates are measured by counting the number of times the screen is refreshed every second. This value is called hertz and given the symbol Hz.*

The graphics adapter also specifies the number and width of horizontal lines, which essentially amounts to specifying the resolution of the pixels that are created. The greater the resolution, the finer the images on the screen appear and the more information can be displayed onscreen. Some of the most popular resolutions are 800 × 600, 1024 × 768, 1280 × 1024, and 1600 × 1200 pixels, with a pixel being the smallest unit of an image that a screen can display. If you take a magnifying glass and look at your screen, you will see the pixels that make up the image displayed on the screen.

In order to work, most graphics adapters have their own memory. This is used to store the screen information and process the refresh. The more memory available, the better quality image you can get, in terms of color depth and size (limited, of course, by the specification of the monitor you are using). The memory available ranges wildly from 1MB (not common nowadays), to 32–64MB (the common range nowadays), through 128MB and beyond.

Onboard Graphics Adapters

Sometimes the graphics adapter isn't a separate card inside the system but instead built onto the motherboard. These are known as *on-board graphics adapters*. This can be great because it makes the system cheaper and also frees up a slot for other cards. However, new drivers might appear only infrequently, and these cards don't usually offer the same quality and performance as a separate card. Also, to save on cost, the card will share video memory with the system RAM (in fact, all AGP cards use some system RAM to function).

All is not lost though if you have a system with one of these and you would prefer to use a separate card. You are not stuck using it; you can add your own graphics adapter to the system and disable the onboard card in the system BIOS. You lose a slot, and you have to remember to plug the monitor into the graphics port provided by the new card instead of the onboard one, but other than that, it is a great solution.

Problems with Graphics Adapters

If your computer crashes often or crashes when running a particular game or application, there is a very good chance that the cause is a problem with the graphics adapter. Crashing isn't the only problem either, but it is the most common.

Here are the top reasons for graphics adapter problems:

- Bad driver
- Incompatible graphics adapter
- Loose fitting graphics adapter
- Broken/damaged/loose connector
- Defective graphics adapter
- Overheating

Bad Driver

If you are having instability problems with your system or, in fact, pretty much every other kind of problem short of it not booting up, the first thing you should check for is updated drivers for the graphics adapter (and sound card while you're at it). A bad graphics adapter driver accounts for well over half the stability and conflict issues with PCs.

Why Graphics Adapter Drivers Cause Problems   Basically, a graphics adapter has grown into more than just a component inside a PC; it is a critical component (like the CPU or RAM). But unlike the CPU or motherboard, it is a component that relies heavily on drivers loaded into the operating system. Anything loaded into the operating system is prone to problems from time to time because of a bad installation, conflict with another driver or software application, or corruption.

There are also many different graphics adapters available, made by many different manufacturers, and these cards conform to different standards. In order to handle this, the driver that controls the card itself, as well as the onboard software that carries out the bulk of the work, are very complex indeed, and complexity can lead to problems.

There is a very good chance that you've already had encounters with graphics adapter problems. Perhaps you installed a game that told you that you need to update your software driver or the operating system you want to upgrade to doesn't support your existing hardware or drivers. The graphics adapter update is one that many of us are forced into, so let's look at that next.

Getting New Drivers   The first and best source of drivers is the Internet. Visit the manufacturer's website and see if they have a "drivers" or "downloads" section that you can browse. Many manufacturers have simplified the driver installation process by bundling all the drivers for their hardware into one package that you can download and install. During installation the program determines which card you have on your system and installs the correct driver. This does mean a larger initial download, but it means that you get the right driver for your hardware. (It will undoubtedly take longer on a dial-up connection than it would to download a specific driver, although you might spend the same amount of time trying to find the right driver!)

If the Internet isn't available to you, you will have to resort to phone support and having the driver sent to you in the mail. It can be an effective option, depending on the hardware manufacturer and the cost of support involved. You will be far better off getting onto the Web (perhaps locate an Internet café or ask a friend with a Web connection).

 NOTE *Waiting for a driver to come by mail can mean a long wait, and you might be charged for it.*

Don't Upgrade Unless You Need To   Upgrading your graphics adapter drivers when you need to because of a problem or conflict is one thing. You have a clear goal in mind (getting your software working). Upgrading when you don't have to is quite another matter, and can cause more problems than it solves.

There are three clear reasons why you should upgrade a graphics adapter driver:

- You are currently having problems.

- The new driver is compatible with an operating system or other software you plan on installing.

- You are installing the new driver because the old driver had known defects that caused instabilities or performance issues.

Be very careful about updating for any other reason. For now, the message is "be cautious," but later on in this book (Chapter 18), we will look at drivers and making the right choices, as well as getting out of sticky situations caused by bad drivers. However, the golden rule applies to drivers, like everything else: If in doubt - Don't!

Incompatible Graphics Adapter

Choice is usually a good thing. The problem with choice is that it leads to a variety of competing and often incompatible standards fighting it out in the consumer arena. This is where choice turns around and bites the consumer, because you either made a bad choice (easily done and not something that you should blame yourself for), or the good choice you made a while back is no longer a good choice!

Maybe you bought a game or some other application that lists on the box that it needs a graphics adapter with a particular capability or functionality (games are most likely to bring graphics adapter issues to a head). Or perhaps the installation halted because the wrong kind of card was detected. Either way, this forces you into the uncomfortable position of not using the software or deciding to upgrade your existing card (which until now may have been trouble free). With this kind of upgrade, you are entering into the unknown.

 FIX-IT-YOURSELF HOME REMEDY *There used to be a saying that went "New game, new graphics adapter!" No single bit of software can highlight a graphics adapter problem more than a game.*

Here are some issues you should consider:

- How will a new card affect your current system?

- What current software might you have that could be incompatible with the new card you get? Check the specification of your games carefully.

There are no shortcuts to research. Also, generally, the more expensive the card you buy, the fewer problems you will get, although there are some great deals to be had by buying an older-specification card that has been superseded by the maker.

 PC DOCTOR'S ORDER! *Steer clear of generic cards. While the chipset of the card (the main onboard chip) might be made by a reputable maker, the rest of the card as well as the driver might be of lower quality.*

The best way to make sure that you understand what graphics adapter you need is to read the specifications—of both the card and the games that you run. They should be listed on the box. If not, it might be a good idea for you to check out the maker's website for details, and if you still are in any doubt, get in touch with them by email.

Two standards you might see are DirectX and OpenGL (Open Graphics Library). These standards both provide an application programming interface (API) that game makers (among others—good graphics are no longer something restricted to games) can use to build on. The standards not only cover graphics but also sound and input devices. DirectX is a Microsoft standard, while OpenGL was initiated by Silicon Graphics but is now an industrywide review board that includes 3Dlabs, Intel, IBM, Nvidia, and Sun Microsystems.

Games are usually built on the DirectX or OpenGL standard, and many problems used to be caused by the fact that graphics adapters only supported one of the standards. This meant that the cards were incompatible with a whole host of games. Nowadays, most cards claim to support both, but that doesn't mean you won't get problems; however, many of these will be fixed by newer drivers.

 WARNING *One problem with buying cutting-edge technology is that if there are problems, you might have to wait a while for them to be fixed. The same goes for buying a game on the day it comes out. If there is a problem, you will have to wait for a fix to be posted.*

Loose Fitting Graphics Adapter

The continual heating and cooling that happens inside a PC during each switch-on and switch-off cycle can cause *joint creep* to occur. This is because as components heat up, they expand. This expansion causes joints to become looser and cards to distort slightly. Slowly, over many on/off cycles, this can cause the cards to work loose, until one day a connection is severed and the system no longer works. It isn't unknown for a graphics adapter, even though it is screwed down on one end, to work loose from the slot and cause the whole system to stop functioning. Graphics adapters are more prone to this kind of problem than other kinds of expansion cards because they themselves generate a lot of heat.

 PC DOCTOR'S ORDER! *Never use any form of thread-locking compound (common in the automotive industry) on any screws on a PC. This can make undoing them difficult and can damage the delicate threads.*

Each time you open the case on your computer, take a few seconds to check the connections and look for any signs of distortion. If you see any, undo any of the connecting screws and remove the card before reseating it.

Also, some graphics adapters have a separate power supply fed from a drive connecting socket. If this is present, check it for signs of looseness.

Broken/Damaged/Loose Monitor Connector

If the monitor suddenly seems to cut out, but the PC appears to be running OK (judging by the lights) and the power light is illuminated on the front of the monitor, check to see if the monitor/PC connection is sound (no pun intended).

Undo the connector and visually check both the plug and the socket (shown in Figure 11-4) for damage such as broken or bent pins. Redo the connection, tightening up the screws hand tight (don't use power tools or cordless screwdrivers here, as any tighter and you might cause damage), and try it again.

If you are unfortunate enough to break a pin, there is little chance that you can repair it. You might be lucky enough to have only broken a part of the pin, and there might be enough left to use. If you bend a pin, you'll be able to fix it. Take a small pair of tweezers and gently grasp the whole of the bent pin in the tip of the tweezers. Carefully squeeze the pin straight, gently working the metal. Once you get the pin to the approximate position that it should be in, try reattaching the connector to it, slowly and carefully easing it onto the pins. If the pin still seems out of alignment, go back to the tweezers and work on the pin again, bending it no more than is needed. Never work a bent pin back and forth, as this will undoubtedly break it off.

FIGURE 11-4   Graphics card connector

PC DOCTOR'S ORDER! *If a device has a broken pin, don't use it, as it may be damaged. Also, if a pin has broken off, check the cable in case the remnant of the pin is still in the connector, as this could damage the pin on the next device you try to connect.*

Defective Graphics Adapter

Nothing lasts forever, and consider that a PC is made up of dozens of interlinked components consisting of thousands of individual parts, each of which plays a key role. If even one fails, the whole component is dead. The fastest, easiest way to test a component is to try it on a known good system. Remove the old card, insert the new one, and see if the system works. You don't need to fully boot up the system; just as long as you see something on the screen, you can be sure that it works.

 NOTE *A great use for an old system left over after buying a new one is for testing. And by keeping the old one, you also have a backup in case your main computer goes down.*

Overheating

A PC creates huge amounts of heat that need to be carried away from sensitive components by ensuring adequate air flow around the system. If this doesn't happen properly, overheating will occur, which may result in intermittent system problems (lockups, crashes, and reboots) or could even damage the components permanently.

It is usually the CPU and hard drives that generate the most heat, but recent boosts in the performance of graphics adapters have added them to the category of "heat generators." Many graphics adapters make use of heat sinks and fans to cool components, but these rely on a constant and ample air supply. This air also needs to be cooler than that of the component; otherwise no cooling will happen no matter how powerful the fans! Always make sure you keep the air intakes on the case clear of dirt and dust and unobscured by books and papers. Also, over time the fans and heat sinks can collect huge amounts of dirt and dust. This can reduce the effectiveness of the heat sinks and fans, and if the buildup is great, it can damage or even completely stop the fans from turning.

Dirt and dust need to be cleaned out regularly. How often you clean your PC depends on how dusty an environment it is in. You will need to clean it more often in a room where there are carpets and pets, compared to a more sterile office environment.

Clean fans carefully with compressed air and a vacuum cleaner. With a little practice, you will be able blow the dust free with the air and catch it with the vacuum cleaner.

While you are working on the fans, remember that they are delicate (an example is shown in Figure 11-3 earlier). You should never press or turn fans by hand, as this will damage them. Don't worry if the air blast causes them to rotate; that's quite safe and won't cause damage.

Doctor's Notes

The monitor is a big part of the whole PC package and unfortunately, because of the high voltages inside it, is a part that should be left to the experts in the event of a problem with it. If you have any reason to suspect your monitor is faulty (you smell a burning smell coming from it or it cuts out or just plain doesn't work), unplug it and leave it to the experts. You can attach another monitor to the system and if that works it should show you that the faulty item is indeed the monitor and that it should be repaired or replaced.

The graphics adapter is a key component of your system and carries out a vital job. It is also a complex job, and things can sometimes go wrong. Fortunately, manufacturers correct and compensate for many of the problems that users come across, and the Internet has made it easy to get new, updated drivers.

The graphics adapter can also need looking after, in the form of making sure that the drivers are the best possible and that it is clean and getting adequate cooling. Make checking the graphics adapter a part of your regular maintenance routine!

Monitors and Graphics Adapters—
Troubleshooting Checklist

- ☑ Never open the case on a monitor; always seek professional help if you have a problem with a monitor.

- ☑ If the adapter is newly installed, have you installed all the necessary drivers and software? Reinstall drivers and software.

- ☑ Check all the cables and connections between the PC and the monitor.

- ☑ Carefully check cables and connectors for signs of damage.

☑ Check that you have all the tools you need before opening the case.

☑ Carry out safety checks (power off, etc.).

☑ Protect against ESD.

☑ Open case.

☑ Check graphics adapter seating. Remove and reseat as required.

☑ Check the graphics adapter cooling system (fan and heat sink).

☑ Start up the system; install any software/drivers.

☑ Thoroughly test the system.

☑ If possible, try the graphics adapter on a different PC.

☑ If all else fails, contact tech support for the device.

Chapter 12

Expansion Cards

Expansion cards offer a way to expand on the capabilities of your PC by adding more circuit boards to the system directly onto the motherboard using preexisting connections (called slots). Every desktop PC and tower offers slots that allow you to add cards. In this chapter we'll examine the different slots that you might encounter inside a PC and look at several different kinds of expansion cards that you can add to your system.

Expansion Slots

There are three different kinds of expansion slots that you are likely to come across when you look at the motherboard of your PC. These are PCI (Peripheral Component Interconnect), AGP (Accelerated Graphics Port), and ISA (Industry Standard Architecture).

PCI (Peripheral Component Interconnect)

Most of the cards you will have in your system will be PCI cards. Network cards, modems, TV cards, and sound cards are all now usually in PCI form, with many graphics cards being made to fit the PCI slot too.

When you look at PCI cards that fit into the slots, you may come across a wide variety of connector numbers. The 32-bit PCI cards (that is, those capable of transmitting 32 bits of information simultaneously) have 124-pin connectors (not just carrying data but also power supply for the card and grounding), while 64-bit cards have 188-pin connectors. Figure 12-1 shows a close-up of a PCI slot on a motherboard, and Figure 12-2 shows a typical PCI card.

Card lengths can also vary. The PCI specifications define two different lengths:

■ The full-size PCI form factor is 312 mm long.

■ Shorter PCI cards range from 119 mm to 167 mm in length to fit into smaller slots where space is an issue.

FIGURE 12-1   Close-up of a PCI slot on a motherboard

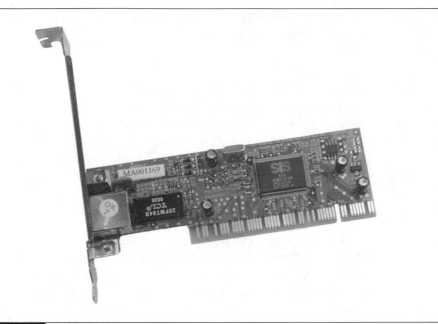

FIGURE 12-2 A PCI card

AGP (Accelerated Graphics Port)

Because of the volume of data that graphics demand, trying to push huge amounts of data through a PCI slot has always resulted in a bottleneck. To alleviate this, AGP was born.

A 32-bit PCI card can handle data rates of 133 Mbps (megabytes per second), but a 32-bit AGP adapter can handle a whopping 533 Mbps, with the future promising in excess of 2.5 Gbps and higher. This means that in the future (as processor power increases), we'll be seeing better and faster graphics on the PC, making games more realistic and general screen viewing more pleasurable.

AGP was designed primarily for rendering onscreen 3D graphics and is ideally suited to gaming, video, and sophisticated scientific/engineering graphics programs. It is a 132-pin connector, 71 mm long, and the connectors are usually brown. Another huge advantage that AGP has is that it can access and make use of main system memory (that is, the RAM installed on your PC). This makes AGP graphics adapters cheaper while not sacrificing power.

PC DOCTOR'S ORDER! *Most motherboards now support AGP, but both the motherboard and the BIOS need to support AGP for it to be available.*

If you take a close look at an AGP card (shown in Figure 12-3), you will notice that there is a slot on the front of the card, or even a clamp. This slot clips into a holder that is present on some motherboards and is used to secure the front of the graphics card, while the clamp actually clamps the card to the motherboard. (The rear is secured using standard screws that we will be looking at shortly.) Be mindful of this when you are removing and replacing AGP cards.

ISA (Industry Standard Architecture)

The ISA is not a commonly used slot nowadays and impossible to find on new motherboards. Figure 12-4 shows what they look like. If you do have a PC old enough to have ISA slots, you are unlikely to be able to get any expansion cards for it. Fortunately, during the transition period, motherboards were manufactured with both ISA and PCI slots. If your motherboard does not have PCI slots, and you want to add something extra, it is probably time to think about buying a more modern system.

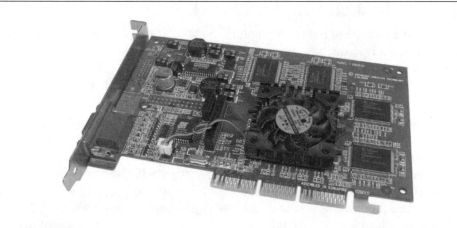

FIGURE 12-3   A PCI expansion card—this one is an AGP graphics adapter, showing a close-up of the connectors and the slot.

FIGURE 12-4   ISA slot

Card Removal and Refitting

Removing and adding cards is a common upgrade and repair task, and like most things in life, there's the right way to do it, the wrong way to do it, and the hard way! I'll cover the right way to remove and add cards to a PC.

Card Removal

Before proceeding with the steps in removing a card, take some time to prepare for the job. Always take the necessary ESD precautions to prevent damage to the system. Even if you are removing an unwanted or defective card from the system, carelessness with ESD can damage more than the case you are working on. Always wear a wrist strap properly grounded, and be careful of loose clothing or hair getting into the system.

Work in a clear area. If you have to, pull the PC away from its working location and place it on a table. Make sure you have good lighting (a plastic or rubber flashlight is ideal—avoid big, heavy aluminum ones that will cause huge amounts of damage should you drop one into the system). Have plenty of free space to work in and freedom from pets and others entering your workplace and distracting you. Get all your tools ready and check them before starting. Usually you will only need a medium-sized crosspoint screwdriver, but some cards might be held in place by little bolts. Also, if you are going to have to remove slot covers, you might need a flat-headed screwdriver.

FIX-IT-YOURSELF HOME REMEDY   *As you get more proficient at card replacement, you'll need less space. Eventually you will probably be able to carry out the job with the PC in its normal working position. However, give yourself the best possible start if it is your first time and prepare the area properly.*

OK, you're ready to begin.

1. Take all necessary safety precautions, and unplug the PC from the power outlet.

2. Carefully open the case and set it aside, away from your working area.

3. Locate the card at the back that you want to remove. Sometimes it can be hard to ID the card by how it looks on the inside, so be sure to visually identify it externally.

4. Give the area around the slot (and the rest of the interior of the system) a darn good cleaning with compressed air.

5. Locate the screw holding the rear of the card onto the PC chassis. Slowly and carefully undo the screw (see Figure 12-5). After the first couple of turns with the screwdriver, it may be easier to finish undoing it by hand. Take care not to drop the screw into the PC! Place the screw on one side for safekeeping.

 PC DOCTOR'S ORDER! *If you do happen to drop a screw into the system, make sure that you've retrieved it before starting the system again, as it could cause a huge amount of damage.*

FIGURE 12-5   Undoing the holding screw at the back of the card

6. Once the screw is out, double-check that you undid all the cables going to the card.

7. Now you can start to work the card loose. Grasp the card by the metal rail on one hand and the far end of the circuit board with the other (avoiding any components on the board), and gently and slowly pull the card free from the slot (see Figure 12-6). Don't use any more force than is needed, and take care not to bend the card, as it could crack the circuit panel.

8. Once the card is free, check it for signs of damage, overheating (scorch marks), missing components, or corrosion on the contacts. Corrosion on the contacts can be cleaned off by very carefully rubbing the contacts with a pencil eraser.

9. Place the card in an antistatic bag for safekeeping.

10. Check the slot for signs of damage (corrosion on the contacts, loose slot, dirt in the slot, etc.).

11. Cover the now vacant slot with a slot cover. (These usually come with a new PC, or you might have one if you removed a slot cover to add a card.) Attach firmly with the screw and hand tighten. If you are replacing the card, you can skip this step.

FIGURE 12-6   Correct removal technique for an expansion card

PC DOCTOR'S ORDER! *Never leave a PC with a slot uncovered, as it allows dirt and dust to enter your system. Also, it disrupts airflow and can cause the system to overheat.*

Replacing an Expansion Card

Replacing an expansion card is a little bit different from simply reversing the removal process.

1. Take all necessary ESD precautions!

2. Read all the instructions and paperwork that come with your new card. Make sure that you have everything you need and that you are familiar with the fitting process.

3. Begin by removing any slot covers that might be present. Some slot covers are separate from the case and have a screw holding them in place (keep the cover if this is the case). Others are a press-out metal blanking cover. Use a flat-headed screwdriver (preferably an old one) to snap out the plate, as shown in Figure 12-7.

 PC DOCTOR'S ORDER! *Take great care not to create tiny shards of metal that can infiltrate the case and cause short-circuits.*

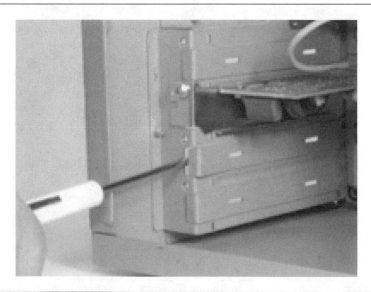

FIGURE 12-7   Removing a metal blanking plate using a flat-headed screwdriver

4. Make sure the expansion slot is free from dirt and dust that will damage the slot when the card is inserted or that might prevent it from making a good contact.

5. Carefully take the card out of the antistatic bag and hold it by the metal end rail. Gently and carefully guide it into the card slot (being careful not to knock components off the circuit board). Get it to the position where it is resting on the edge of the slot.

6. Now, place one hand on the end of the metal end rail of the card and the thumb of the other hand on the top edge of the card about a quarter of the way from the end, as shown in Figure 12-8. Taking great care not to press on any components, apply gentle pressure on the card. It will slowly sink into the slot. Work slowly and try not to rock or bend the card. Watch out for the metal rail at the end catching on the motherboard. If it looks wrong, remove the card and try again.

7. Once the card is correctly and firmly seated, secure the rail of the card with the screw. It can sometimes be tricky to get the screw to bite into the metal, so first give it a half turn counterclockwise while in the hole before turning it clockwise to tighten it. Never overtighten the screw.

 PC DOCTOR'S ORDER! *Never try to use the screw to work a card into a slot. If the card is not firmly seated, pull it out and try again. Tightening the screw on an improperly seated card can break the card.*

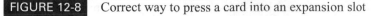
FIGURE 12-8   Correct way to press a card into an expansion slot

8. Visually check the connection and ensure that the card is still correctly seated. (Sometimes the card can be distorted when the screw is tightened.) Check all the other connections for signs of them coming undone or in case you dislodged something while working.

9. Do up the case on the system (making sure you haven't left anything inside), and plug it back in.

10. Switch the PC on and boot up the operating system. Install any software or drivers that the card needs in order to operate. (These should have been provided to you with any new card that you received.)

Special Considerations for Other Cards

What we are going to do for the remainder of this chapter is look at a few special considerations you have to bear in mind when installing certain cards in your system.

 FIX-IT-YOURSELF HOME REMEDY *Since cards and systems vary enormously, some of these considerations may not apply to you.*

Graphics Cards

The cable from your monitor to the card might cause you some grief, especially if you have a lot of other wires at the back of your PC. Monitor cable is very thick and pretty inflexible, and if you are installing an AGP card, you won't have any choice as to where the card goes. You'll only have one AGP slot inside your system. What you might have to do is move other cards to make sure that the cable has an unhindered path from monitor to card.

TV Cards

TV cards, again, have a thick coaxial cable going to them, feeding in the TV signal. Figure 12-9 shows the connectors on a TV card.

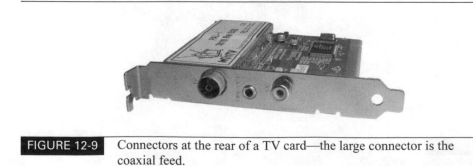

FIGURE 12-9   Connectors at the rear of a TV card—the large connector is the coaxial feed.

TV cards also usually have a TV card-to-sound card line-in bridging cable to carry the sound directly to the sound card. This means that the gap between the two cards cannot be too big.

Modems

One of the main problems with internal modems is that they can pick up interference from other components (such as fans) and other cards within the PC. With this in mind, it is always better to try to place a modem card so that it has a free slot on either side of it. This isn't always possible though, especially if you have a number of expansion cards installed. A modem card looks like the one shown in Figure 12-10.

Sound Cards

There are two main issues with sound cards: first, they are the potential source (or destination, depending on how you look at it) of a lot of cables. Cables usually mean tangles unless properly looked after. Add to the cable frenzy all the cables originating from other cards and peripherals, and you have an enormous scope for tangling and mess.

 PC DOCTOR'S ORDER! *Keep cables as tidy as possible all the time. The more mess they get into, the harder it will be to sort them out and the greater the potential scope for damage.*

Second, most systems still have the sound connectors at the back. Some have them at the front now, but most systems older than six months or so will most likely have the ports at the back. If you've added a different sound card, this will almost certainly mean that the connectors are on the back of the machine. This means that if you want to change speakers or temporarily connect a microphone or headphones, you are going to have to go climbing around the back to plug in the jacks.

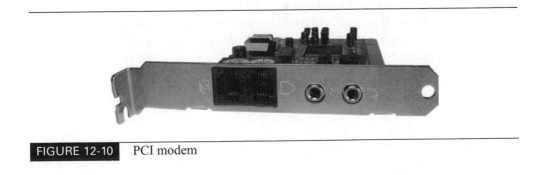

FIGURE 12-10   PCI modem

If you habitually use headphones or microphones, you might want to consider adding a third-party extension cable to the ports to bring them to a more convenient location. There are many different types (most sold to make video conferencing easier), and they are available at most computer outlets. The adaptor might look something like this:

 PC DOCTOR'S ORDER! *Take special care when using headphones on your PC. If you forget to remove them before getting up, you could seriously damage your headphones and even the sound card.*

Doctor's Notes

Because so many devices can be added to a PC by connecting to one of the various ports on the outside, you could be forgiven for thinking that you'll have no need to open the case when you want to add anything new to your system. Not true!

As you become more confident in working on your PC (rather than with it), you'll find yourself looking at where it is lacking or how it can be improved. As you think of new things you want your PC to do, you will eventually need to add or replace an expansion card that it contains. And this is where this chapter will be useful to you.

Whether you are removing an unwanted or defective expansion card, or replacing a card, the key is to work methodically and carefully, and take your time. Make sure that you work in a clear space and that you are free from distraction and others moving about in your workspace.

Keep all new cards in their antistatic bags before use, and place the old cards in the bags as soon as possible to protect them. ESD is one of the biggest dangers to cards while you are working on them.

Expansion Cards—Fitting/Removal Checklist

☑ Read all instructions and paperwork relating to your device, and keep all the paperwork and drivers for future reference.

☑ Work methodically, taking all necessary safety precautions and protecting against ESD.

☑ Clean the area around the card so that it is free of dust and dirt before removal and refitting of the card.

☑ Never force a card in or out of a slot. Never bend the card or hold it by components.

☑ Make sure that cards are correctly seated in the slot before attaching the holding screw.

☑ Take care not to drop screws into the case. Immediately retrieve any that are dropped, and keep track of how many you have undone—count them in and out!

☑ Check the contacts on cards that you are removing and adding for signs of damage or corrosion.

☑ On restarting the system after adding a new expansion card, install any drivers or software required.

Chapter 13

Networking

S uch is the desire to have instant access to a PC when necessity or the desire takes us, that many homes and most offices now have more than one PC available. It's therefore natural that people want to take these separate resources and link them together in order to share information and attached resources, such as printers and modems.

One thing that has become easier with every release of each new operating system is the ability to connect PCs together via a network. The software side might have become easier, but folks who have a couple of PCs and want to establish a link between them often don't find that the hardware side has improved. In this chapter we'll be looking at the hardware that you need to connect PCs and how that hardware comes together to create a network.

What Is a Network?

A *network* is a way to connect PCs so that data and resources can be shared. If you have two PCs at home and one or both access the Internet, you are already connecting to a kind of network (albeit on a massive scale). If you want to establish a link between your PCs, you'll need to create a small network of your own. Once you have done this, the resources (printer, modem, hard drives, etc.) on both PCs can be made available to each user, and you can share information between the two and even send each other messages across the network. If you are into gaming, setting up a network will allow two people to play games "head-to-head" (if the game allows network play, which many do). This can add a new dimension to game play that is a lot of fun!

There are dozens of different kinds of networks, ranging from small, two-PC outfits to the massive network that makes up what we call the Internet. Do a search on the Web for "networking," and you will come across terms like WAN (wide area network), PAN (personal area network), MAN (metropolitan area network), LAN (local area network), Ethernet, and many more.

The two terms that we are concerned with here are LAN and Ethernet. A local area network is a group of computers and associated devices that share a common communications line or wireless link. Contrary to what most people think, you don't need to have a single "dedicated" computer running as a server to have a LAN network; the minimum you need is two standard PCs and a method of connecting them.

NOTE *That is not to say that a LAN couldn't be scaled up to include thousands of users, but if you are looking to do that, you're reading the wrong book!*

Ethernet is the most widely used LAN technology. It has grown from a standard that dates back several years, and it gives you the easiest, most flexible way to connect PCs.

Let's look at some decisions you'll have to make before you know what hardware you need.

Decisions, Decisions, Decisions…

As always, what hardware you need depends on what you want to do with it. You have some decisions that you need to make before you begin buying bits. Doing this now will save you a lot of time and money later, so don't skimp on this step.

Before you go to the PC store or fire up your browser and visit your favorite online retailer, spend a few minutes going through the following:

1. How many PCs do you want to connect? Is it two or more? If it is currently two, is there a possibility that you'll want to add another to the network soon (within 3 to 12 months)?

2. What are you going to be using the network for? Is it occasional file transfer and printer use, or will you be playing games or connecting to the Internet via the network?

3. Do you have any network hardware in any of the PCs already? If you are unsure, check! Some PCs have network adapters built onto the motherboard. Take a look at the back of the system for the port (or consult the manual). If you do have the hardware, it might need a software driver installed to bring it to life.

4. How spaced out are the PCs you want to connect? Are they side by side or in different rooms? Are they all desktops, or are there laptops/mobile devices in the equation?

Answer these questions as honestly as possible, and then go through the following to analyze what this means.

1. OK, are you connecting two PCs or more than two? The reason for asking this is that if you are only going to be connecting two, you might be able to join the two together directly, adding a network adapter to each and using a cable known as a *crossover cable*. Not every network adapter supports this (so if you have existing hardware, this could be a problem), but it is a cheap

and easy way of connecting two PCs. However, if you plan on adding more PCs to the network at a later stage, *do not* take this option now, and instead build a proper network foundation early.

2. Honestly, how much data are you going to be pumping through the network? The occasional file transfer and printer use, or something more sustained? If you are going to be making more than just the occasional use of the network, you are better off looking at the 100Base-TX high-speed Ethernet standard that transmits data at 100 Mbps (megabits per second) as opposed to the slower 10Base-T standard, which only operates at 10 Mbps. Make sure that the hardware you have (or purchase) supports the speed that you require. If you want even more speed, look for the latest gigabit Ethernet equipment that supports 1 Gbps transfer (1000 Mbps). This will give you an ultrafast network that will support many users and network-intensive activities such as gaming.

3. Hardware that you already have installed might affect your purchasing choices. Check all your PCs (desktops and laptops) for any network adapters, and find out their specifications (probably in the documentation).

4. Are the PCs you want to network side by side or in different rooms? If they are in different rooms, consider how you are going to route the cabling from one to the other. Are you happy drilling holes in the walls? Would a wireless solution be a better option for you? Also, consider the cost of the wiring. With networking hardware being quite cheap nowadays, the cost of the cabling that you will need may add significantly to the cost of the job.

Network Hardware

Let's now begin our tour of the hardware that you need to set up a home network. We'll begin with the trusty network interface card.

The Network Interface Card

Also known as an NIC, the network interface card is the mainstay of most networks. They are so generic nowadays that to almost all intents and purposes people just call them "network cards."

The most popular network card is the PCI network card that fits into the expansion slot in a PC. They have a port in the back for the network cable and usually a couple of lights indicating that the card and network are working properly (handy place for the lights at the back of the PC!).

You plug this kind of card into a free slot, reboot the machine, load the drivers, and you're off!

If you have a laptop and it doesn't have a built-in network adapter (not all do in order to keep the price down and to offer a wider "range"), you can add your own network adapter. However, you won't be able to add one in the form of an expansion card. Instead, you can add one in the PCMCIA (Personal Computer Memory Card International Association) or PC Card slot present on most laptops:

If you don't have a PCMCIA/PC Card slot on your laptop, you might be able to add a USB network adapter that does the same thing.

Once you have a network adapter, you need to think about how things are going to connect together. One thing you are going to need to connect things together is cabling.

Network Cable

The cable you are most likely to come across in LAN networking is called the CAT 5 (short for "category 5") UTP cable (UTP stands for unshielded twisted pair).

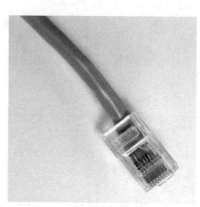

This cable is approximately 6 mm in diameter and has on each end a connector called an RJ-45. Here's a close-up:

This cable can be the snagged type (it has a small plastic retaining clip to keep it in the port on the network adapter) or snagless (which also has the clip, but the clip is protected from snagging on things by small plastic guards that cover the clip). As you can see, the one pictured above is snagless. In areas where you might want to pull the cable through holes in the wall or through a lot of wiring, use the snagless type, as this reduces the risk of damage to the clip and other cables.

 PC DOCTOR'S ORDER! *Along with the CAT 5 cable, you might come across network equipment that uses coaxial cable with BNC bayonet connectors at the ends. My suggestion to you is that you steer clear of this stuff because it is far more trouble than it's worth. The connectors are very hard to get right and continually fall off or become loose and break the network connection. Go with the modern, better CAT 5, and you'll save yourself a lot of headache and trouble!*

A cable solution for a network is a common way to create a network because it is cheap and relatively easy. However, because you are using cables, there are a few considerations to bear in mind:

- Be careful not to damage the cable by pulling excessively on it, and don't be unduly rough with the connector.

- Never crush the cable with filing cabinets or desks. Never put cable where it can be walked on. (If it must cross traffic areas, install cable guards to prevent damage to the cable and to eliminate the risk of tripping over it.)

- Don't create loops of cable that are too tight or pull the cable too tightly around corners. The minimum bend radius for CAT 5 cable should be no less than eight times the diameter of the cable (about 50 mm or 2 inches).

- If you are making holes in the wall for cables, make them no smaller than 15 mm (5/8 inch) in diameter. Take care when pulling cables through walls that they don't get damaged.

- Support hanging cables with broad supports, not on narrow hangers, as this can damage the cable.

- Keep cabling at least 6 inches away from fluorescent or HID (high-intensity discharge) light fixtures.

- Don't use metal cable staples or staple guns. Instead, use plastic stand-off cable staples.

- Use cable ties to keep cable bundles together. Don't overtighten the ties (they should rotate freely on the bundle) or install them at regular intervals. (As the bundle sags, regularly spaced ties can stress the cable and damage

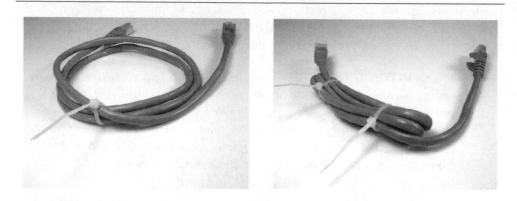

FIGURE 13-1   Cable on the left is looped properly

the delicate internal wires.) Figure 13-1 shows cable looped properly (on the left) and improperly (on the right).

- Reduce possible electrical interference by making sure that CAT 5 cable doesn't go through holes with electrical cables or cross them at right angles.

- Do keep installations as neat as possible and document connections carefully.

- Never try to repair damaged cable. Replace the whole thing.

- The longest length of cable that you should use is 330 feet (100 meters). If you want to span greater distances, use extra network hubs. The longer the cable, the greater the risk of slowing the network down.

 NOTE *The connectors at each end of the cable are identical.*

Types of Cable

There are two kinds of cable you can use to connect a 10Base-T or 100Base-TX network adapter:

- Straight-through cable
- Crossover cable

PC DOCTOR'S ORDER! *Visually, straight-through and crossover cable look the same (the markings might betray it, but they can be hard to read), so make sure you get the right cable.*

If you are connecting more than two PCs together (or you are connecting two but want to have room for future expansion), you need another piece of kit that we haven't looked at yet—a network hub.

Network Hub

So far, you know that one end of the CAT 5 cable is connected to the network adapter. But what about the other end? The other end of the cable is connected to a device known as a network hub (or sometimes a switch). The hub performs the function of the crossover cable and allows one PC to communicate with all the others connected to the hub.

The network hub then takes over the job of allowing a PC to communicate with the rest of the PCs on the network. The network hub itself will be powered and will need to be close to a power supply. (It is best if the power supply has a lightning surge protector or UPS protecting it.)

Most network hubs are compatible with both 10Base-T and 100Base-TX network adapters, and you can mix and match adapters on the hub. However, remember that when communicating with a computer that has a slower 10Base-T adapter, the speed of the connection will be at the slower rate.

Setting Up a Network Hub

Setting up a network hub is simplicity itself: take the device out of the box, wall mount it with screws or place it on a desk (not as good an idea as wall mounting because it can be dragged about by the wires connected to it), plug all the network cables (that originate from the PCs you want to connect together) into the back of the hub, and hook it up to the electrical outlet. Try to place it in a clear, well-ventilated area, and ensure that it has adequate airflow around it to keep it cool. Network hubs don't require any installations or drivers.

FIX-IT-YOURSELF HOME REMEDY *Earlier I mentioned the fact that crossover cables are used to network two PCs together, while straight-through cables are used to connect PCs to a hub. Well, that's an oversimplification. Most modern network hubs can automatically detect what type of cable is being used to connect a PC to it and modify automatically, allowing you to make further use of any cables you've already bought. Consult the manual that comes with your network hub.*

Hubs can come equipped with different numbers of ports—4, 8, 12, and 16 are the most common.

You can also connect a number of hubs together by different means. One way is to use hubs that come with a special port known as an *uplink port* that allows the hub to be connected to another network hub, expanding the number of connections available. Other hubs have a switched uplink port that can be switched from being an ordinary port to an uplink port. Finally, on the higher-end hubs, you can have autodetection on all the ports. This type detects whether the port is connected to a network adapter or another hub and reconfigures automatically. This can be a real time-saver.

Adding hubs is not limitless though! Depending on your network type, you can have up to four hubs on the network:

■ 10Base-T supports four hubs.

■ 100Base-TX supports two hubs.

■ 1000Base-T (gigabit Ethernet) supports only one hub.

Your Hub Tells You About the Network

Don't just wire up the network hub and forget about it! Take time to look at it and familiarize yourself with the lights on the device and what information they are communicating to you. There are usually a lot of lights on a network hub. Here are some of the most common:

■ **PWR/Power**   When illuminated, indicates the device is powered

■ **ACK**   Acknowledges the receipt of data

■ **Speed**   Indicates the speed of the adapter connected to the hub

■ **Col**   Indicates that there has been a data collision on the network

■ **Err**   Indicates an unspecific error

There will also usually be a separate light for each port on your hub. This light will illuminate when a cable is connected to the port. This light might be combined with the ACK and speed lights.

 PC DOCTOR'S ORDER! *Read the documentation that comes with your hub carefully and familiarize yourself with what all the lights mean on your hub.*

Surge/Lightning Protection

Because you have both wires and power going into a hub, you have the scope for a voltage surge or lightning damaging your devices. Both of these can either damage or destroy your equipment and can also present a fire hazard. A voltage surge is only likely to damage your hub and take the network down, but a lightning strike on a PC or cable or the hub is likely to damage or destroy not only the hub but also the PC connected to it. For security and peace of mind, I suggest protecting networks fully from both.

For protection from voltage surges, I suggest that as a minimum precaution you should put a surge protector between the hub and the power supply. This will filter out damaging voltage before it has time to damage your equipment. For greater protection, install a battery backup UPS system (shown in Figure 13-2), which will feature surge protection.

Protection against lightning, especially if you live in an area prone to thunderstorms, is also valuable. Because of the interconnection that the network gives and the massive cable lengths sometimes used, lightning strikes on the cables become not only more likely but also more damaging.

FIGURE 13-2   UPS device

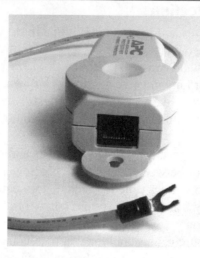

FIGURE 13-3   Network surge protector

The best cure is prevention, and prevention in this case comes in the form of a network surge protector (see Figure 13-3).

Usually you install one of these at the PC end of the network cable and attach the grounding cable to a suitable grounding point nearby. However, for complete protection, add one at both the PC end and the hub end. It might seem like overkill, but it's far better than having all your equipment damaged by a single lightning strike.

PC DOCTOR'S ORDER! *Never underestimate the damage that a lightning strike can cause. If you have no protection on your network currently, I strongly suggest that you disconnect the hub from the power supply and all the cables during a thunderstorm. Move the cables away from the hub/PC by about 45 cm (18 inches) to create an air gap that the lightning is unlikely to jump.*

Troubleshooting Network Hardware

If you have a network with a hub and the hub stops working, so does the rest of your network. Follow this simple hardware troubleshooting guide for home networks:

1. How many PCs are involved? Are all the PCs unable to communicate, or is the problem isolated to just one? If the whole network is down, check the network hub and go to step 2, otherwise go to step 6.

2. Check that the network hub is powered properly and that the power light is illuminated. If it isn't, investigate why.

3. Even if the hub appears to be working, internally it might have a glitch. To clear this, unplug the hub from the power source and wait 30 seconds before reconnecting it to the power, after which, try it again.

4. If you have connected two hubs via an uplink port, check to see that the connection cable between them is sound, and if present, check the uplink switch.

5. If none of the above helps, switch off all the PCs and disconnect all the connections from the hub. Then reconnect them all and retry.

6. If the problem is confined to one PC, check that the cable connection between the PC and the hub is sound, and retry.

7. Check that the network card is properly seated. Remove and reseat if in doubt.

8. Check that the software is properly installed for the device and that the operating system is properly set up. (Consult the documentation that came with your hardware for assistance.)

Dealing with Collisions

When you set up a network, one thing you'll notice is that the collision light doesn't light up very often (if the network is set up correctly at least), but sometimes you might find that it flashes on and off often or even stays on all the time. This will be accompanied by a slowing down of the network, because two or more devices are trying to communicate with each other simultaneously, causing the two devices to wait before trying to talk again. If this happens often enough (a few times a second), the network will slow down. If it becomes more frequent, the problems will get even worse. However, there are a few things you can do to eliminate the problems.

1. Is the network under an excessive load? This is unlikely to be a problem with a home network, unless serious gaming is going on, and you might either want to upgrade the speed of the network adapter you use or maybe even split the network into smaller units.

2. Shorten any excessively long cables. Get the shortest cable possible to do the job. The longer the cables, the greater the chance of electrical interference.

3. Remove any knots or excessive loops from the cables.

4. Check for cable damage and replace any suspect cables.

5. Make sure cables are plugged in properly at both ends.

6. Check drivers installed on the PCs. Upgrade any old drivers with newer ones downloaded from the Internet.

7. Check in case the cables are going by any noisy (from an electrical point of view) devices, such as fluorescent lights, power supply units, and power lines, and reroute the cable if you need to. Electrical noise in the cable can cause the hub to think that data is being transmitted when it is in fact just interference.

8. If all the above fail to bring a resolution to the problem, it's possible that the noise is being generated by a faulty network interface card or even the hub. Disconnect each PC in turn from the network, and see if you can isolate the card/PC/cable causing the problem. Replace any adapters or cables that appear to be causing the problem. If none of the PCs appears to be the source of the problem, assume it is the network hub and replace.

Wireless Network Solutions

No longer do you have to use masses of cables or drill massive holes in walls and ceilings or crawl about in lofts and crawlspaces trying to feed cables around your home. By installing a wireless network you can do away with the need for wires—very handy indeed!

Going wireless allows you to connect to the network from a distance of up to 540 meters (1800 feet). This is the maximum distance that you can connect from, and walls, floors, and ceilings will reduce this. However, distances of at least 100 meters (330 feet) are easily achieved.

Let's take a look at what you need to set up a wireless network.

Wireless Hub/Router

The core of most wireless networks is the hub, or router, which takes the place of the network hub and controls how the PCs communicate with one another. There are many different types of wireless hubs/routers on the market, and what you get depends on your needs and budget.

■ Make sure that whatever you get conforms to the latest high-speed 54g 802.11g standard, which offers wireless speeds up to 54 Mbps. This is reasonably fast, but only just over half the speed of a wired 100Base-TX network. Normally, this drop in speed isn't noticeable, but if you want the fastest possible home network, you should, if possible, still opt for a wired network. There are slower standards (such as the 802.11b standard that offers speeds up to 11 Mbps), but these are rapidly becoming obsolete. Don't skimp on the router you use!

NOTE *The 54g standard uses the 2.4 GHz radio frequency to communicate. This is a license-free band, and you don't have to pay any fee in order to use it (apart from purchasing the equipment).*

- Do you want to connect your wireless network to a broadband Internet connection? If so, you might want to consider getting a wireless router that allows you to connect the router directly to a broadband modem. (The modem will need an Ethernet port on it to allow this to work.)

- Do you want to connect wired devices to your wireless network too (such as desktops)? Many wireless access points have built-in ports that take the place of a wired network hub. This allows you to integrate wireless and wired in the same network (say, wired for the desktops and wireless for laptops and mobile devices).

- You actually don't need to have a wireless router or access point in order to create a wireless network. It is possible to create a network known as an *ad hoc network* that allows PCs to communicate directly with one another.

Router Placement Tips

Because your router is the hub with which all of your other wireless devices must communicate, it is important to choose its location well. Here are the top wireless router placement tips:

- Try to place your router centrally in the building. This way you will be able to roam around and work in different rooms. Don't fall into the trap of thinking that you only want good reception in your study or office, because as soon as you have wireless, everywhere will become your study! Placing the router against outside walls might be a necessity though, so be aware that your network could be broadcasting well outside the boundary of your property.

- Be aware that walls, doors, ceilings, and floors all reduce the signal strength and quality. The thicker the material the signal has to travel through, the weaker it will become.

- Choose a dry, well-ventilated area for the wireless router. Kitchens and bathrooms are a bad location, as are small cupboards or pigeonholes.

- As with most devices, keep them away from windows where strong sunlight can cause overheating. This is especially important for wireless equipment because overheating can lead to electrical noise and slower speeds.

- If possible, place the router higher than head height. This will give you the best possible reception.

- In a two-story building, a good place to put the router is centrally somewhere above head height on the second story.

- If your router has two antennas on the back, orient them so that one is pointing up and the other down. This seems to offer the best all-around reception.

- Test your reception for signal strength in various areas indoors (and outdoors, if you plan on using it outside). Aim to have signal strength/ quality above 35–40 percent everywhere you will be using the wireless network.

- If possible, surge-protect the power supply to the router and any wired network connections to it.

Wireless Network Interface Cards

In addition to a router, you'll need a wireless network interface card to allow you to communicate with the router (if you're not connecting to it with a wired connection). This will need to be able to communicate with the wireless hub using the same or compatible standard. (The best way to get a compatible card is to get one from the same manufacturer and preferably the same range.) There are several types of network interface cards that you can get, depending on the device you want to connect:

- A PCI wireless network adapter for a desktop PC

- A PCMCIA/PC Card network adapter for a laptop PC

- USB network adapter

- Small, Compact Flash wireless card for handheld devices

Desktop PCI Wireless Card

The desktop PCI wireless card is a replacement/substitute for a wired network adapter that you might have or want in a PC. These cards basically look like a standard network adapter but without the port; instead they have an antenna on the back.

This type of wireless card gives good radio reception and allows normal network activity to be carried out.

PCMCIA/PC Card

Laptops are enormously popular nowadays, and because of the nature of a laptop (a mobile device that you carry around with you), tethering it to a fixed network point seems odd. In the past, several companies had network points scattered around their offices (some even having a few outdoors!) to allow employees the freedom to roam and still be hooked up to the network. Well, wireless networking technology makes this really easy.

Installation is a snap: just install the drivers, and insert the card in a spare slot.

You will need to set up the card to detect the wireless router, but this is generally easy to do with setup wizards and the new Wireless Zero Configuration service available on Windows XP.

 PC DOCTOR'S ORDER! *A word of caution when using wireless PCMCIA/PC Card cards: they generally stick out of the PCMCIA/PC Card slot by 1–1 ¼ inch (25–30 mm), usually because of the antenna. This can be a weak point. Take care when using your equipment that you don't knock or hit this when moving the PC around, as serious damage can occur to both the card and the slot on the laptop.*

Compact Flash Wireless Card

If you have other mobile devices (such as a Pocket PC, powered handheld devices, or palm devices), you will also probably (eventually!) want to connect these to your wireless network. In some cases you might be lucky and find that the device you have already has built-in support for connecting to a wireless network, in which case you are pretty much ready to go. However, if your device doesn't have support, all is not lost, as you can usually add support in the form of a wireless card.

The most common way to add this kind of support is through the addition of a Compact Flash wireless card. While a few of the handheld devices come with support for Compact Flash, those that don't can usually have support added through the addition of a Compact Flash adapter or "expansion sleeve," such as those commonly available for the iPAQ range of handheld devices.

The range on these devices isn't as good as what you get with a full-sized card, but you can still roam easily 50-75 meters (160–250 feet) away from the wireless router.

Wireless Security

Wireless networking isn't without risk. Because you are theoretically creating a network without the use of a physical wire, it does mean that other people you might not want on your network could gain access to systems (such as hard drives), devices (such as printers), and resources (such as your Internet connection) without your knowledge. Never skimp on wireless security.

 PC DOCTOR'S ORDER! *Read the manuals that come with your router and other wireless equipment carefully and familiarize yourself with the setup and security features. Thankfully, most driver installation programs have an easy-to-follow wizard to make setup easier.*

Wireless network security revolves around creating a station ID (called an SSID) and a passphrase. Several different kinds of wireless network security are possible nowadays. The two most common are

- WEP (Wireless Equivalent Privacy)
- WPA (WiFi Protected Access)

WPA is better than WEP, but currently there isn't widespread support for it.

Here are tips for good network security:

- Use the best security possible. What this is will depend a lot on the hardware you use and software available. You might have to experiment to get a level of security that works and is workable for you.

- Choose a good, long SSID (up to 32 characters), and set the hardware not to broadcast this as the default (although in the beginning while you are setting up the network, it might be easier if the system is set to broadcast the SSID until you are happy with the setup). Consult the manual on security. Don't rely on the default SSID; these are known to people who might want to try to access your system.

- Choose a good passphrase, and keep it secret.

- Change the SSID and passphrase regularly (every other month is ideal; change it more often for extra security).

- Most wireless routers let you control which devices are allowed to connect to it by using a system called MAC ID (Media Access Control Identification). Each network adapter has its own MAC ID, and you can enter this into the router and block any other adapters. It's not foolproof (because it is possible to copy or clone MAC IDs), but it is another layer of security and worth implementing.

These are just the basics of wireless security. Using a good passphrase and SSID and changing them regularly are adequate measures for most users. Setting deeper security is just adding needless complexity to the setup. By following these guidelines, you keep it simple, yet secure.

Doctor's Notes

With homes and offices installing more PCs, the desire to link them together and have them communicate with one other and share resources is great. If you have more than one computer, you should consider the advantages of creating a network.

Networks are what you make them, but the hardware side isn't as complex as it seems, and what I've tried to do in this chapter is dispel some of the fog that seems to surround networking.

The main choice you have to make is whether your network should be wired or wireless. Each has advantages and disadvantages. Weigh up the pros and cons (roaming versus security, setup time versus cost), and come to the decision that is right for you. Or you can mix and match (desktops on the wired network, laptops and mobile devices on a wireless). The choice is up to you!

Networking Checklist

☑ If you are planning on creating a network, check your existing PCs and laptops for network adapters.

☑ Decide on how many users you want to cater to on your network.

☑ Should your network be wired or wireless? If it is going to be wired, how will you route the cables? Plan and investigate *before* you invest in hardware!

☑ Keep cabling to a minimum.

☑ Take care of the cable: prevent excessive looping and routing too close to electrically noisy devices.

☑ Protect your network with surge protectors.

☑ If you are using a wireless network, make sure you take steps to secure it.

Chapter 14

Connections

There are two ways that you can connect additional devices to your PC system in order to expand upon what it can currently do:

■ Devices can attach to the PC inside the case, usually onto the motherboard in the form of an expansion card, or more memory, or a new CPU.

■ Devices can connect on the exterior, using one of the many ports available for connections to devices in the outside world.

In this chapter we concentrate on the connections that your PC makes to the outside world and look at how you can go about solving problems relating to devices connected to your PC via these ports:

■ Serial port

■ Parallel port

■ USB port

■ FireWire port

You might be wondering why there isn't just one "standard" type of port that is used to connect all devices to a PC, rather than the variety of ports on a single machine, as shown in Figure 14-1. Well, the answer to this question lies in the past and the gradually evolving standards over the years. As PCs have improved and become faster, so have the connections that connect them to the outside world. Gradually the COM port has given way to the faster and more versatile USB and FireWire ports.

Another change is that we are now connecting more and more devices to our PCs, and we expect them to work much faster now too. With a COM port, you were restricted to a slow data transfer rate and one device per port, but with a single USB port on a PC, you can connect up to 127 devices (by using USB hubs that let you make four or eight ports from a single port, and even some devices, such as keyboards, that themselves have ports, enabling you to daisy-chain them to another device). Speed though, is the ultimate driving factor behind new ports. If you compare a scanner that connected to the parallel port (popular maybe six years ago) with a scanner that connects to a USB 2.0 port now, you see a huge difference in scanning time and data transfer speeds, with a reduction in waiting time from several minutes to a few seconds. We want more and more speed to do more things at once and to do them faster, and the hardware manufacturers are certainly doing their part in giving this to us!

FIGURE 14-1   There are a lot of ports on the back of the most basic PC.

But why still include all the older, now inferior connectors? The reason is simple: broad appeal to consumers who have already invested in peripherals and want to upgrade their PC but not all of their peripherals. For manufacturers, the cost of adding a serial port and a parallel port is small indeed, and it means that a PC is backward compatible with the hardware the customer already has. (The operating system support or drivers might not be there, but the hardware manufacturers have at least done their job!)

If your devices are all modern, it is likely that you will only be making use of the latest ports—USB and FireWire. Using only these fast ports means that you have greater flexibility and scope for more devices, as well as all the speed advantages. However, if you have older devices that don't support the latest ports (these are generally called *legacy* devices), you'll be making use of other ports.

The Serial Port

The serial port is most certainly a legacy port on PCs nowadays. However, it is still a well-used legacy port, and many devices, from external modems to graphics tablets, make use of this port, so knowing how to troubleshoot problems with it is important.

A serial port on the back of your computer allows for the input and output of data. There are two different types of serial ports: 9-pin and 25-pin. Here is a 9-pin serial port and the plug that goes in it:

You might have a device that makes use of 9 pins and only have a 25-pin port on your PC (or vice versa), in which case you will have to buy a 25-pin female–to–9-pin male adapter. These adapters can be purchased at most computer stores.

FIX-IT-YOURSELF HOME REMEDY *Be sure not to confuse a parallel (LPT) port, which has 25 female pins (sockets), with a 25-pin serial port, which has 25 male pins.*

Signs of Trouble with Serial Ports

The main sign of trouble is when a device connected to a port suddenly stops working (or a newly acquired device doesn't work when you connect it). Either the device (and/or its controlling software) or the port itself could be the problem. Always thoroughly troubleshoot the device first, as this is far more likely to be the cause of the trouble than a defective port. If the device checks out OK, then check all the cabling between it and the PC, and (if applicable) also check its power supply and outlet for signs of trouble. (Not all PC problems are a result of a problem with the PC!)

Physical Check of the Serial Port

If you have problems, and troubleshooting the affected device leads you to believe the ports or cables are to blame, you will need to thoroughly check the cable, the port, and the connector. Look for the following:

■ Is the cable connected properly to the port, and are any retaining screws properly done up? If not, this might be the cause of the problem. Reconnect the connector and retry.

■ Is the cable obviously damaged (cut sheathing, for example), or has it been crushed by a heavy weight? If this is the case, replace the cable and retest.

- Check the pins on the port. Are any showing obvious damage (bent/missing)? If pins are bent, carefully straighten them with tweezers or needle-nosed pliers. If pins are missing, you will have to replace the port. The easiest way to do this is to add a serial port expansion card.

- Check the connector for damage. Does the connector seem damaged, or are there any signs of debris in the connector (paper, gum, dirt)? If you find that this is the case, clean out the port carefully (with tweezers).

After carrying out any of the above, retest the device to make sure all cable connections are OK before switching it on.

Software Check of the Serial Port

It is possible that your port is suffering from a misconfiguration of the operating system.

A COM port is a software "port" configured in Windows. Each physical serial port on your PC (and your internal modem, if you have one fitted) is assigned a unique COM port. IRQ (Interrupt Request) channels are used by the COM port to request time from the CPU. If the device needs processor time, it notifies the CPU by sending a signal on its IRQ channel. Because there are so many devices inside a computer, and very few IRQ channels, COM ports share IRQ channels by default, as the following table shows. (It is possible to have two COM ports sharing the same resources if only one is in use at any one time.)

Port	IRQ Channel
COM1	4
COM2	3
COM3	4
COM4	3

Changing IRQ Channels

Devices that share an IRQ address cannot communicate with the processor simultaneously. It is possible to share IRQ channels, but this should only be done when no other IRQ channels are available.

PC DOCTOR'S ORDER! *If you use a serial mouse, do not configure its port to share an IRQ address with anything else, as this would cause you no end of problems.*

In general there will be two serial ports on the back of a computer, although since the appearance of USB and FireWire ports, some manufacturers now only include one serial port.

To test for COM port conflicts in Windows 95/98, carry out the following:

1. Right-click on the My Computer icon and choose Properties.

2. Switch to the Device Manager tab.

3. Expand the Ports (COM & LPT) tree by clicking on the [+].

4. Select the serial port, and then click the Properties button.

5. Switch to the Resources tab.

6. If the Conflicting Device List field displays "No conflicts," your COM port is free; otherwise, there is a hardware conflict with this port, and you will need to manually reassign resources. This is a trial-and-error fix, and you will probably have to make several attempts to resolve the conflict. If a resolution does not seem possible, either look for an updated driver or replace the device.

To see if you have a COM port conflict in Windows NT:

1. Open the Start menu, click Programs, and choose Command Prompt.

2. Type **winmsd** at the command prompt.

3. Switch to the Resources tab.

4. Make sure that the device named Serial is using a unique IRQ. If it is not, try assigning it a different one.

To see if you have COM port conflicts in Windows 2000 and Windows XP:

1. Right-click on the My Computer icon and choose Properties.

2. Switch to the Hardware tab.

3. Click the Device Manager button.

4. Expand the Ports (COM & LPT) tree by clicking on the [+].

5. Select the port, and then click the Properties button.

6. Switch to the Resources tab.

7. If the Conflicting Device List field shows "No conflicts," your COM port is free; otherwise there is a hardware conflict with this port.

Repairing Serial Ports

If you have a damaged serial port (usually in the form of damaged pins), you won't be able to use the port.

PC DOCTOR'S ORDER! *Never use a damaged serial port, as this might damage your hardware.*

There are two possible avenues open to you:

■ **Replacing the port**   On some of the older motherboards the port is replaceable because the ports are on a card in the expansion bay and have leads that plug onto the motherboard. However, most modern motherboards have the ports built directly onto the motherboard, meaning that they aren't replaceable.

■ **Adding new ports**   See the next section!

Adding Serial Ports

If you have more devices than ports, you'll either have to remove devices and only hook them up when required or add more ports. Adding ports isn't difficult, and you can do it one of two ways:

■ Add a USB–to–serial port adapter.

■ Add a serial port expansion card.

Both of these solutions are available from PC outlets. Both are good solutions, but an expansion card is a more permanent solution. The adapter solution is more short term or suited to situations where you might want to move the device from one system to another.

The Parallel Port

The parallel port is the port that connects most printers to PCs. The port and connector look like this:

Again, USB has in some ways taken over from the parallel port because it is both faster and more flexible. However, for most home needs, connecting a printer to the PC via the parallel port is an ideal setup. (Generally printers don't come with cables, and if you had an old printer, you'll have a cable available; if you want a USB cable, you'll have to buy one.)

 FIX-IT-YOURSELF HOME REMEDY *If you are finding that the transfer of files to the printer from your PC is slow and you have the option to use a USB connection on your printer, then change to using USB for better performance!*

Signs of Trouble with Parallel Ports

The sign of trouble is similar to that of problems with serial ports: a printer that is connected suddenly stops working, or a new printer won't work. Generally you will only find out that there is a problem when you try to print, so the problem may go unnoticed for some time.

Physical Check of the Parallel Port

Not much can go wrong with parallel ports. Here's the routine you should adopt in the event of a suspect parallel port:

- Thoroughly troubleshoot the printer. (Try it on a different PC first if possible; if not, reinstall any software that came with the printer.)

- Check the cable for signs of damage or being crushed by a heavy weight (filing cabinets and desks). Replace any suspect cables.

- Check the cable for sound connections at both the PC end and the printer. Normally the PC end of the cable is screwed to the connection to the PC, but the printer end is normally a wire clip that can slowly, over time, work its way loose.

- Check for bent pins. Straighten if necessary and retry.

- Check the cable connectors for damage or debris. Replace any damaged cables.

The USB Port

Currently, the USB (Universal Serial Bus) port is the most popular port on modern PCs. Here's a close-up of the port and connectors:

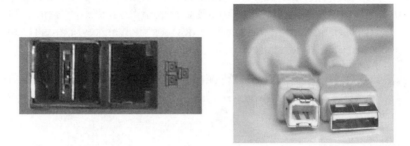

It is fast and versatile and offers greater scope for connecting hardware to a PC than any other port. USB comes in two flavors—USB 1.1 and USB 2.0 standards. USB 1.1 operates at a speed of 12 Mbps, while USB 2.0 can run at a whopping 480 Mbps.

In terms of compatibility, USB 1.1 and USB 2.0 are completely interchangeable. The USB system will run each device at its optimum speed, but the speed of the USB controller on the computer will determine the overall speed of the device. For example, if you plug a USB 2.0 device into a computer that makes use of USB 1.1, the USB 2.0 device will run at 12 Mbps, and if you plug a USD 1.1 device into a computer that is USB 2.0 compliant, the device will again run at the USB 1.1 speed (12 Mbps). However, if you plug a USB 1.1 device and a USB 2.0 device into a computer that is USB 2.0 compliant, each will run at its maximum speed.

In addition, be aware that all USB ports are not created equal—there are two different kinds of USB ports:

- Powered USB port

- Unpowered USB port

This means that there are two types of USB devices—those that need a powered hub and those that don't. Smaller devices such as USB flash memory, PDAs, and digital cameras can all use both powered and unpowered hubs. But when it comes to bigger devices such as scanners, these might need a powered hub because they not only use the USB port to communicate with the PC, but also draw power from it.

Any USB port directly on your PC will be powered and can take any device that you care to attach. However, as you add USB hubs to the system to give yourself more ports, you will have the option of adding powered or unpowered hubs. The easiest way to tell the difference is that a powered hub will come with a power adapter to plug into the power outlet. This provides the power for the hub, allowing it to power devices that need to draw current from the USB port. Many expansion USB ports that come installed on devices such as keyboards (to allow you easy access to a USB port) are unpowered.

 FIX-IT-YOURSELF HOME REMEDY *Always check the specification of any device you buy to see whether it requires a powered or unpowered USB hub.*

Signs of Trouble with USB Ports

Basically, if you add a new device and it doesn't work, check that you're not trying to connect a device that needs a powered hub to an unpowered hub. Nine times out of 10 the problem with new devices is just that. Reconnect the device to a USB port that is on the PC directly and retry.

First Connection of USB Devices

We are all accustomed to "plug and play," where all you need to do is plug in a device and the operating system picks up on it and guides you through the software installation process. It is sometimes easy to forget that there is a driver installation step. If you attach a new USB device to your PC, don't expect it to work immediately; there will be a lag between connecting it and the operating system picking up on it. This can sometimes be quite long so leave it for a good few minutes (five minutes maximum). Also, with some devices, you are required to install drivers manually before connecting the device. This is where reading the manual and installation instructions pays off dividends!

Physical Check of the USB Port

Because of the simplicity of USB connectors, there is little chance of connecting them the wrong way. In fact, the connectors are so good that they don't require the use of any retaining screw to hold the connection in place. However, there are a few things you can check for:

- Undo and redo the connectors (both at the PC and the device) and recheck.

- Try a different USB port. Sometimes this makes the system redetect the device, and things start working again—seems odd, but it works often.

■ Check the USB cable for any signs of damage.

■ Undo the connector and check for any debris that may be present. Sometimes a bit of paper can make its way into the connector, and you need to remove it with tweezers:

 PC DOCTOR'S ORDER! *Never grease or lubricate any connector on your PC, as this can severely damage it or cause a short circuit that could cause a fire.*

Software Check of the USB Port

Make sure that all the drivers and software needed for your device are installed. If you are in any doubt, reinstall the drivers, or check for updated drivers. If possible, test the hardware on a known good machine.

The FireWire/IEEE1394 Port

The FireWire port is quickly becoming a contender with the USB port. It's fast and versatile. Its major advantage over USB 2.0 is the future speed capability. Currently the speed is at 400 Mbps, but this can be expected to rise to an amazing speed of 1600 Mbps!

Major manufacturers of multimedia devices are already adopting the FireWire technology. FireWire speeds up the movement of multimedia data and large files and enables the connection of digital consumer products, including camcorders, videotapes, DVDs, set-top boxes, and music systems, directly to a personal computer. All this and you can have up to 63 devices attached to a FireWire port. The FireWire standard requires that a device be within 4.5 meters of the connector. Using a simple daisy chain, up to 16 devices can be connected in a single chain, each with the 4.5 meter maximum (before the signal begins to weaken). This means that, theoretically, you could have a device as far away as 72 meters from the PC.

Eventually, FireWire is expected to replace the parallel and serial ports, as well as SCSI interfaces.

Signs of Trouble with FireWire Ports

FireWire does away with the concept of unpowered hubs, which in itself makes things easier for the consumer—all ports are created equal. When problems occur with a FireWire port, the process you have to go through is similar to the one for USB ports. Reconnect the device to a FireWire port that is on the PC directly and retry.

Physical Check of the FireWire Port

As with USB, because of the simplicity of the FireWire connectors, there is little chance of connecting them the wrong way. As with USB, the connectors are so good that they don't require the use of any retaining screw to hold the connection in place. However, there are a few things you can check for:

- Check that the device is working. Replace or recharge any batteries that it uses and try again.

- Undo and redo the connectors (both at the PC and the device) and recheck.

- Check the FireWire cable for any signs of damage.

Software Check of the FireWire Port

Make sure that all the drivers and software needed for your device are installed. If you are in any doubt, reinstall the drivers or check for updated drivers. If possible, test the hardware on a known good machine.

Doctor's Notes

In this chapter we've looked at the most popular ports that are present on today's PCs:

- Serial port

- Parallel port

- USB port

- FireWire port

Some of the common problems that plague ports and the devices attached to them have been covered. Generally, the rule of thumb is to first make sure that the device itself isn't faulty before laying blame on the port or connection cables. Once you're sure it's a port issue, and not a software, driver, or device issue, the next thing to try is the cable connectors. You will find that this is the most common cause of device problems and that once you redo the connection, things will work.

Ports—Troubleshooting Checklist

☑ Check that the device is working properly, and make sure that drivers and software are properly installed. Reinstall if in doubt.

☑ Replace any batteries in the device and retry.

☑ Undo and redo the cable connectors, doing up any retaining screws if present.

☑ Check the connectors and socket for signs of damage (such as bent pins). Also, check the cable for signs of damage.

☑ With a USB device, if it doesn't work in one port, try another.

☑ Also with a USB device, check that it doesn't require a powered USB hub.

Chapter 15

Input Devices

Without input devices, your computer would just do its own thing with you being cut out of the loop. Most devices have a way for you to input commands and information: TVs allow you to change channels, adjust the picture, and change settings such as volume and brightness; a microwave oven allows you to set the cooking time and power; a cell phone lets you input numbers and store contacts. But a PC is remarkable in that it has so many different input devices available to use with it. You can pick and choose the best device to do what you want.

In this chapter we are going to take a tour of input devices and look at how they connect, how you maintain them, and how to diagnose problems based on symptoms in order to come up with a remedy.

The Keyboard

The main input device that most people associate with a computer system is a keyboard. The keyboard started life as a method of data entry but then expanded to have function keys (the keys along the top marked F1 to F12), a control key (CTRL), ALT key, and more. Nowadays keyboards can have all sorts of buttons and features (for example, scrolling wheels; buttons for cut, copy, and paste; and buttons to bring up and control your media-playing software). They also come in a variety of shapes and layouts, like the one shown in Figure 15-1, to make typing easier and less exhausting. But the primary function of the keyboard remains the same—to let you input alphanumeric data into the PC.

FIGURE 15-1　An ergonomic keyboard designed to reduce fatigue during typing

Hooking Up a Keyboard

How you hook up a keyboard depends on what connectors are on the keyboard and what connectors you have available on your PC. There are three that you can choose from:

- PS/2 or mini-DIN connector

- The larger DIN-5 connector

- USB connector

Most personal computers have a specific PS/2 connector at the back of the system ready and waiting for you to connect the keyboard, and usually this is the quickest and easiest way to hook it up.

Some keyboards also come with additional USB ports attached that make plugging and unplugging your temporary USB devices (external memory, digital camera, portable music device, etc.) a lot easier than having to climb around the back every time to do it. If you want this function to work, you'll have to plug the keyboard into the USB port too.

FIX-IT-YOURSELF HOME REMEDY *You might have a keyboard that itself can work off the USB port, which means you'd only have to connect it to the USB port, or it might be a PS/2 keyboard with USB ports on it, in which case you'll need to connect both connectors to get the USB ports to work.*

Keyboard Maintenance

Primary keyboard maintenance consists of two things:

- Keeping the keys clean and free from dirt, dust, and muck

- Keeping the keyboard away from liquids

Cleaning Your Keyboard

Computers attract a lot of dust, a lot of which falls onto the keyboard. Combine this with oils from skin and hair (human and pets), and you have the perfect recipe for a natural cement that will clog up your keyboard.

Keep your keyboard clean! Over time, dirt and dust can build up and accumulate around and under the keys and cause them to stick or become hard to press down. In extreme cases, the dirt can build up to levels where keys no longer work. At this stage, cleaning becomes difficult, and damage to the delicate keys might have already occurred.

 PC DOCTOR'S ORDER! *Always clean your keyboard while the PC is off. You could be pressing a lot of keys, and if the PC is on, you could be creating, modifying, or even deleting files randomly.*

Cleaning a keyboard is a two-stage process:

1. With a clean, dry, soft cloth, give the keyboard a thorough wipe down to remove any surface dirt, dust, and hair. While you are doing this, test each key in turn to see if it works freely and can be pressed down all the way and springs back up properly.

2. The second stage of cleaning is to use a vacuum cleaner to remove dirt from deeper inside the keyboard and under the keys. Work carefully with the crevice tool, and try to get in around the keys and at the edges of the keyboard.

 PC DOCTOR'S ORDER! *Don't use powerful "industrial" vacuum cleaners to clean a keyboard, as they can suck the keys straight off! If you are concerned that the vacuum cleaner you are using is too powerful, place a light sock or net over the nozzle. This will both reduce the power of the vacuum cleaner and also catch any keys that might come off.*

It might be tempting to use compressed air to clean a keyboard, but this isn't recommended because it can push dirt deeper into the keyboard and cause keys to jam.

Cleaning Schedule   For best results, wipe your keyboard down weekly, and give it a thorough cleaning with a vacuum cleaner on a monthly basis. Adjust these if the system lives in a dusty environment or experiences a lot of hard use.

Keyboard Care

Keyboards are quite cheap nowadays, but that's no reason not to take care of them. (If your keyboard is on your laptop, a replacement could cost hundreds of dollars.)

The following are just a few hints and tips that can help you get the most out of your keyboard.

■ Never keep drinks near a keyboard. Spilling coffee or soda into the keyboard is a guaranteed way to damage it. Even having a can of soda near your keyboard is bad because the bubbling in the can causes particles of acidic drink to fall onto your keyboard, which, over time, can damage it.

PC DOCTOR'S ORDER! *If you are unfortunate enough to spill a drink into your keyboard and it stops working, you might be able to save it if you are fast enough to carry out the right first aid. Quickly turn the system off and unplug the keyboard. Once unplugged, rinse the keyboard out with cold water (preferably distilled water that's had all the minerals removed—the same stuff you put in car batteries if they aren't sealed). Once you have rinsed out the spill, allow the keyboard to dry. You can help this along with cool air from a hair dryer (but not a hot paint stripper gun or anything like that). Once it is completely dry, hook it up again and see if it works. This does not work on laptops or wireless keyboards! If you spill anything into those, you are looking at a new keyboard/laptop.*

■ Never eat over a keyboard. Food particles can easily jam the keys.

■ Smoking near a PC is bad for it too. The smoke and ash is corrosive, and the ash will damage the delicate circuitry.

■ Pets are also not good for keyboards. Pet hair can work its way deep into the system and is very hard to remove.

Signs of Keyboard Trouble

Here are the signs of keyboard trouble and how to deal with them:

■ Keyboard not working at all or not detected during system startup (you see the error message "Keyboard not detected"): check all the connections and try again. If this doesn't make any difference, either try the keyboard on another PC, or try a known good keyboard on the affected system.

WARNING *Never plug or unplug a keyboard while the system is switched on, as this can seriously damage the system. Always switch the system off first.*

■ Stuck key: this can betray itself during system startup by giving you either a "Stuck key" error or a more generic "Keyboard error." The first thing to check is that there is nothing lying on the keyboard causing the error—simple, but it does happen. If this isn't the problem, press all the keys to see if they work properly. If this fails, give the keyboard a good cleaning. Usually a stuck key error can be fixed, but it might take a few attempts at cleaning.

■ Key not working: your first indication of this will either be that you cannot enter your password because a key for one of the characters doesn't work, or generally when you are typing text. Clean the keyboard and see if this helps. If it doesn't, replace the keyboard.

If you have a wireless keyboard, it might also contain batteries to provide power. If a wireless keyboard stops working, check the batteries, replace, and retest. Another problem with wireless devices is that they can sometimes lose contact with the radio signal used to communicate with the receiver. Consult the documentation that came with your device for information on how to reestablish a lost signal. (Usually there is a button on both the device and the receiver that needs to be pressed.)

The Mouse

Next to nearly every keyboard you'll find a mouse (or as some now call it, a rodent). The purpose of the mouse is to allow you to move the pointer around the screen and click on elements, and in turn cause something to happen. Figure 15-2 shows three different mice.

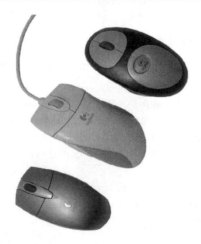

FIGURE 15-2   Selection of PC mice

There are many different kinds of mice available, but they can be categorized as mechanical, optical ball, or optical no-ball. The three mice are shown upside down in Figure 15-3 so that you can see the differences.

Hooking Up a Mouse

There are three ways that a mouse can be connected to a PC:

- COM port (Mice were originally connected via a COM port using a connector called a DB-9—a 9-pin connector that was once common.)

- PS/2 connector (the Mini-DIN-6)

- USB port

Mechanical Mouse

A mechanical mouse contains a weighted ball that moves across the surface that the mouse is moved on. Inside the mouse are rollers that detect the movement of the ball and translate it into electrical signals that the PC can understand.

Mechanical mice are the most susceptible to problems related to dirt, dust, and hair, which can make their way into the device and clog it up, causing the pointer to move erratically or even stop altogether.

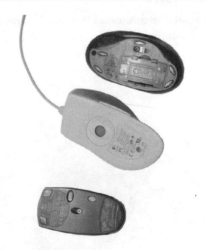

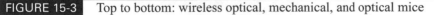

FIGURE 15-3   Top to bottom: wireless optical, mechanical, and optical mice

Cleaning Mechanical Mice

Switch off the PC and disconnect the mouse. Turn it over, and you should find a plastic ring that is used to hold the ball in the mouse body. Rotate this ring counterclockwise by hand (or if there is a hole in the ring, use the tip of a dried-out ballpoint), and pull the ball out (see Figure 15-4). Wash the ball with soapy water, rinse in clean water, and dry it.

After cleaning the ball, turn your attention to the inside of the mouse. Remove any dirt or hair that is present, and clean the rollers with Q-Tips or tweezers. Remove any remaining dirt particles with a vacuum cleaner and reassemble the mouse. Clean the mouse mat (just wipe it with a dry cloth), attach the mouse back to the system, and check to see if it is working.

Cleaning Schedule   To keep the mouse in good working order, clean it thoroughly on a monthly basis.

Optical Ball Mouse

An optical ball mouse still contains a ball, but the rollers that detect the movement are replaced by an optical system that shines a beam of light onto the ball. Movement of the ball causes the light to be scattered by the surface of the ball, and this is detected by an optical "eye" and translated into electrical signals that move the pointer. Fewer moving parts mean it is more robust and less prone to problems caused by dirt and dust.

Cleaning Optical Ball Mice

Cleaning is similar to that of a mechanical mouse. Disconnect it from the PC, open it up, and give the ball a good clean. Remove any dirt and dust inside the mouse and reassemble.

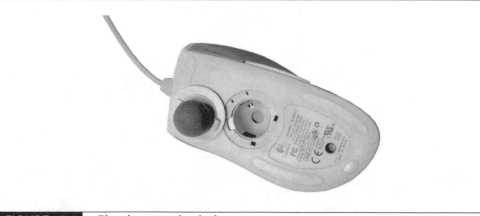

FIGURE 15-4   Cleaning a mechanical mouse

Cleaning Schedule   To keep the mouse in good working order, clean it thoroughly on a monthly basis.

Optical No-Ball Mouse

The optical no-ball mouse does away completely with the ball and uses an electronic eye to detect the movement of the mouse across any patterned surface (such as a mouse mat). From a user's point of view, this is a much simpler and more robust system.

Cleaning No-Ball Mice

Cleaning is simple. Turn the mouse over and give it a quick wipe with a dry, soft cloth. From a technical standpoint, there is no need to switch off the system or disconnect the mouse from the PC. However, be careful if you click on the mouse buttons as you clean. You could end up copying, pasting, or even deleting files this way. To be on the safe side, switch off!

Cleaning Schedule   The cleaning is so simple that you can carry it out on a weekly or monthly basis.

Signs of Mouse Trouble

Mice are quite robust, and usually most problems are cured by a thorough cleaning. If the mouse isn't working, the main suspect is always the connectors. Check the connections and retest.

   If your mouse is wireless, it might also contain batteries to provide power. In the case of a wireless mouse ceasing to work, check the batteries, replace, and retest. Another problem with wireless devices is that they can sometimes lose contact with the radio signal used to communicate with the receiver. Consult the documentation that came with your device for information on how to reestablish a lost signal. (Usually there is a button on both the device and the receiver that needs to be pressed.)

Graphics Tablets

You use graphics tablets to move and manipulate the pointer using a pen, which is far more intuitive and precise than using a mouse. It is a very popular device among artists and graphic designers.

Hooking Up a Graphics Tablet

The usual way to hook up a graphics tablet to a PC is with one of the following:

- COM (DB-9) port
- USB port

The device may also come with a *tap* that goes between your keyboard and the connector. This is for the tablet to tap the power from the keyboard connector (this has no effect on the keyboard).

Maintenance of Graphics Tablets

Maintaining your graphics tablet is a simple case of making sure that all the connectors are sound, the surface clean, and the pens you use are all in good condition. Check the tips of your pens regularly. Damaged pen tips need replacing; otherwise they might feel "scratchy" and hard to use, or could even damage the surface of your tablet. (They pull out easily, and you should have been supplied with some replacements when you bought the tablet.)

Cleaning Graphics Tablets

Cleaning is easy. Just give the surface of the tablet a wipe down with a dry, lint-free cloth. Don't use any liquids or solvents on the tablet, as this can damage the plastic.

Cleaning Schedule   Because the tablet is exposed and has a large surface area, it will gather a lot of dirt and dust, so give it a wipe over weekly.

Web Cams

Being able to video conference with your family and friends from the comfort of your office or home is compelling, and this accounts for why web cams are so popular. All you need is a web cam and an Internet connection, and you can see friends and relatives (who may be on the other side of the globe).

Hooking Up a Web Cam

Hooking up is easy. You load the drivers and plug the camera into an available USB port, which it uses both to transfer data and to draw power from. USB ports allow for *hot plugging* (plugging in the device while the system is switched on).

Maintenance of Web Cams

Web cams contain no "user-serviceable" parts. That means if something goes wrong with the device, there is no point in dismantling it. All you can check are the obvious:

- Check the drivers in the operating system.
- Check the connections.
- Try it on another PC.

Cleaning Web Cams

There are two elements to cleaning a web cam:

- Cleaning the camera as a whole
- Cleaning the camera lens

To clean the camera as a whole, use a clean, dry, lint-free cloth to remove accumulated dust. To clean the lens, use a proper lens cleaning kit to prevent any damage to the lens. If the lens has a cover, use it to protect the lens when the camera is not in use.

Cleaning Schedule   Cleaning of the lens need not be done too often, unless the camera is in a particularly dusty location. Twice or three times a year should be sufficient.

Digital Video (DV)

Recording video on a video camera and sharing it on the Internet or by email with friends and family are easy to do with the latest recording devices. You record the video, either on tape or on memory cards or sticks in the camera, and then either connect the camera to the PC or slot the card into an appropriate reader and transfer the files.

Hooking Up DV

Digital video requires a fast connection. The best way to connect a video camera is to use a USB 2.0 or FireWire connection, if you have either, and your camera supports one or the other. If your video equipment supports FireWire or USB 2.0 and your PC doesn't have an appropriate port, consider adding a port—usually on an expansion card. Video transfer will be faster (and the faster it is, the more you are likely to use it), and you will encounter fewer problems in using it.

 FIX-IT-YOURSELF HOME REMEDY *Although you can connect many video cameras to a USB 1.1 port, the data transfer rate will be low and the transfer will take a very long time.*

Troubleshooting DVs

Problems with connecting video cameras generally fall into three categories:

- Communication with the camera cannot be established: this can happen for a variety of reasons. Start with the simple and most obvious: a bad connection at the PC end or camera end, or the wrong cable used. Then

308 The PC Doctor's Fix-It-Yourself Guide

progress to other issues, such as a dead battery in the camera or incorrect setting on the camera. Check all the settings within the actual program used to access the camera too (although if the camera was working and then stopped and you changed nothing, it is unlikely to be a bad setting).

■ The data transfer is slow: don't underestimate the amount of data involved in video data; even a few minutes can easily run into hundreds of megabytes. The speed of the data transfer will be determined by the port you are using, and there's not much you can do to improve on this. If the speed is too slow for you, the best solution is to connect using a faster port (if your camera supports it).

■ The transferred data is poor quality: the usual cause of this is that frames from the video are lost during the transfer process. The most common reasons for this are that the port, the PC, or the software doing the copying are too slow; you have other programs running and causing the data to be lost; or it is a connection issue. Check all the connections first and make sure they are sound. If all seems in order and the problem remains, it is likely to be a PC or software issue. If you are not using USB 2.0 or FireWire, then upgrading to this may help. However, it may be the software that you are using, and nothing short of changing software will help—not a cheap option, as most video editing programs are very expensive.

Digital Cameras

Digital cameras are widespread, and to make use of one you don't need a computer anymore. You can either take your camera memory along to a photo store for printing, or plug it directly into the newer types of printers. However, most digital camera owners also own PCs, which they can use to get more out of their investment in the camera. You can also use it to keep your photos in digital form (as opposed to printing them out and storing them in albums).

Hooking Up a Digital Camera

The usual way to connect a digital camera to a computer is with a free USB port. However, instead of connecting the camera directly to the USB port, what normally happens is that the camera comes with its own docking cradle that connects to the PC, and you slot the camera into the cradle. This makes for a simpler connection and also reduces the risk of damage to the device by repeated connections. Using a docking cradle also means that buttons can be added to the docking station to allow one-button transfer of images from the camera to the PC or printer.

But this permanent connection does mean that you have a device plugged in continuously. If you are short on ports, this can be a major downside. The best way to overcome this limitation is to add more USB ports by adding another USB hub to the system. See Chapter 14 for more details.

Troubleshooting Digital Cameras

Once you have the hardware and software installed for your camera and docking cradle and have it working, there are a few things that might cause the setup not to work. Here are some troubleshooting suggestions:

- Check for a bad connection somewhere. Maybe the data cable or a power cable has become detached. (Well over 50 percent of hardware issues are solved by checking all the connections!) Check all of them carefully, and then recheck. Also check that you are seating the camera properly in the docking cradle and that nothing is fouling the connections (such as a bit of paper).

- Check the settings on your camera (refer to the manual for details). It is possible that you have altered a setting somewhere on it that prevents connection. Reset to defaults if possible (refer to the manual on how to do this).

- Was any new software or hardware installed that might conflict with the camera? Uninstall or remove the last thing added, and see if that helps. If there is a conflict, this is the time to look for a new driver or patches. Remember, if you are having the problem, more than likely someone else is too! The last resort is to contact the vendor and see if they can shed light on the issue or offer a solution.

- Check the batteries in the camera. Many cameras will not connect properly if the batteries are low or dead. Replace the batteries and try again.

 PC DOCTOR'S ORDER! *If possible, run your devices on rechargeable batteries. (Check the device instructions carefully to see if they will work.) Not only will you save stacks of cash, but you will also be doing a little bit to protect the environment!*

Slow Transfer

By far the biggest complaint with a digital camera is that the transfer of images from the device to the PC takes so long. If you are transferring data via the device itself, there isn't much you can do about it. However, more and more devices have removable memory, and if your digital camera has removable memory (most do), there is something you can do to speed things up.

FIX-IT-YOURSELF HOME REMEDY *Slow data transfer isn't limited to digital cameras. Most devices suffer from this problem (portable music players, GPS receivers, PDAs, etc.). If you are using a USB port, there isn't much you can do about this because it is the circuitry within the device that is the bottleneck. This is likely to become less of a problem over time as new devices get faster, but don't expect miracles!*

The fastest way to transfer data from your digital camera to your PC is to remove the memory card (if it is removable) and use a suitable card reader to read the card through the operating system and copy the data off it that way. This way, you remove all bottlenecks in the digital camera and get a far better rate of transfer. Figure 15-5 shows a card reader and various digital media.

The type of card reader you get depends on the type of memory card your digital camera uses. There are nine types of memory that you are likely to encounter in digital devices:

- CompactFlash Type I
- CompactFlash Type II
- MicroDrive
- SmartMedia
- xD-Picture Card
- Memory Stick
- Memory Stick Pro
- Secure Digital
- MultiMediaCard

You can buy cheap card readers for all of these formats that plug into your USB or USB 2.0 ports and allow you to access the card and navigate the file structure just like any other drive on your system. This is quick and easy and allows you to be in complete control over which items are saved and where they are saved.

If you have devices that use more than one type of memory or you just want to buy something that is future-proof, you can get card readers that will read more than one format. (One multicard reader is the 6-in-1 reader that reads the six most popular formats—CompactFlash Type I/II, MicroDrive, SmartMedia, MultiMediaCard, Secure Digital, and Memory Stick.)

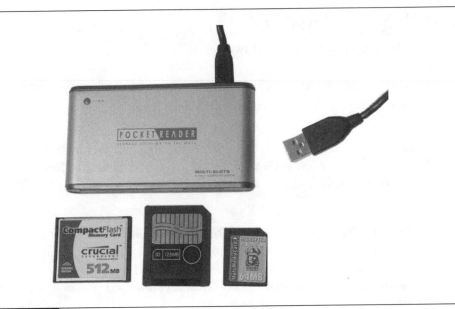

FIGURE 15-5   Card reader and various digital media

PC DOCTOR'S ORDER! *Take care when handling removable memory. Although you don't need to take the same level of care as you do when handling circuit boards and CPUs, you should still keep the card in the supplied case when not in use and not expose it to heat or damp. Also, protect the memory from impacts and falls, and don't bend the card or be rough with the connectors.*

Joysticks

A joystick is similar to a mouse, but it allows you to navigate within the three-dimensional world of computer games. The joystick is based on the flight controls of an aircraft, although significantly simplified, allowing you to input movement in 3D, back and forward, side to side, and combinations thereof. Joysticks also host a staggering array of buttons and levers, allowing you to have full control in a game all in one place and easy access to most of the functions with one hand. If you play a lot of games (especially flight simulators), you probably have a joystick, as these kinds of games are extremely difficult to play without one.

Hooking Up a Joystick

Joysticks hook up to a PC in one of two ways:

- A 15-pin game port, which is normally on the back of your sound card
- USB port

An advantage to continuing to use a game port joystick over a USB version, is that if you play games a lot, you can leave the joystick connected. However, over time the game port will disappear and be replaced almost completely by USB devices.

 FIX-IT-YOURSELF HOME REMEDY *Be careful not to dislodge the game port connector when working at the back of the PC. Many joysticks do not have a screw-secured game port connector, and it can easily become detached (even midgame, causing either the system or the plane you were flying at the time to crash).*

Maintenance of Joysticks

Opening a joystick isn't for the fainthearted. Taking it apart for cleaning or repair is a major task best not done. There is a staggering array of wires, levers, and pivots in them, and the scope for losing a part or forgetting how to put it back together is huge!

Because of the internal complexity, and delicate parts and switches it contains, joysticks are also very susceptible to damage from impacts or being dropped. Take care when handling and moving them.

 PC DOCTOR'S ORDER! *Never squirt or spray oil or grease into a joystick. This will not only damage the electronic components inside, but also strip away the special grease used to cover the moving parts. Also, adding extra oil or grease encourages dirt and dust to build up, leading to a possible jamming of the device.*

Cleaning Joysticks

With a joystick, prevention is better than cure, and it is a good idea to keep a dustsheet over your joystick when it isn't in use. That way you keep it cleaner far longer, and the actions will remain smoother and work better.

Wipe the exterior of the joystick carefully with a dry, lint-free cloth, making sure that you clean all the joints and moving parts. (These are the areas that allow the dirt to work its way into the joystick.) Carefully clean around all the buttons too, as dirt making its way into them can jam and cause problems.

Compressed air is handy for cleaning a joystick, but take care that you don't force dirt into the joystick. Aim the nozzle so that you direct the dirt away from the device.

Cleaning Schedule   If you keep your joystick covered, you can get away with giving it a clean once every 6 to 12 months. If you keep it uncovered, consider cleaning it on a monthly basis.

Other Input Devices

There are dozens of other input devices available for computer systems. Here are a few that you might be aware of:

- GPS receivers

- Game input devices (usually, elaborate keyboards)

- Voice recorders

- PDAs

- Musical keyboards and other musical instruments

- Radio receivers

I don't have the space to cover all these devices in any detail, so what I'm going to do here is condense all the important facts into simple points that you can check against if you have any problems with any of them.

- All these devices connect to your PC and allow data to be passed to and fro. As with most things to do with PCs, there are a lot of variations in them; even similar devices from different manufacturers can behave and act differently. Don't assume that similar devices operate similarly. Always consult the manuals that come with your device.

 PC DOCTOR'S ORDER! *When it comes to computer devices, never make guesses as to how the device works. Consult the manual if in any doubt. Damage can occur if a device is improperly used, and your warranty can also be invalidated.*

■ Keep all your connections sound. Also, if you have many different devices, you might like to stick labels on the cable connectors so that you know what they all are. Nothing is worse than trying to connect the wrong connector into a device!

■ Check your batteries if you are having problems. In most cases if the batteries are low or completely discharged, the device won't communicate with the PC. Replace them and see if it works.

 PC DOCTOR'S ORDER! *Check the expiration dates on batteries in devices regularly. If they get old, they can ooze corrosive chemicals and damage your device. For added protection, use only high-quality batteries.*

■ If you are having problems getting the PC to establish a connection with the device, disconnect any other unnecessary devices from the PC and try again. If the device doesn't work, you are looking at a conflict with another device or driver. If you have removed multiple devices, reattach them one at a time and check that the devices all work. This way you can narrow down the problem.

 FIX-IT-YOURSELF HOME REMEDY *You might find that a conflict resolves itself simply by going through the process of disconnecting and reattaching devices one at a time.*

■ If you have more than one computer, consider which system you want to install your device on. Think about which PC you'll want to use with which device. The more you burden a PC with drivers for devices that you don't use, and the more you add onto a system unnecessarily, the more problems you'll have (not to mention the fact that each driver you install will consume valuable system resources).

 PC DOCTOR'S ORDER! *If you disconnect a USB device and plug it back into a different USB port, there is a very good chance that you will need to reinstall the driver; so have the disc close at hand and ready, in case.*

Doctor's Notes

In this chapter we've looked at the common and not so common input devices that you might come across or want to add to your PC. We've also looked at how you care for these devices and troubleshoot the problems that make them unusable.

So that you can effectively take care of your devices, you should make a list of all the devices that you have installed on your PC and from this create an effective regular maintenance schedule that you can follow. Regular maintenance prolongs the life of your input devices and also makes them easier and more satisfying to use.

Input Devices—Troubleshooting Checklist

☑ Clean all your input devices on a regular basis.

☑ With any problem with an input device, check all the connections before doing anything else.

☑ Reinstall any software or drivers associated with the suspected defective device.

☑ Check the batteries in any cordless/wireless device. Replace if old.

☑ If possible, connect a suspect device to another port on the PC, or a different PC.

Part III

The Details: Software and Data

Chapter 16

File System Care

The file system of your PC is like the long-term memory of the brain (the short-term stuff is handled by the RAM). Usually, thousands of millions of bits of information are written to your hard drive, and it is done without any problems. But, for one reason or another, a problem can happen—the wrong information is written to the disk, or a piece of it is missing or damaged because of a "glitch." In this chapter we are going to look at how to use tools (some provided by your operating system) to run preventative maintenance on your PC's file system, what you can do to pull yourself out of these kinds of problems, as well as ways to help prevent such problems from happening in the future.

Taking Care of the File System

In much the same way that you need to clear out the dirt and dust from your system every so often, you need to do some housekeeping on the file system of your hard drive.

Hard Errors and Soft Errors

There are two kinds of errors that can affect the data on your hard drive: hard and soft.

Hard errors are caused by a hardware problem that affects the data. The most common reason for this kind of error is a physical error on the hard drive platters (the part where data is written to). These errors can mean the data either wasn't written to the platter properly or that an area on the platter has become unreadable since the data was written. Either way, your data is lost, and the chances of recovery by using software are determined by the scope of the damage—what part of the data was damaged and how big the damaged area is. Recovery might be possible if you send your drive to a company specializing in data recovery, but that is likely to be costly.

Hard drives showing any signs of hard errors need to be replaced with the utmost urgency. These kinds of damage do not get any better over time, only worse.

 FIX-IT-YOURSELF HOME REMEDY *The damaged areas on a hard drive are commonly known as* bad sectors.

Soft errors are data errors caused by glitches in the software. Maybe the operating system crashed, or the program hung just as it was saving a file to the hard disk, or most commonly, you switched your PC off without shutting Windows down first. These kinds of problems can cause all kinds of unpredictable soft errors on the hard drive. And there can be all sorts of side effects from this kind of problem too. Data can be lost (if writing the data to the disk was interrupted and it wasn't actually written to the disk, then it won't be recoverable), but also the file system itself can become compromised and damaged. Many of these problems are fixable using disk scanning and recovery software.

Before we go on to look at checking the drive for errors, let's take a look at the most common file systems currently in use.

Types of File Systems

The two common file systems used to structure and control the way data is stored on your hard drive are the FAT (File Allocation Table) system and NTFS (NT File System).

The FAT system has been around since the early days of PCs and has gone through many different incarnations and vast improvements over the years, since the early days of the MS-DOS operating system. (The first version, called FAT16, was introduced in 1981.) It was originally designed to handle files on a floppy drive and has had minor modifications over the years so it can handle hard disks.

PCs running Windows 95, 98, 98SE, and Me will all run a form of FAT called FAT32. This version improved speed and made better use of the hard drive overall, but it was still sorely lacking in support for security and compression. However, FAT is now outdated. This is because it is very basic and has no real tolerance for faults, which means that data loss can be more frequent than it should be. Recovery of lost data is also more difficult, and it has no built-in form of data access security. Add to this the fact that FAT could only support drives smaller than 2GB (small by today's standards). FAT32 under Windows XP can support 32GB, while NTFS supports nearly 256 *terabytes* (a terabyte being a thousand gigabytes)!

The other option, NTFS, has been the file system of choice for professional versions of Windows operating systems for years. Windows NT, Windows 2000, and Windows XP (both Professional and Home) all give you the option of using NTFS as well as converting hard drives using the inferior FAT file system to the more robust NTFS system.

Apart from being more robust, there are other huge advantages to using NTFS:

- Increased security

- Support for larger hard drives, volume sizes, file sizes, and more files per volume

- File-by-file compression (which means that you can compress individual files to save disk space)

- Encryption

- Disk quotas (allowing you to assign a specific amount of disk space for users to use on any particular PC)

Conversion of FAT to NTFS

NTFS is the default file system for new installations of Windows XP, and if you are carrying out an upgrade from a previous version of Windows, you will be asked if you want to convert your existing file systems to NTFS during the installation process.

But what if you've already upgraded to Windows XP and didn't do the conversion during installation? Not a problem! You can convert FAT16 or FAT32 volumes to NTFS at any point.

 PC DOCTOR'S ORDER! *Remember that you can't easily go back to FAT or FAT32 (without reformatting the drive or partition); not that I think you'll want to, as long as you are aware of the limitations of it initially.*

There are many third-party utilities on the market enabling you to convert from FAT16 or FAT32 to NTFS (these normally have a jazzy interface and cool graphics), but you don't really need anything special to carry out the conversion. The program required is included on your hard disk as part of the Windows XP installation.

To use this utility to convert your D drive, for example, carry out the following steps:

1. Close all open applications. This process may require a reboot, so be prepared.

2. Click Start, then Run, type **cmd**, and press ENTER. You will be in the command-line interface, as shown in Figure 16-1.

3. In the command window, type

   ```
   convert D: /FS:NTFS
   ```

4. Press ENTER.

It's as easy as that! If any files are open, you'll have to reboot the system. I don't recommend that you use your system for anything else while the conversion is in progress.

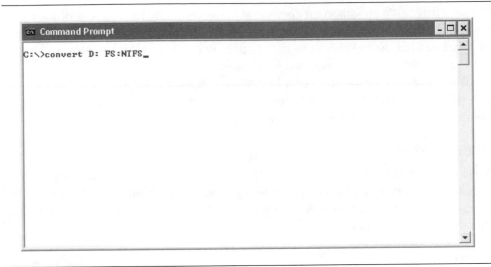

FIGURE 16-1   Carrying out the conversion of FAT to NTFS

NTFS Limitations

The NTFS file system might not be compatible with other operating systems installed on the same computer (Windows 95, 98, Me, OS/2, Unix, or the Linux flavors of Unix, although some Unix and Linux distributions do support read-only access to NTFS drives and volumes); nor is it usually available when you've booted a computer from a floppy disk (unless you are using a special utility).

Be extra careful using old disk tools and utilities on an NTFS system that you used on a FAT system—running these can damage the file system and make the data or the operating system unavailable. Always check, and apply the golden rule: "If in doubt - Don't!" Utilities in question can include (but aren't limited to):

- Disk defragmenting utilities
- Disk formatting utilities
- Utilities to recover lost or deleted files
- Antivirus tools and utilities

Checking the Drive for Errors

When your system boots up, one of the checks that it performs on the attached hardware is normally a S.M.A.R.T. check. (S.M.A.R.T. stands for Self-Monitoring Analysis and Reporting Technology.) This test checks the health and well-being of the hard drive. It's an important check that helps eliminate the chances of data loss through hard drive failure because of predictable wear and tear. However, the system does not do any checks as to the integrity or validity of the data on your hard drive. For that, as always, you have choices!

If you are willing to spend a bit of cash, you'll have a number of utilities to choose from. If you don't want to spend any extra cash, you'll have to use what comes built into your operating system.

Free Tools

Most operating systems come equipped with tools and utilities that allow you to check and optimize the hard drive for best performance. Windows XP comes with two important tools that allow you to gauge the health of your hard drives and keep them running at peak efficiency:

- Chkdsk

- Disk Defragmenter

Chkdsk

The Chkdsk utility is the tool that you use to check the integrity of the data stored on the hard drive. It comes in two different flavors:

- A command-line tool that you use through a Command Prompt window like the one shown in Figure 16-2.

- A Windows-based utility (This is in fact just an overlay to the command-line tool.) A screen is shown in Figure 16-3.

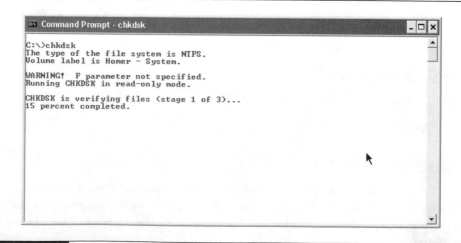

FIGURE 16-2   Chkdsk through the command line

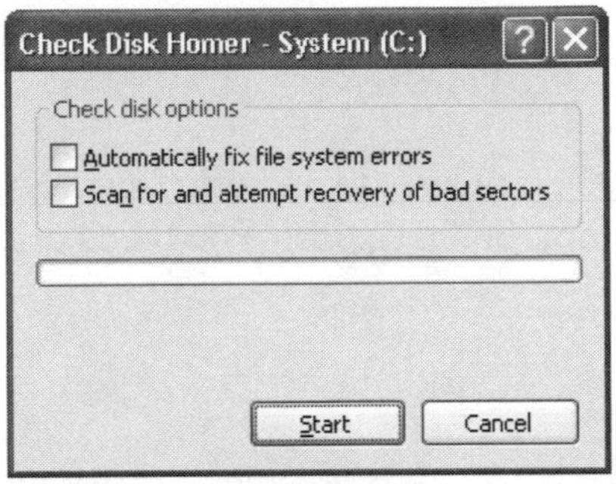

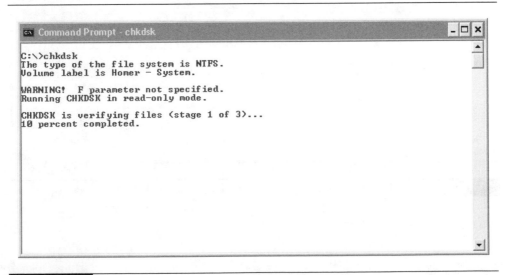

FIGURE 16-3   Chkdsk—the Windows-based utility

Both tools are identical apart from the interface that they offer you. Which one you choose is up to you. I'll cover both here.

To use the command-line version of Chkdsk to carry out a check on the C drive without any attempt at a repair, go to the command prompt and type

```
chkdsk c:
```

Note the warning in Figure 16-4 about Chkdsk being run in read-only mode. This tells you that no attempt at a correction will be made if an error or errors are found.

FIGURE 16-4   Chkdsk checking the C drive for errors

To check the D drive, type the following at the command prompt:

```
chkdsk d:
```

If you want to fix errors, you have to add the /f switch to the command you type at the command prompt. So, to fix errors on the D drive, you'd type the following:

```
chkdsk d: /f
```

Doing this will give you a message about unmounting the drive for carrying out the check, as shown in Figure 16-5. You can choose yes (Y) or no (N). Generally, it is better to choose no, because if open files are forcibly unmounted, a whole host of problems can occur. Also, if system files are open (files relating to the operating system and other applications running), the check cannot be carried out. As you can see in Figure 16-6, Chkdsk asks if you want to schedule the check for when the system is restarted.

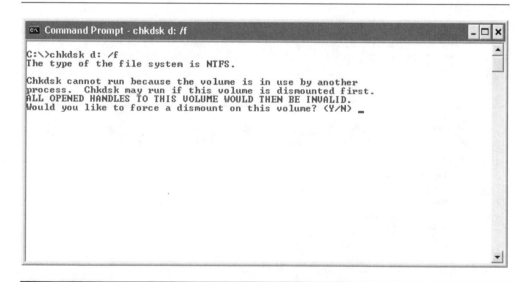

FIGURE 16-5   Chkdsk offering you the option of unmounting the drive

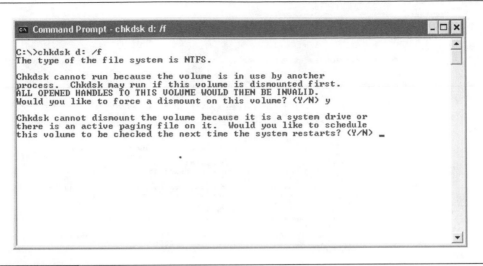

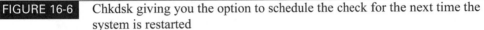

FIGURE 16-6   Chkdsk giving you the option to schedule the check for the next time the system is restarted

There are other command-line switches that you can supply to the Chkdsk application. Some are shown in Figure 16-7, and here are a few more:

/v   (For *verbose*) Gives you greater feedback

/r   Locates bad sectors and recovers lost data

/x   Forces the system to dismount

/i   Skips certain checks on the system to make the check faster

/c   Skips certain folder checks to make the check faster

/?   Provides help on using the application

The Windows version of Chkdsk is simple to use. However, finding it might be a little tricky. Run Windows Explorer (press ▦ along with E to bring it up quickly), and right-click on the drive you want to check; then choose Properties from the context-sensitive menu. A dialog box will appear, and you should click on the Tools tab at the top, and then click on the button labeled Check Now under the error checking section. You will see the dialog box shown earlier in Figure 16-3,

```
Command Prompt                                          _ □ ✕

C:\>chkdsk /?
Checks a disk and displays a status report.

CHKDSK [volume[[path]filename]]] [/F] [/U] [/R] [/X] [/I] [/C] [/L[:size]]

    volume          Specifies the drive letter (followed by a colon),
                    mount point, or volume name.
    filename        FAT/FAT32 only: Specifies the files to check for fragmentation
    /F              Fixes errors on the disk.
    /U              On FAT/FAT32: Displays the full path and name of every file
                    on the disk.
                    On NTFS: Displays cleanup messages if any.
    /R              Locates bad sectors and recovers readable information
                    (implies /F).
    /L:size         NTFS only:  Changes the log file size to the specified number
                    of kilobytes.  If size is not specified, displays current
                    size.
    /X              Forces the volume to dismount first if necessary.
                    All opened handles to the volume would then be invalid
                    (implies /F).
    /I              NTFS only: Performs a less vigorous check of index entries.
    /C              NTFS only: Skips checking of cycles within the folder
                    structure.

The /I or /C switch reduces the amount of time required to run Chkdsk by
skipping certain checks of the volume.

C:\>_
```

FIGURE 16-7   Using command-line switches

where you can check the option you want. You will be given further options similar to those offered by the command-line version. For example, if system files are currently in use, a check can be scheduled for when the system is restarted. The Windows version prompts you with the following dialog box:

```
Checking Disk Homer - System (C:)                            ✕

ⓘ   The disk check could not be performed because the disk check utility needs exclusive access to some Windows files on
     the disk. These files can be accessed only by restarting Windows. Do you want to schedule this disk check to occur
     the next time you restart the computer?

                    [ Yes ]        [ No ]
```

In order to carry out a check that's been scheduled to occur at the next restart, you'll obviously need to restart the system.

PC DOCTOR'S ORDER! *Be careful about scheduling a check for the start of the day, as it can take a long time. Far better to carry it out at the end of the day.*

Whether you choose the command-line option or the Windows interface option, check your hard drive on a regular basis (weekly if at all possible, monthly if time is tight).

Disk Defragmenter

Another tool that you can use on your hard drive to improve performance is the Disk Defragmenter. But there remains a lot of mystery about what it does and what the gains are. Before you can appreciate why you need to run a disk defragmenter, you need to consider why it's needed in the first place.

When your PC saves data on your hard drive, it doesn't do it in neat and tidy blocks. This would take a lot of time and effort and slow the system down. Instead, the system writes the data to the closest patch of free space on the hard drive. Sometimes the portion of free space it chooses isn't large enough to write the whole file, so it breaks up the file into smaller pieces, spreading them over the whole hard drive. This makes writing a file a quick process. However, when it comes to reading a file, having it spread all across the hard drive and in any number of different parts slows things down again (so that what you gain on the saving speed, you lose on the reading speed).

OK, it's important for the system to get the data safely written to the hard drive as fast as possible because once on the hard drive the data is safer than in RAM. (If it's in RAM and the system is switched off or crashes, the data will be lost.) But over the days and weeks, this fragmentation of that data all over the hard drive can contribute significantly to the time it takes to open or read a file. When you run a disk defragmenting tool, you are in effect taking all the data on the hard drive and writing it in such a way that the files are in one piece on the disk. This dramatically improves the speed of file access.

 PC DOCTOR'S ORDER! *Never defragment a laptop PC while it is running on battery power, as a power failure can result in loss of data or damage to the file system.*

Just running a disk defragmenter once isn't good enough, as files will grow and change. It will need to be done on a regular basis (weekly or monthly is a good interval).

 PC DOCTOR'S ORDER! *Because disk defragmenting involves moving a lot of your files around on the hard drive, it is recommended that you carry out a disk check before doing a disk defragment.*

You can access the disk defragmenter that comes with Windows (rather unimaginatively called Disk Defragmenter) by clicking on Start and then All Programs | Accessories | System Tools | Disk Defragmenter. The main screen is shown in Figure 16-8, and you can see it in action in Figure 16-9.

Disk Defragmenter has limitations, but they aren't usually much of a bother:

- You can only analyze or defragment one drive at a time.

- Reporting is primitive. (A report is shown in Figure 16-10.)

- The tool cannot be set to defragment drives automatically and has to be run manually.

- You have little control over the defragmenting options.

PC DOCTOR'S ORDER! *When you choose to defragment your hard drive or drives, leave your PC alone while it is doing this and don't try to work with it. The more you use it, the more files are being changed, and the longer it will take. Also, it is best to switch off screensavers and close any applications that are running. The more you have running, the slower it will work, and the less efficient it will be. (Open files and those of running applications cannot be moved.)*

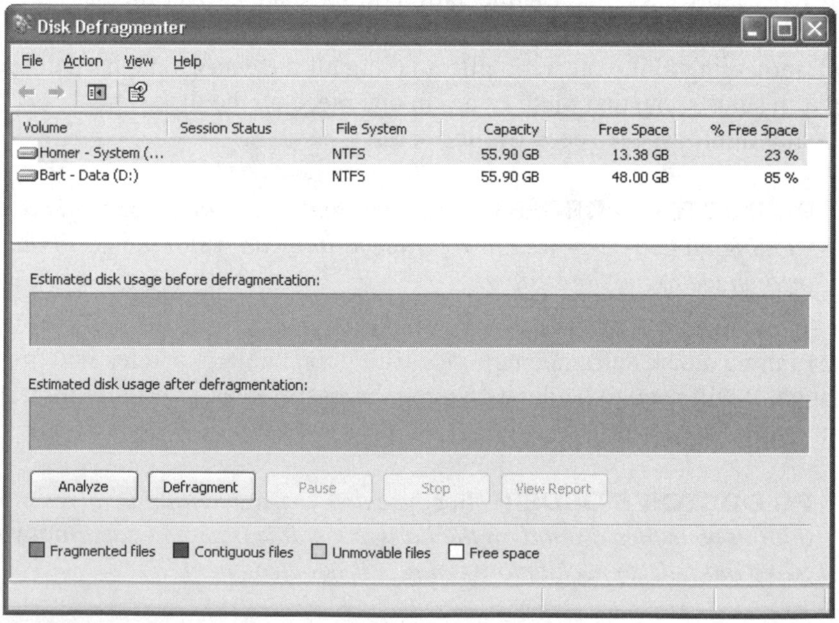

Volume	Session Status	File System	Capacity	Free Space	% Free Space
Homer - System (...		NTFS	55.90 GB	13.38 GB	23 %
Bart - Data (D:)		NTFS	55.90 GB	48.00 GB	85 %

Estimated disk usage before defragmentation:

Estimated disk usage after defragmentation:

Analyze | Defragment | Pause | Stop | View Report

Fragmented files ■ Contiguous files □ Unmovable files □ Free space

FIGURE 16-8   The Microsoft Disk Defragmenter

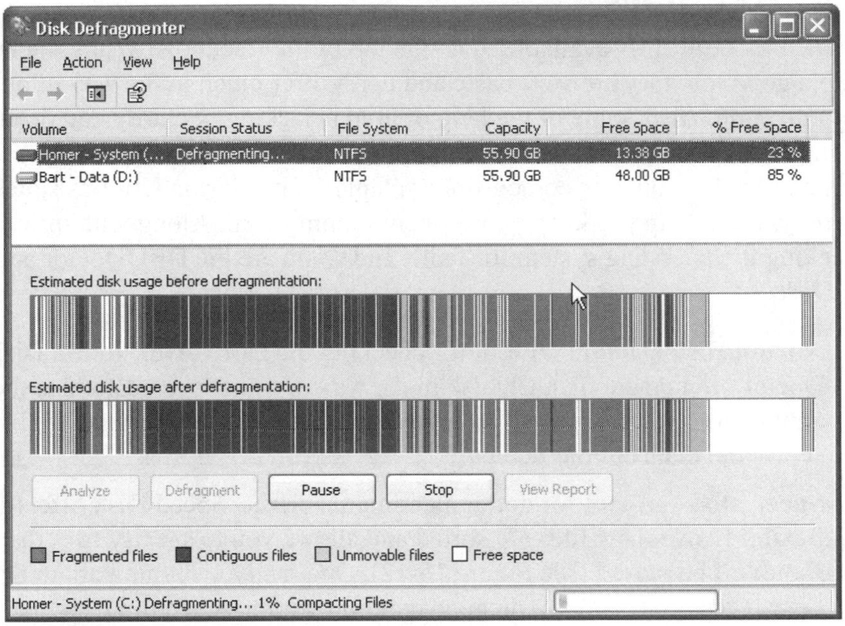

FIGURE 16-9   Disk Defragmenter in action

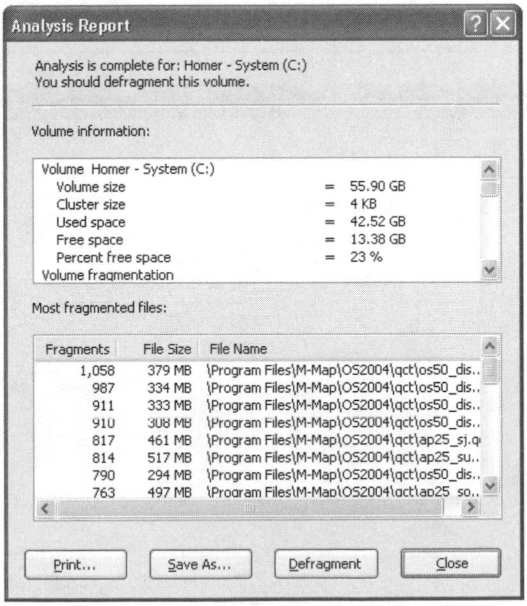

FIGURE 16-10   A report on hard drive usage

Not So Free Tools

There are a lot of utilities available to do the job of the free tools. While the free tools do a good job, they are very basic and don't offer much in the way of options or customization. Also, some of the help offered is lacking in clarity and detail (the idea being that if you can find the tools, you must know what to do with them!).

Some of the best utilities come from Symantec. The Norton Utilities suite of tools offer a lot to help you keep your system running well. Along with utilities for checking the operating system for faults and so on are the Disk Doctor and Speed Disk.

- **Norton Disk Doctor**   A tool for checking the hard drive, Norton Disk Doctor offers more than Chkdsk in the way of options to customize the application (some of which are purely cosmetic though). Figure 16-11 shows the main options screen.

- **Speed Disk**   A tool for defragmenting the drives, Speed Disk offers flexibility over how files are sorted and allows you to specify files that shouldn't be moved (see Figure 16-12). One really nice thing about Speed Disk is that you can have detailed control over the scheduling, so that you can defragment when you want to. And Speed Disk not only gives you details of how the files are sorted but also details of how files and folders are organized on the hard drive and how the space on your hard drive is utilized (see Figure 16-13).

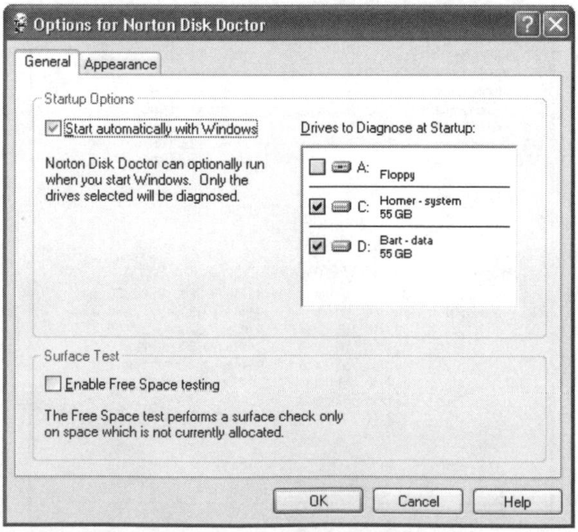

FIGURE 16-11   Some of the options offered by Norton Disk Doctor

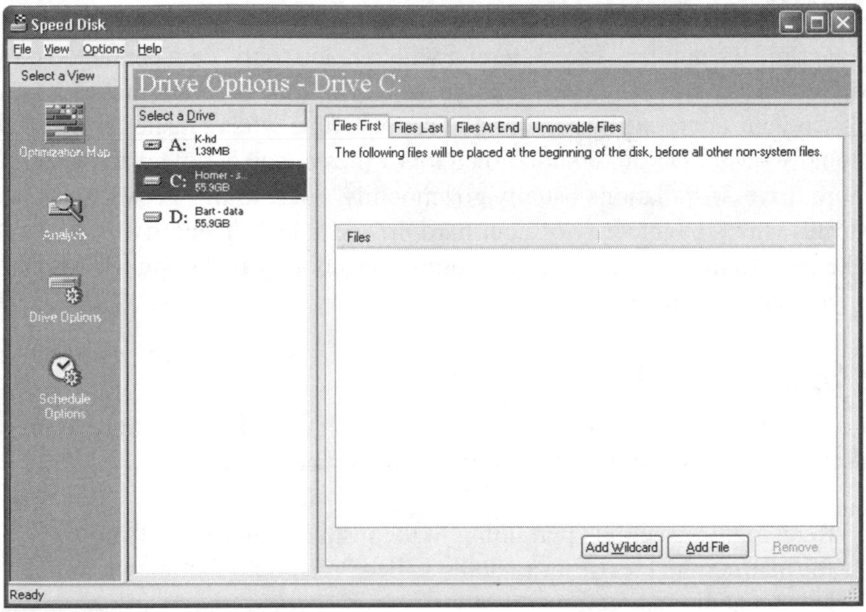

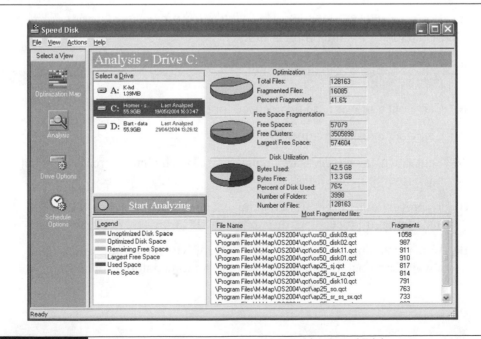

FIGURE 16-12   Some of the options offered by the Speed Disk utility

FIGURE 16-13   Hard drive utilization report generated by Speed Disk

Safe Install of Software

The main time when things can go wrong with relation to the data contained on your hard drive is when you are installing software. Installing software makes a lot of changes to your operating system, and it can be a time when crashes and lockups occasionally occur. During installation a lot of files are also moved and altered on your hard drive. Installations usually go smoothly, but if things go wrong, it is at these times when the integrity of your hard drive can be in jeopardy.

Take time to make sure that installations go smoothly by laying the foundation *before* you carry out an installation.

The Groundwork

Don't just drop the CD in the drive and start installing. Take some time to prepare so that it will go as smoothly as possible. Here are the top tips:

1. Read any instructions pertaining to the installation. Check the disc for instructional text files (usually called "readme") that may contain late-breaking instructions.

2. Never reinstall software over the top of defective software. This can cause major problems. Uninstall the defective software, and then reinstall.

3. If your system appears unstable, don't carry out any unnecessary installations. Fix the problem first!

4. Carry out a virus scan of your hard drives and any CDs used for installation.

5. Carry out a proper hard drive check for errors.

6. Carry out a disk defragment.

7. Shut down any unnecessary applications. This includes screensavers but not antivirus applications.

8. To prevent other users from making changes to the system while installation is proceeding, disconnect the PC from any network.

9. When installing on Windows NT, 2000, or XP Home and Professional, always carry out installations using the Administrator account.

The Install

After preparing the way, you can start the installation. Still, there are things that you can do to ensure that it goes smoothly:

1. While your computer is carrying out the installation, leave it alone. Don't try to use it during installation.

2. Don't take any shortcuts. Follow the installation instructions to the letter.

3. Read all onscreen instructions carefully.

4. If the installation uses multiple discs, make sure to install them in the right order. Getting them in the wrong order shouldn't crash the system, but it might.

5. If your system is on a UPS, so much the better, as you'll be protected from a power cut.

6. Keep children and pets away from the PC at this critical time in case they accidentally switch it off or change a setting.

7. If the installation appears to have hung, give it time. If the disc light is flashing, leave it for a while. Allow 15–20 minutes of inactivity before attempting to abort a "stuck" install.

Safe Uninstall

When you install software, you are adding a lot of files to the system and making enormous changes to settings within the operating system in the process. When you uninstall an application, you are doing the reverse—removing a lot of files and folders and undoing significant changes that were made to your operating system.

This means that if the uninstall halts partway through, it's equivalent to an installation not making it all the way through and leaving the system in limbo. However, if an installation halts partway, you can normally start it again, and hopefully, it will continue and install properly. (Keep all the settings the same if you do this.) An uninstall is different because files are removed and settings undone on the system by files and applications on the computer. Take care and follow the guidelines in the next sections to help make things run smoothly.

How to Do an Uninstall

A few words of advice first: don't install software that you don't think you need in the first place. An installation isn't a minor thing, and neither is an uninstall, so keep them to what's necessary. Also, be careful about time-limited software and trialware (software that you can download and try for a limited period). Support for these (especially getting rid of them!) can be limited if not nonexistent.

 PC DOCTOR'S ORDER! *Be careful about littering your system with trialware and shareware that you don't need. Many people look at this kind of software as "free," but you should consider carefully whether you actually need it.*

1. Before carrying out any uninstallations, reboot the system and shut down any unnecessary applications.

2. For added safety, carry out a disk check before the uninstallation.

3. If you are going to uninstall an application, check the manual/help files as to the best way to uninstall it. Most applications have one or both of the following:

   ■ A link to an uninstaller in the same program group as the application in the Start menu

   ■ An entry under Add/Remove Applications in Control Panel. Generally, an uninstall is carried out by clicking on one of these links and following a wizard.

4. On Windows NT, 2000, and XP Home and Professional, carry out the uninstall process through the Administrator account.

5. If you can't find an uninstall link, have another look through the manual/ help files. (Check the disk or CD if the application came on a floppy or optical disc.)

6. Follow any uninstall instructions given by the uninstall program to the letter—no shortcuts.

7. If you are uninstalling drivers for hardware, consult the instructions as to whether the driver should be uninstalled before or after the hardware.

8. While an uninstall is in progress, don't use your system for anything else.

9. Carry out uninstalls separately; reboot between each.

If the uninstallation fails, try it again. (Fortunately, this doesn't happen too often nowadays, and if you take the additional precautions listed above, it is even less likely.) If it fails again, and the program is in a state of partial uninstallation, try reinstalling the application and then uninstalling it again.

How Not to Do an Uninstall

Just as there are right ways of doing things, there are wrong ways too. Here are a few no-nos when it comes to uninstalling software:

■ Don't uninstall applications unnecessarily. If they are giving you problems or you are really low on disk space, you might have to. However, it is better not to have installed the application in the first place.

■ Don't delete applications manually off the hard drive using a file explorer (like Windows Explorer).

■ Never carry out any kind of uninstall from a user account, always from the Administrator account. If you don't have access to this, ask your network administrator.

■ Give the uninstall plenty of time. Even if it appears to have hung or crashed, be reluctant to reboot the system or fiddle with it in any way while it is working.

Call for Backup!

If things go wrong—and I mean wrong, such as an application not uninstalling properly and the system becoming unstable or no longer working properly—your final hope (short of wiping the system and starting again) might be to use a full system backup (if you have one). With this, you can reload everything back onto your system and bring it to a state that it was in before the uninstall. Now, you'll still have the program installed, but that might be better than having an unstable system as a result of a partial uninstall.

FIX-IT-YOURSELF HOME REMEDY *A working system is better than one that isn't working. In the same way, it is better not to install applications that you don't need and then need to uninstall them. Take care of your system, and be discerning as to what goes onto it and what doesn't. "If in doubt - Don't!"*

The Operating System

Probably the biggest part of your system, from a software perspective at least, will be the operating system. It is, after all, the control center for all the other software that you will be installing and running. It also determines what software you can run and how the system represents itself to you.

There are a lot of operating systems around, some free, some expensive, and those in between. There are also a wide variety of support levels, ranging from telephone support to web community only. Choice is a good thing. However, too much choice can put you on a quest for perfection. The PC is ultimately a tool that does a job, and no tool will ever be perfect; but as long as it does the job well "most of the time," that's good enough for most.

Because you may have one of a myriad of operating systems installed on your PC and may be wanting to upgrade to any one (or more) operating system, I would have to fill the whole book if I tried to cover repairing operating systems and upgrading from one operating system to another; and then only a small part of the book would be applicable to you and your situation. So, instead, what I'm going to do is lay out for you a general road map that you can use to help make the transition from one operating system to another more enjoyable and less painful to you.

Repair of the Operating System

There are several different ways that you can repair an operating system, depending on how involved you want to get and what the problem is.

1. First, you can restore the system to a previous state using a full system backup. The older the backup, the older the state to which the system will be restored. Remember that if you haven't kept a more recent backup of your data, your data too will be rolled back to the time of the last backup.

2. You can try to fix the problem yourself. How successful you are depends a lot on the problem and whether it is a documented one with a documented solution. You might have to do a lot of digging on the Internet, or you may

need to contact tech support. It might not be a quick fix, but it is the best because you are improving your operating system and learning in the process. By taking the "wipe and start again" route, you are not really learning from the problem but rather choosing to avoid it. You might come across that same problem again, possibly sooner than you expect. If you solve the problem and the system seems stable, make another full system backup.

PC DOCTOR'S ORDER! *Document the problem you had and the solution you found. In that way, if you come across the problem again in the future, you'll have the answer close at hand (which will save you both time and money). Don't trust it to memory.*

3. You can reload the operating system over the top of the existing installation. What this does is take most of it back to the original state but keep all of the program settings in place. If the problem is with the operating system, this will fix the problem, but if it is with an associated application or driver, it might not. Also, when you do this be aware that some settings and customizations you have made might be undone. (It is common to see shortcuts that you deleted reappear or settings you have changed revert back to the default.)

4. Operating systems such as Windows XP have a repair feature that accomplishes a reinstall, but quicker and with less fuss. When you try to reinstall the operating system you will be presented with this option.

5. After any repair, carry out a disk check and disk defragmentation to optimize performance.

Update of the Operating System

Updates to operating systems are commonplace today because of the need to bring out security patches and improvements on a regular basis. These updates can come in a variety of ways, the two most common being from the operating system itself or from a CD.

The Windows operating system is now updated using a single Windows Update system. To begin Windows Update, open the Internet Explorer browser and click on Tools | Windows Update.

You can also set Windows to automatically update the system on a regular basis (see Figure 16-14). Click on the Start menu, then Control Panel. Choose

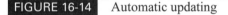

FIGURE 16-14   Automatic updating

Performance and Maintenance, and then choose System. Select the Automatic Updates tab. From there you can control how automatic updating is carried out.

Updates can also come in the form of downloads off a CD. Service packs for operating systems that contain major updates are usually big (several tens if not hundreds of megabytes) and might come in the form of a CD. These are tested fixes for problems and become a permanent part of the operating system (although they can be removed). The alternative is a *hotfix*, for which a temporary update is released. These are worth installing only if you are directly affected by the issue that they are designed to fix.

Carry out a disk check and disk defragment before installing major updates, and remember to check the CD for viruses before installing.

Upgrade of the Operating System

Inevitably, there will come a time when you'll want to change the operating system, either so you can upgrade it to the latest one or try a different one. Trying a different operating system can be fun and seem like a change, but it can also be hard work and time consuming. Also, the software that you have for one operating system might not work for another. The same goes for drivers and even hardware. Here are my tips for a smooth, successful upgrade.

First, research the upgrade before carrying it out:

- Is it what you really want?

- What additions does it give you? What do you lose?

- What will it cost you?

- Will the PC need any upgrades? Find out if your hardware and software will work with the new operating system. Check to see if you have a PC of the right specification for the new operating system that you have in mind.

OK, so you've done your research and you're ready to carry it out. If you are upgrading to an operating system in the same "family" (such as Windows Me to Windows XP Home), you can go directly from your old operating system to the new one (as long as your PC can handle it). Usually all you need to do is start the setup process, and the wizard will guide you through the steps. This seems simple but hides complexity and also potential problems:

- Always keep a backup aside. Don't assume that it will all work OK. Be prepared!

- If your system is currently unstable, don't expect an upgrade to be the solution. In fact, I'd suggest that you either fix the problem and get the system working or install the new operating system from scratch. If the installation doesn't go right, you could still be stuck in a situation where the old operating system won't work either.

Finally, the following general guidelines are useful for any type of upgrade:

- Don't carry out an operating system upgrade until you have enough time to do it. Give yourself a good space of free time (a day or a weekend if you are new to upgrading).

- Make sure that you have a recent backup of your data.

- Have a full system backup (just in case things go wrong or you aren't happy).

- Get all the additional drivers and software that you'll need beforehand and have them ready.

- Uninstall any applications that won't work on the new operating system before carrying out the installation. Be especially wary of applications such as drivers, antivirus and firewall software, as these can cause you substantial grief.

- If you are at all uncertain, consult the help files or manuals. Don't make guesses, as this is how things go wrong.

- Once you have the system running the way you want it, make another full system backup ... just in case!

Taking Care of the Operating System

Operating systems don't need a lot of care and attention to work properly. But a little care and attention goes a long way.

- Regularly update that full system backup.

- Run antivirus regularly. Update it regularly.

- Install a firewall application and keep it updated to protect against new vulnerabilities and exploits.

- Check the hard drive regularly.

- Carry out a disk defragment regularly.

- Apply any available updates often—weekly or biweekly.

Care and Feeding of the Windows Registry

The Windows registry is a central location where Windows (and other installed applications) stores configuration information about the system. It is being constantly read, altered, and added to. All this changing makes the registry prone to problems, and because it is such an important part of the operating system, it needs protecting. Figure 16-15 shows a small part of the registry.

The easiest way to take care of the Windows registry is to use the Microsoft Backup Utility.

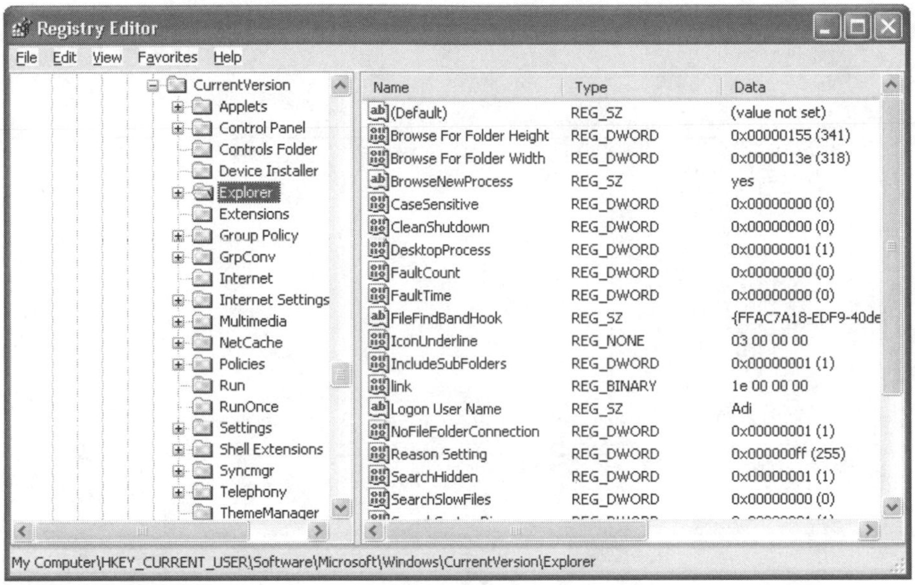

FIGURE 16-15 A small part of the Windows registry

1. Click Start, then All Programs | Accessories | System Tools, and then click Backup.

2. After the Backup and Restore Wizard starts, click Advanced Mode.

NOTE *If the Backup and Restore Wizard does not start automatically, click Backup Wizard on the Tools menu to back up files.*

3. Click the Backup tab.

4. Click New on the Job menu.

5. Click to select the check boxes next to the drives you want to back up. To back up the registry and other important system files, select System State (see Figure 16-16).

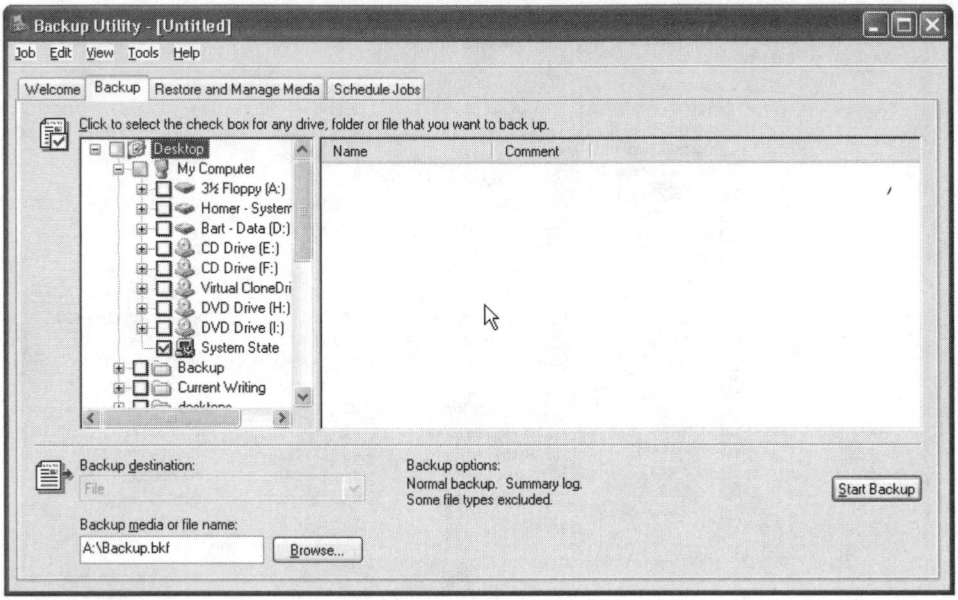

FIGURE 16-16 Backing up the system state

From this point on it's the same as a normal backup. Done this way, the Windows registry backup can form part of the full system backup easily.

Lost Files

Most of us have been there. We've been working on a file or set of files for a few hours (or even days). You've finally finished work on a file, so you save it. Next morning you go to the PC and look for the file, and you can't find it! You're sure you left it on your desktop, so you have another look … but it's not there. You check a few more folders on your desktop.

Nothing!

You start to feel the sweat popping up on the back of your neck. Is someone playing a prank on you? Did you delete it by accident? You check some more, but you soon begin to realize that the file that you worked on for so long has vanished.

What do you do? Start again from the beginning? Well, you might have to, but it's too early for that just yet.

1. Don't panic! The more you panic, the longer it will take to find the file you are looking for.

2. Check the Recycle Bin. Did you delete it by accident? If so, it might be there.

3. Think—are you on the right PC? If you have more than one, perhaps you were working on the file on the other computer. This is quite likely and has happened to me before.

4. Carry out a search for the file using the search facility on the operating system. (In Windows, click on the Start menu, and then click on Search. You will see the screen shown in Figure 16-17.) It helps if you know the name you gave the file (hopefully you made it descriptive and unique).

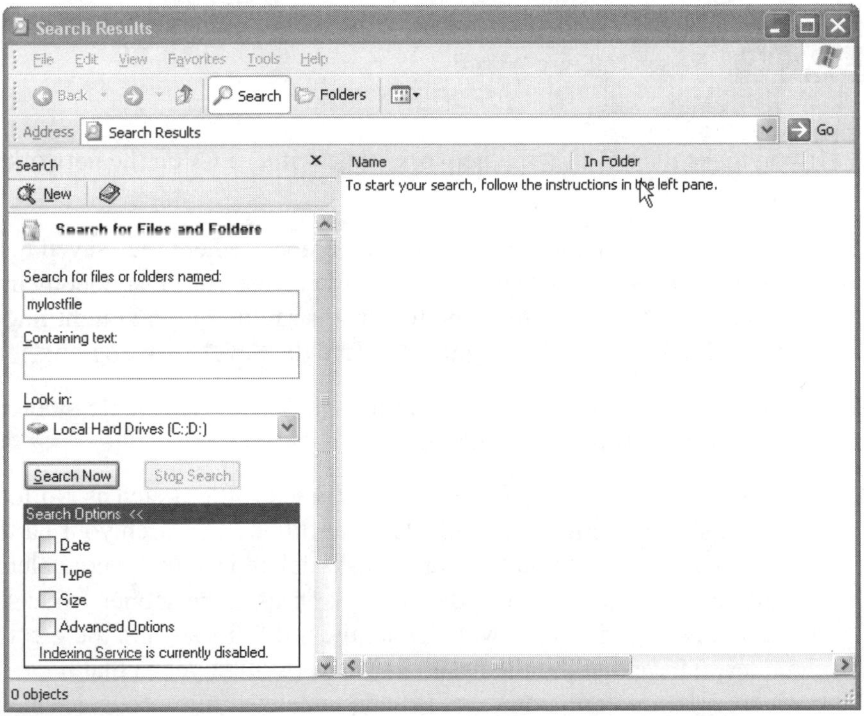

FIGURE 16-17 Searching for lost files in Windows

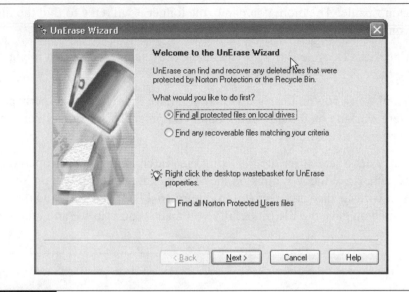

FIGURE 16-18   Norton UnErase Wizard

5. If you make a lot of use of a network, check other PCs on the network. Do a search.

6. One handy tip: sometimes programs "remember" where they saved the last document; so open the program you used to create your lost document and click Save As. Make a note of the folder it is saving to; you might find that your lost file is there. (Click cancel to leave the Save As dialog box.)

7. Think again. Did you save the file onto some sort of removable memory (floppy disk, USB flash memory, etc.)?

8. Do you have access to any undelete or unerase utilities (such as Norton UnErase, shown in Figure 16-18)? These utilities can search your hard drive, looking for files you have previously deleted (or that were deleted by another user or maliciously deleted by a virus). The sooner you discover files are missing, the sooner you can let the utility loose, and the greater chance you have that the file hasn't been overwritten yet so that it can be recovered. If you don't have access to an undelete utility, consider the value of your data. Does it justify the cost of buying the software?

9. If all else fails, go to your backups and recover your most recent copy.

Doctor's Notes

In this chapter we've looked in some detail at the precautions you can take to protect the integrity of your data while it is on the hard drive. Not only have we looked at how to check the disk for errors and correct them, we've also taken time to look at ways for you to manage your data and protect it against damage and corruption.

I've shown you how to take care of the operating system you have installed, plus given you tips on repairing it and on carrying out a pain-free upgrade. Finally, should you ever need it, you'll know how to recover files that have been lost or accidentally deleted.

File System Care Checklist

☑ If possible, use the NTFS file system.

☑ Check the file system regularly using Chkdsk or another available utility.

☑ Defragment your data regularly.

☑ Take precautions to protect your data during installs and uninstalls.

☑ Uninstall software properly.

☑ Back up the Windows registry before making changes.

☑ Files you think are missing may in fact not be missing at all. Check for them in the Recycle Bin. If all else fails, carry out a search.

Chapter 17

Backup

Go to almost any computer technician, repair center, technical support engineer, or even a PC Doctor with a problem involving loss of your precious data, and the first thing you will be asked is "Do you have a backup?" And this won't just be a casual question; we will all assume that you've got one!

But what is a backup? How do you make one? What does it contain? How does it help you when you've lost your data?

Read on!

What Is a Backup?

OK, start with the basics. What is a backup?

A backup, put in the simplest terms, is a copy of your important data. However, it isn't just a copy that you make and keep on the same computer. No, no, no. A proper backup is a copy of the data that is kept somewhere other than the machine where the original data is kept. There are many different types of backups, and they vary from the very simple to the very complex. As a home or small-office PC user, you are unlikely to want or need a complex backup solution, so we are going to concentrate on the solutions that will most likely be of use to you.

People are using their PCs more and more, and in the process, they are creating vast amounts of data. A modern PC has about 10,000 times the storage capacity of a PC available 10 years ago, and this space isn't just left blank; we are using it!

Think about the kind of data you have on your machine. Which of the following do you routinely use or create?

- Word processor files (letters, poetry, work files, etc.)

- Spreadsheets

- Digital images

- Digital photographs

- Video

- Email

- Web downloads (paid for and freeware)

- Financial information

- Game profiles

- Music

- Internet favorites

Now think about how you'd feel if, through hard drive failure or virus, you lost the lot. Some of it you could replace. You could probably download anything that came from the Internet again, and you may be able to reenter any lost financial data from paper records. It wouldn't be easy, but it's not the end of the world. (Well, it could be if it's tax time, or you needed something in a hurry for a client or colleague.) But what about the other stuff. Perhaps it's data that has less financial value, but instead has a lot of sentimental value. For example:

- Baby photographs

- Wedding videos

- Emails from grandchildren

- A game profile from a game you've been progressing through for months

This kind of data isn't as easy to replace. Lose some of this, and it could be lost forever.

PC DOCTOR'S ORDER! *If you've already lost a lot of data and you don't have a backup, all might not be lost. It depends on how you lost the data. If you deleted it by accident, there is a good chance that the data actually just went into the Recycle Bin. If you were hit by a nasty virus or the files didn't go into the Recycle Bin, you can get software that scans for and recovers deleted files. (Switch off the PC and get the software before doing anything else, as the more you use your PC, the greater the chance that the operating system will overwrite the deleted files with new files, thereby making their recovery more difficult.) Finally, you can always turn for help to data recovery specialists who can (for a price—usually a high one) recover deleted files or data from a dead hard drive. Details of software and companies are in Appendix B at the end of this book.*

Backups are important—don't neglect doing them! If you don't have a backup, there will come a point where you *will* lose data that is important to you!

Let's take a look at the types of backups that you can do.

Types of Backups

Broadly speaking, there are three types of backups:

- Local backup
- Off-site backup
- Internet backup

Let's take a look at the pros and cons of each of these and investigate the type of user each is suited to.

Local Backup

With a local backup, you make a copy of your important files and move them to a storage medium large enough to hold them, and keep those files in your home or office. Here are some ways you can do this, starting with the smallest capacity and cheapest method:

1. Copy the files onto a floppy disk, as I'm preparing to do in Figure 17-1. This is a fast and cheap method but also limited in capacity. You might get

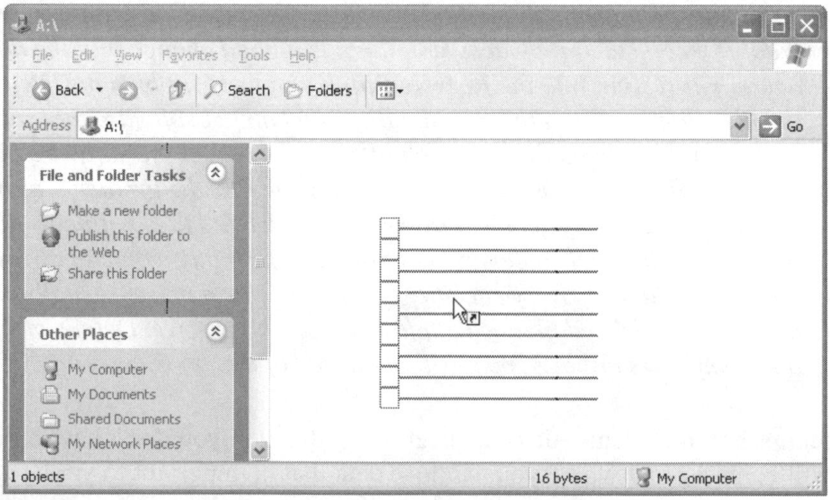

FIGURE 17-1   Copying files to a floppy disk

dozens of word processor files onto a floppy disk, but not be able to get a single image from your digital camera onto one. (Digital camera images can be massive nowadays, anything up to and over 20MB. One good-quality image is unlikely to fit on the 1.44MB available on a floppy disk.)

2. Going up in capacity and complexity, you can copy files onto USB flash memory. For under $50 you should be able to get 128MB of USB flash memory that will hold a lot more than a floppy disk. You can get a lot of files and data onto one of these, but not many digital images and very little video.

3. If you have a writable CD or DVD drive, you have a good method of backing up files, and it's easy to do (see Figure 17-2). With a CD you can back up as much as 700MB, while with a DVD you can back up a massive 4.7GB of data. This sort of capacity can allow you to back up vast amounts of digital images and video, and combine that with the fact that the discs are very robust, you have an ideal long-term storage method.

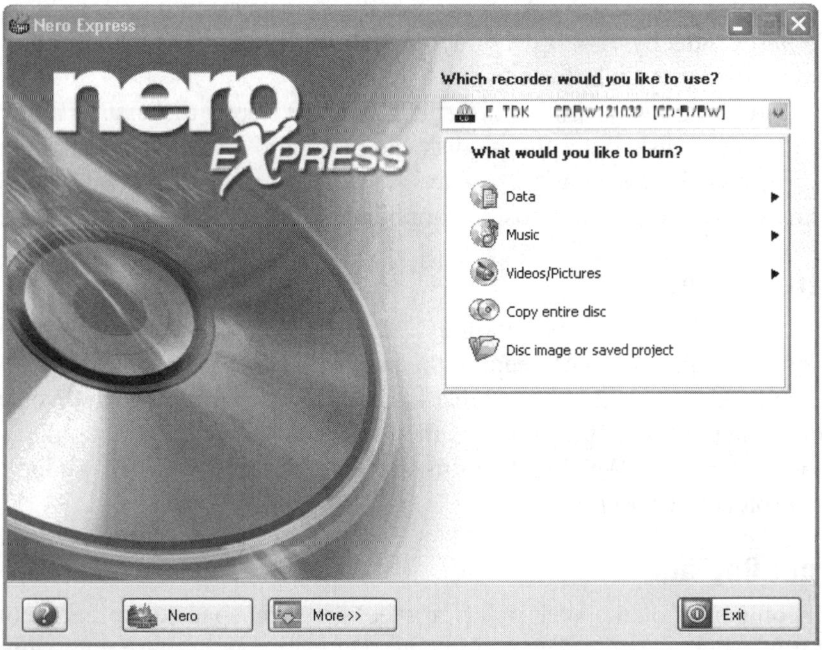

FIGURE 17-2   Burning a CD is easy nowadays with step-by-step wizards.

PC DOCTOR'S ORDER! *Nowhere here have I mentioned backing up your data from one hard drive to another on your system. Generally, this is a bad idea. You can (safely) back up your data onto a removable hard drive or an external hard drive that you disconnect once the backup process is finished. But by writing a backup to a hard drive that remains connected, or to a hard drive inside the computer, it is no safer than the original data from problems such as power glitches, theft, or fire. Keep the backup separate from the PC!*

Basically, the deciding factor for you will be how much capacity you need. If you only need a little space, go for floppy disks or external USB flash memory; if you want a lot of space, go for a CD writer. For high capacity, go straight to a DVD writer!

Take a look at the costs of different media. It's easy to calculate the "cost per megabyte" or "cost per gigabyte" of the various media. Let's compare a few costs.

You can pick up 100 CD-R discs for, say, $40 at a store. That works out as 40 cents a disc. Each disc has a capacity of 700MB. Divide 40 cents by 700MB, and you find that the cost per megabyte is about 6 cents—pretty cheap!

Do the same with DVDs. A 10-pack of discs costs around $20, or $2 a disc. A DVD has a capacity of 4.7GB, or 4700MB. Despite the higher cost of the discs, the cost per megabyte is only four cents.

Compare these two to floppy disks. A box of 10 floppy disks costs about $4. This is 40 cents a disk, but a floppy disk can only hold 1.44MB, which means that the cost per megabyte is nearly 28 cents! A stack of floppy disks that would hold the same as a $2 DVD would cost a whopping $1300.

Off-Site Backup

Off-site backup is more a methodology than a way of creating a backup. With an off-site backup, instead of keeping the backup in your home or office, you take it somewhere else. You might send that information to a computer that you can connect to via the Internet, or take the media you've saved your data onto and keep them somewhere else. We'll look at this in greater detail later when we look at ways to protect your backup.

Internet Backup

Several companies on the Web will (for a fee) give you space to upload your data so that it is kept safe and off-site all in one. (I'll list a few of these companies in Appendix B at the end of the book.)

There are two parts to a good Internet backup service:

 The space that you are going to be sending your data to: this needs to offer enough capacity to store your data and be secure (from prying eyes and hackers).

■ The client program that you install on your PC, which controls the uploading of your data to the host: usually, this encrypts your data before uploading it.

Depending on your budget, you can get a lot of additional services from your host. For example:

■ Large capacity

■ The ability to view stored files

■ Robust, reliable system (backups kept of the backups, 24/7 availability)

■ If you ever want your data, there might be an option that allows you to have it sent/couriered to you.

If you will be backing up a lot of files, you are going to need the speed or transfer offered by a broadband Internet connection; otherwise the process will take a long time.

 FIX-IT-YOURSELF HOME REMEDY *Remember that you ultimately get what you pay for. The more you pay, the better service you should get. Read the details of the products available carefully, and take advantage of any trial periods available so that you can test the service and see if it is suited to your needs.*

What to Back Up

Once you've decided what type of backup you are going to do, the next question is "What data am I going to back up?"

Several levels of backup are possible:

■ Individual files: if you only have a few files on your system that you need to back up, doing these individually isn't going to be a major hassle. This is a great way to back up small numbers of files that don't change often.

■ Whole folders of data: this is easier for sure, because you only need to remember which folders you store your data in. However, the more data you have, the longer and more complicated this job will be.

■ Entire system: this means everything—applications, data, everything. Depending on the volume of data you have and how many applications you have installed, this might run in many tens of gigabytes.

■ Something in between all of the above.

Consider what level of backup you want. But, how do you decide on the level of backup that you want? To answer this question you'll need to do some more thinking.

■ How much space do you have available for backup purposes? Do you have enough to back up the whole system or just to back up important files?

■ Do you think that the amount of space you have available for backup purposes is enough? Do you have to pick and choose what you keep and not keep a backup of?

■ How valuable is your data? How much time and effort do you want to invest in backing it up? Decide on a system that you will actually use to carry out a regular backup so that you have one when trouble strikes. Never underestimate how much work any particular system will actually be.

 PC DOCTOR'S ORDER! *Stick to your backup routine. Don't let the time you need the backup be the time that you forgot to do it!*

■ Do you have a lot of applications installed as well as customized settings of those applications and the operating system? If you do, how much trouble is it going to be to redo all of this in the event of a system catastrophe? If you have a lot of applications and custom settings, you might be better off making what is known as a "complete system backup" (which we'll come to in a moment), where you copy and keep everything. This can result in enormous backups but is the easiest way to recover a system after a problem.

How to Do a Backup

Almost as important as what files you choose to back up is how to actually carry out the backup. You have three options:

- Copy the files manually.

- Use a utility to back up files.

- Use a disk cloning utility.

The Manual Method

The manual method is by far the most work, especially if you have a lot of files that you need to keep track of or that change often.

This method is really only viable if you keep your data in a few known places. The more scattered your files, the harder they will be for you to keep track of and the greater the risk that you will forget and so omit them from your backup.

The Utility Method

If you have a lot of files, you really need to investigate backup utilities. There are many to choose from, and they can range from free to costly. If you use Windows XP Professional, you already have a backup program installed. This tool is called Microsoft Backup Utility. You can find it by clicking on Start | All Programs | Accessories | System Tools | Backup. Figure 17-3 shows the welcome screen.

Click on the Backup Wizard (Advanced) button, and you will be guided through a process that allows you to back up specific files and folders on a regular basis. You can also specify different styles of backup:

- Normal backs up selected files and marks them as backed up by clearing a value known as the "archive file attribute." The value will be reset if the file is later modified (edited and saved).

- Copy makes a copy of the selected files but does not mark them as backed up.

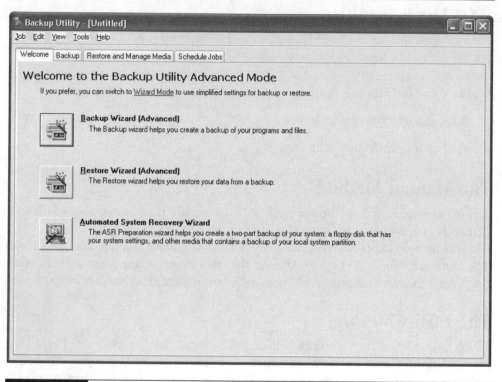

FIGURE 17-3 First screen of the Microsoft Backup application

- Incremental makes a backup of the selected files only if they were created or modified since the last backup.

- Differential is the same as incremental but does not mark the files as backed up.

- Daily creates a backup only of the files edited or modified today.

The Microsoft Backup Utility saves the backup to a specific file (with the *.bkf* file extension), which can be password protected to prevent unauthorized access. The program can also be instructed to carry out scheduled backups automatically; so you can schedule the process to run at the end of the working day or when you are not using the system.

The Microsoft Backup Utility also allows you to create a set of backups known as Automated System Recovery (ASR) backups. This process creates a two-stage backup:

1. A floppy disk that holds your system settings

2. Other media (such as a CD) that contain parameters of the hard drive that contains your operating system

This backup set is kept until needed by the Windows XP operating system in the event that it stops working properly. One thing to bear in mind is that ASR doesn't back up your data files, so you need to do that separately.

For XP Home Users

If you are running Windows XP Home, you won't have the Microsoft Backup Utility installed on your PC. The program was not included by Microsoft. However, you can still install it; you just need to know where to look for it!

Simply insert the XP CD, and run *ntbackup.msi* (you might just see *ntbackup*) from the folder *D:\Valueadd\msft\ntbackup,* where D: is the letter of your CD drive. This will launch the Windows Backup Utility Installation Wizard, which will install the utility automatically. When it is finished, click Finish and you're done. Now you can use the backup utility just like Windows XP Professional users.

 PC DOCTOR'S ORDER! *Do not use the Automated System Recovery on Windows XP Home, as it is not supported. All the other features work normally however.*

Disk Cloning

The easiest way to copy everything on your hard drive is to use a disk cloning utility, such as Norton Ghost, pictured in Figure 17-4. This takes all the data and parameters on your hard drive and saves them to a file (or files) that can be used later to re-create the exact data structure of the hard drive copied. Because today's hard drives are massive, the size of this backup will also be huge, although many disk cloning applications offer compression as an option to make the final backup somewhat smaller than the original data.

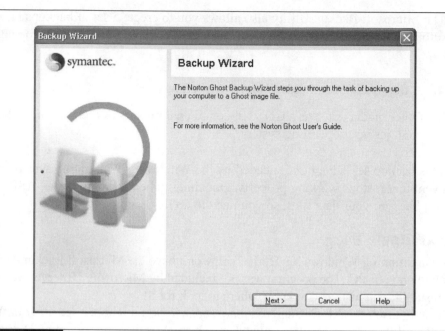

FIGURE 17-4   Hard drive cloning with Norton Ghost 2004

To properly take advantage of disk cloning, you will need a storage medium capable of high capacity—CD or DVD. Even using these methods, you can still expect to use multiple discs to store the data, even if you have the "normal" amounts of data on your PC.

 FIX-IT-YOURSELF HOME REMEDY *The "average" user has between 5GB and 10GB of data and files on his or her PC. Even at these levels, you can expect a disk clone that uses compression to need about three DVDs.*

Disk cloning needs special software, and you are going to have to pay for this—shortcuts aren't recommended or desired! There are lots of different kinds of disk cloning software available (see Appendix B for details on vendors), but most operate in pretty much the same way:

1. You load the software onto the system. Generally this then allows you to create a floppy disk or CD to start the system with and loads the cloning software. This is so that the operating system is bypassed, allowing it to be copied.

2. You select what you want to be copied, from certain files and folders or the whole hard drive.

3. You choose the options related to the backup (password protection, compression, etc.).

4. You choose a destination—another hard drive or removable media such as a writable CD or DVD.

5. You start the backup. Expect it to take about one to three minutes per gigabyte of data you are backing up.

6. Once the backup ends, you're done, although you might be given the option to verify that the backup is readable and correct. (This may be an option that you have to choose at step 3.)

How Often to Back Up

One of the hardest questions to answer is how often to back up because the answer is a combination of

- How often do your data and system settings change?

- How valuable is your data?

Again, you are on your own in deciding the value of your data. It's not easy, but a good way to think about it is to come at it from the point of view that you've lost everything already. Ask yourself:

- What have I lost?

- Can it be replaced?

- How long will it take?

- Is there anything I can't replace?

- How much have I lost from a sentimental standpoint?

- How much have I lost from a financial standpoint?

Be honest. Feel the pain of having lost your data; then come back to the reality that you haven't and you are in a position to do something to prevent it from really happening. Answering these questions will help you decide on the true value of your data.

If your data is really valuable and it changes often (maybe you're a writer working on your book), you might want to have a regular backup that copies your important files daily, if not more often. If you don't use your system much, other than play some games and surf the Web, then a weekly or monthly backup might be more suited to you.

 PC DOCTOR'S ORDER! *There is one time when you should always do a backup—before doing anything major on your system. Don't carry out major upgrades or repairs without first making sure that your data is safe.*

How Long to Keep the Backup

If you were in a position of continually making backups and keeping them, you would eventually get to the point where you were hip deep in them. So, how long do you keep them?

A common strategy for backups is the "son, father, grandfather" approach in which three generations of data are available. There are many different ways to do this, but say that you do a weekly backup of your important files. The system would work like this:

- **Week 1: Backup to Disc 1**   Disc 1 becomes the "son" backup because it is the youngest.

- **Week 2: Backup to Disc 2**   Disc 2 becomes the "son," with Disc 1 now being the "father" backup.

- **Week 3: Backup to Disc 3**   Disc 3 becomes the "son" backup, Disc 2 becomes the "father," and Disc 1 is now the "grandfather."

- **Week 4: Backup to Disc 4**   Disc 4 becomes the "son," Disc 3 the "father," with Disc 2 now becoming the "grandfather." Disc 1 is now redundant.

 PC DOCTOR'S ORDER! *Carefully label and date the discs so they don't get lost among other discs. If you have a set of discs for a backup, number them clearly, something like "04/22/04 – Disc set 1 – No 2/5." Here you have the date, the disc set number, and which disc of how many it is (disc 2 of a set of 5).*

The reason for keeping so many backups might not be immediately obvious; after all, wouldn't you always go for the latest backup? Well, perhaps not. What if you had a virus problem and you wanted to go back to a point that predated that? Or you installed a driver or applications that made the system unstable? This is the kind of situation where having a backup that goes back more than a week or so might be useful. Also, although unlikely (especially if you tested them), you might find that your latest backup is corrupted or unreadable.

Writable CDs and DVDs are cheap but not so cheap that you want to throw them away too often. Also, the system that I gave you assumes that your backup fits on one disc, but it might actually span many discs. This is where rewritable CDs and DVDs come in handy, giving you the ability to erase an old disc and use it again. This will save you a lot in dollars but also in waste. Just be extra careful not to erase the wrong disc!

 PC DOCTOR'S ORDER! *If you are not going to be using rewritable discs, also consider the security issues related to their disposal. If possible, shred any unwanted discs, dispose of them in a fire, scratch off the reflective top layer, or at the very least cut them in half before throwing them in the trash.*

Protecting Backups

Once you've made a set of CD or DVD backups and labeled them clearly, how do you protect them so that they will be working when you need them the most?
Here are the top tips for keeping your backup safe:

- Do not write on the disc with a ballpoint or pencil. Use only pens designed for discs.

- If you have created floppy disks, store these away from magnetic fields (away from speakers, for example).

- Keep discs in the proper cases.

- Keep them in a clean, dry place.

- Do not expose them to direct sunlight or high heat (near heaters or radiators, for example).

- For the complete protection of your backups (and of CDs/DVDs) from fire, heat, dirt, and magnetic fields, consider investing in a fireproof data safe. These safes are designed to protect your data from the worst that a house fire can throw at them. They are also a security measure, keeping your data and software discs safe from theft.

Taking these precautions will give your backups the best chance possible of working when you actually need them. However, there's another step that you can take: keep the backup off-site.

Keeping Backups Off-Site

If you are worried about fire or burglary, the best place to keep your data is well away from your home or office. It is an off-site backup. This can vary in scope from just keeping a few CDs or DVDs over at a friend's house, to installing a fireproof safe at home for the office data, to having a bank safe deposit box, or to signing up for a full-featured business solution where you send your backups over the Internet to a safe location.

What do you choose? Well, I doubt you need a paid-for solution (unless the value of your data warrants it), but keeping a backup at the office or a friend's house isn't a bad idea, especially for important data such as tax and other financial records. After all, there could be financial penalties involved for not keeping proper records.

Backup Media Pros and Cons

So, what's the best backup media to use? CD? DVD? Removable/external hard drive? Web-based service?

Like most things, it depends! What do you want out of it and how much data do you have? A web-based service is useful if you have a very fast Internet connection, but it is only as good as the service you choose. If the company disappears at the same time you want your backup, you are going to go without your data. On the other hand, it's a great way to have an off-site backup of your important stuff.

CDs and DVDs are great because they are cheap and relatively robust. As long as you take proper care of them, they'll last a very long time. All you need is a good supply of discs, a CD or DVD burner, and a safe place to keep them. Just like a web-based backup service, where you can access your data from another PC, you can use CDs and DVDs on different systems (or on a new system).

Another good thing about a disc-based backup solution is that you have a lot of capacity that you have control over. You decide what's on the discs, and you can easily create another backup quickly if you need to. Also, there is no reliance on having an Internet connection to use it; so you can create backups while on the move with a laptop, as long as you have a CD/DVD burner.

Disaster Recovery

Making backups is one thing; using them is quite another. You hope that you are never going to use them, but you make them just in case. If you have to use them, the process is commonly known as disaster recovery—you are recovering data after a disaster. (It's not the only time you might want to recover data. You might be changing computers or moving to a different office, but cleanup after a disaster is the most common reason.)

The types and scope of disaster you are recovering from can vary dramatically, depending on cause and severity, and the type of recovery varies accordingly.

- Accidental deletion of an important file or folder: this is usually the easiest to recover from. If you can't recover the file from the Recycle Bin or by using an undelete utility, recover the last copy you made from your latest backup. You will lose any changes made since the last backup, but the rest of your system will be unaffected.

PC DOCTOR'S ORDER! *Only recover the files and folders that you have lost. Don't overwrite other files, as these will also be taken back to the state they were in at the time of the last backup.*

- Virus attack: many viruses are designed to cause mayhem by damaging and deleting files. Make sure that you regularly scan your system for viruses using an up-to-date virus scanner. Then, as a precaution, scan your backup discs too. Now comes the really tricky part: knowing the point at which you actually got the virus. If you were to recover a backup that was itself infected, obviously, you would still have a problem. However, since the latest backup has the latest files, this is probably the best place to start. Recover the files and scan again for any viruses.

- Hard drive/system malfunction: it is after one of these kinds of problems that you will fully begin to appreciate having a full system backup of the entire hard drive. You fix the problem and load the data back onto the system from the discs. If you only have a copy of your data, you'll have to go through the whole process of installing the operating system, setting up the network and Internet connection, and loading all your applications before the system is back on the road. This can be a long haul for some and a short trip for others.

■ Moving data to a new PC: this is where you shouldn't use your full system backup, as too many of the drivers and parameters will be different. It will actually cause you a lot of problems and is unlikely to work. In this kind of situation don't be tempted to cut corners and use a backup to load your applications and operating system. Instead, load everything yourself, and get the system working before loading only your data from a backup.

Doctor's Notes

This chapter has focused on how you can keep a safe copy of your data on a different medium from your PC, just in case something goes wrong. A backup isn't a perfect solution to the problem of data loss, but it is one that balances the time and effort needed to make copies against the value of the data itself. What puts most people off about backups is thinking that there is only one kind. In this chapter I've shown you the different kinds of backups that are possible and that you don't have to copy everything. Not only that, but recovering everything isn't always the best option!

Backup Checklist

☑ Get a clear idea of the data you have that's important to you.

☑ How often does this data change? How much could you afford to lose?

☑ Does your system come with a device you can use for backup (such as a CD or DVD writer)?

☑ If it is a CD writer, is it adequate for your needs?

☑ Do you have backup software?

☑ Do you have a method of keeping your backups safe?

☑ Would an off-site backup be advantageous to you?

Chapter 18

Improving Performance and Stability

Stability and performance are cornerstones of happy computing. Stability means you can work with your system and be confident in the knowledge that it's not going to crash. Good performance means you get more done in less time.

PCs are usually in their fastest and most stable configuration when they are in an "out-of-the-box" state (meaning the condition of a PC that is new, with just an operating system and minimal hardware and software installed). As you install more and more hardware and software, the system has to cope with a greater workload, and these continual changes to the operating system parameters can, over time, introduce instabilities. So, you have two choices:

■ Leave the PC in the out-of-the-box state and sacrifice functionality for stability.

■ Add more hardware and software to your system and deal with any resulting stability and performance issues.

As idyllic as the first option sounds, it's not really possible (unless your system came with everything you could possibly want—in which case it's probably at the second option anyway!).

In this chapter we'll be looking at ways to improve on the performance and stability of your PC system without having to leave it in pristine condition.

Getting the Best Out of Games

Most people enjoy playing games on their PC. Whether it's a card game like Windows Solitaire or FreeCell, or a role-play strategy game, or a first-person "shoot-'em-up," games are the second most popular use of a home PC (after the Internet).

There is nothing like playing a game on your PC to test it to the limits, and the bigger and more sophisticated the game, the more it will test your system. When it comes to game playing there are four factors that combine to affect system performance and stability:

1. System resources: the faster the processor you have installed and the more RAM and hard drive space you have available, the better games will run. Consider the minimum system requirements listed for a game as the

absolute minimum, and never buy a game on the off chance that it will work on a lower-specification system.

PC DOCTOR'S ORDER! *Check the specifications carefully. If you buy the wrong game or software, you may not be entitled to your money back.*

2. Overall system quality: that is, the quality of the parts used. Lower-quality components, especially graphics adapters and sound cards, will result in poorer performance and stability.

FIX-IT-YOURSELF HOME REMEDY *Remember that you ultimately get what you pay for. A low-cost graphics adapter might well be false economy when you have to replace it because of system performance.*

3. Drivers for the hardware: any game requires input from you, and the quality of the hardware—especially the hardware for the drivers—is of the utmost importance. In a lot of ways, this again boils down to quality. The better the quality of the hardware, the better the drivers will be, and the faster the manufacturer will respond to any problems by bringing out new drivers to solve them.

4. Other installed/running software: conflicts between software aren't uncommon. The less you have running at any one time, the better things will be. Another advantage to this is that the less you have running, the more system resources you'll have available.

Signs of Problems with Games

Fire up a game and start playing. If it works fine, great! If not, here are some common symptoms along with step-by-step solutions.

If the game hangs during load-up, and you get a black screen, try these steps:

1. Check system requirements.

2. Check the game distributor's website for updates or patches to the game. Many games are released and then subsequently refined based on user feedback.

3. Check for updated drivers for the graphics adapter.

4. Check for updated sound card drivers.

If the game hangs during load-up or play, and the audio stutters or repeats:

1. Check for an updated driver for the sound card.

2. Check for an update to the game.

3. If the game makes use of Microsoft's DirectX, make sure you are using the latest version (check for updates at http://www.microsoft.com/directx).

If the game reboots the PC during play, take the following steps:

1. Check for an update to the game.

2. Check the system requirements of the game, and make sure your system is up to the standard needed.

3. If the game makes use of Microsoft's DirectX, make sure that you are using the latest version (check for updates at http://www.microsoft.com/ directx).

4. Check for updated graphics card adapter.

5. Disable screensavers and temporarily disable antivirus applications. Check to see if the problem remains.

Finally, if game play is slow or erratic, try these remedies:

1. Check the system requirements. If your system is borderline when it comes to RAM or processor, consider an upgrade.

2. Reduce the screen size/graphics quality and try again. Check your game manual for information on how to do this.

3. If the game makes use of Microsoft's DirectX, make sure that you are using the latest version (check for updates at http://www.microsoft.com/ directx).

4. If you only did a minimal install (when there was an option to install all of the game to the hard drive), and you are running the game off the CD, try installing the game fully. It will take up more hard drive space, but it will also make game play faster.

PC DOCTOR'S ORDER! *Even after doing a full install, many games will require you to have the original CD in the CD drive as a form of copy protection. So keep the game disc handy!*

Tips for Better Gaming

To make your system more stable for playing the latest games, check out the following tips on getting your hardware and game settings to their optimum levels.

System/Hardware

First, get good hardware. Don't skimp on quality—you'll regret it! Then only install games that are suited to the system you have. If the game requires 128MB of RAM and you only have 64MB, don't be surprised if it doesn't work. The same is true of CPU speed and hard drive capacities. (Don't be surprised to see hard drive requirements for new games running into gigabytes!)

NOTE *Expansion packs for games usually increase the system requirements and affect the load time. System requirements for an expansion pack might be very different from those of the original game. Check the box carefully.*

Check that you have the proper drivers. If you have problems, check for the latest drivers for the sound card and graphics adapter, and replace them if necessary. If problems persist, you may need to replace the hardware.

Installing the Game

Shut down any unnecessary applications that are running. If you have enough hard drive space, carry out a full install of the game. This will make the game faster and more reliable. (When you run a game from the CD or DVD, the game may hang or the system may crash if the system is unable to read from the disc when needed.) If you cannot, or do not wish to, fully install a game on your system and you have a choice of optical drives from which to run the game, always choose the fastest drive for the best possible game play.

Game Settings

Many games offer different levels of graphics quality and game running speed. Experiment with these settings to get the ideal setting for you and your system. The same goes for the audio. Background music might be unwanted, and it also takes system resources. Many games have settings to change how much music or sound effects you can hear. Reduce audio to what you want.

Screen resolution can also have a huge effect on the game. Running a word processor at a screen resolution of 1024 x 768 pixels demands a lot less from the system than running a game at that resolution. If you find that a game is slow at one resolution, try it at a lower screen resolution. Under Windows, screen resolution is controlled by the Display applet in Control Panel. Generally, the lowest screen resolution supported by a game will be 800 x 600.

Network/Internet Games

Hosting a network-play game or an Internet game means that the PC hosting the game will need greater system resources than usual, so use the more powerful system for this.

If you are playing a network game, be aware of the speed of the network and how much other traffic the network is carrying in addition to that of the game. If possible, play network games when the network is otherwise quiet.

 PC DOCTOR'S ORDER! *For more information on games, check out the game maker's website. If they have a forum, check out what others say about the game. Look for problems that people are having and whether they find resolutions to them. The more problems people have, the greater the chances of your experiencing problems. If possible, do this before purchasing the game!*

Improving Your Online Experience

Online is becoming just as important as offline, and with the interactive experience becoming increasingly sophisticated and enthralling, the pressure on PCs to deliver is greater than ever. Getting performance and reliability from the Internet isn't all within your control because the Internet is a vast array of interconnected computers and telecommunication devices. Problems can and will happen, but there are a few things you can do to minimize these problems and maximize your online experience.

Tips for Optimum Online Performance

Get the fastest possible Internet connection that is within your budget. In many places, unfortunately, this is still a dial-up connection, but if a DSL/cable connection is available, consider getting it. The faster your connection the better. Also, having an "always-on" connection reduces many of the problems that you get with poor dial-up connections.

If you use a modem, here are my recommendations:

- Internal modems that fit in a PCI slot are by far the best because they consume fewer system resources than external modems on COM ports or USB ports.

 FIX-IT-YOURSELF HOME REMEDY *Many USB modems are plagued by problems relating to poor use of available system resources (especially consuming CPU resources). They are easy to install, but you pay in other ways for this convenience. If you do choose a USB modem, check carefully as to how it affects your system performance.*

- Get a high-quality modem. Even high-end modems don't cost much these days, and it pays in the long term to get a good brand as opposed to a generic.

- Steer clear of "WinModems" (also known as "soft" or "controllerless" modems). They are cheaper because they don't have the physical communications port controller circuitry that traditional hardware-based modems have, and they can suffer severe performance issues.

- Use the best possible cables you can find. They might not look important, but they are. The quality of your connection relies on the quality of the cables, the connectors, and their ability to shield from interference.

Browsers

Use a variety of browsers. If you use Microsoft Windows, install the Opera and Mozilla browsers alongside the installed Microsoft Internet Explorer. This will give you a browser for every opportunity, and if one browser doesn't work (maybe because the site you are visiting doesn't support it), you can try another. Keep your browsers up-to-date. Check regularly for updates that improve functionality, performance, speed, and security.

If your ISP has provided you with a proxy server, enter this information into your browser, as this will speed up your web browsing as well as offer a measure of privacy to your browsing (because many Internet servers log the address of the proxy server and not that of your PC).

Security Issues

Install a software firewall (see Appendix B for details) and an antivirus program, and keep your antivirus program up-to-date. Running a PC connected to the Internet without an antivirus program and firewall is asking for trouble. Don't do it!

If you use a wireless router to allow mobile devices to connect to the Internet, make sure that you use security to protect your connection from bandwidth thieves. (Refer to Chapter 4 for details on threats and how to combat them.) Also, if you have a network of PCs all connecting to the Internet via a router or gateway, make sure that the network can handle the speed. Use 100 Mbps network equipment for best results.

 PC DOCTOR'S ORDER! *If you suspect a problem with your Internet connection, get the phone company to carry out tests on it. The results of this will tell you what you should be looking for to solve problems.*

Consider getting a spam filter if you get a lot of unwanted email. Spam email can be offensive and will consume a lot of your time. Installing a spam filter or switching to an ISP that scans incoming emails for spam will save you a lot of time and effort. It won't eliminate all spam, but it will dramatically reduce it.

Hardware Drivers

If there is one thing that has the greatest effect on the stability and performance of your system, it is the software drivers that control the hardware attached to your system. There are four different sources for these drivers:

- **The operating system**   More and more drivers are now supplied by the operating system. The advantage of this is that you don't have to bother finding floppy disks and CDs. It also means the drivers supplied have been tested with that operating system and found not to cause problems (at least under normal conditions).

- **Windows Update** Windows comes complete with a feature known as Windows Update (see Figure 18-1). This allows the operating system to check a special website for important updates and drivers. Drivers are often made available for download. The fastest way to get to Windows Update is to fire up Internet Explorer and click on Tools | Windows Update.

- **With the hardware you bought** This is the most common source of drivers. Most hardware comes with a floppy disk or CD that contains all the necessary drivers for a variety of operating systems (as well as manuals and other goodies—check the discs thoroughly, as there is usually a lot of information there).

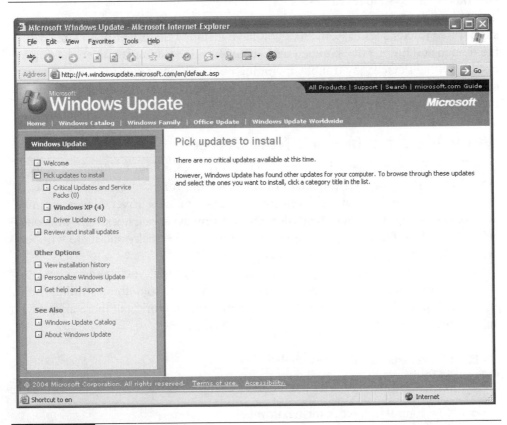

FIGURE 18-1 Windows Update

■ **Internet download**   Although most hardware comes with a driver, and operating systems also come with some that you can use, the Internet is a great source for new and updated drivers from the hardware manufacturers themselves. If you are having problems with your hardware or want updated drivers, this is the best source for new ones.

What driver you choose is really up to you. The drivers that come on a CD or floppy disk are likely to be more full featured than those that come with the operating system. For example, a printer driver that comes with the hardware might have additional functionality, such as cleaning printer heads and aligning the paper, when compared to the generic operating system driver. The downside of such drivers is that they normally have more settings and features, which also consume more system resources.

One guide is that if you want technical support for a hardware device, the support technicians will assume that you have installed the driver that comes with the device and not the one bundled with the operating system. If you are having trouble with a device (any trouble, including not working or causing a system crash, etc.), install the original driver (or an updated version of the driver from the manufacturer's website) and check to see if that makes a difference.

When It's Time to Get a New Driver

There are a few signs that it is time to get new drivers for your hardware: a device may stop working or intermittently crash or lock up, for example. But also be aware that changing operating systems often calls for a new driver. Never assume that the old driver will work on a different operating system. Check for a new one on the manufacturer's website. Failing that, you might be lucky and there will be a driver included with the operating system.

There are many reasons why a device can stop working: you've added new hardware or software, or made a change to the system, or something similar, for example. You could reinstall the old driver, and it might work, but there are a few unknowns:

■ Will reinstalling the driver help?

■ What went wrong? Why did the device stop working?

■ How long will it work the next time?

If you are unsure about the answers to these questions, installing a new driver might be far better than using the old one. Installing a new driver is also the best solution for any of the following problems:

- A device seems unstable (working intermittently, crashing, or locking up). Games are good at finding and highlighting the weaknesses in hardware, especially graphics adapters and sound cards.

- You get odd error messages relating to the hardware or the driver.

- A driver is discovered to have a security issue (maybe it allows others to access the system or compromise security). In this time of hacking and increase in viruses, you need to take security seriously.

Windows XP—Signed Drivers vs. Unsigned Drivers

Windows XP (and Windows 2000) offers vendors the ability to sign drivers with a digital certificate. This guarantees to end users that the driver they have is from the source it claims to be from and that it has not been corrupted or altered in any way. Figure 18-2 shows a signed driver (notice the entry for Digital Signer). Currently, Windows XP doesn't prevent the installation of drivers that aren't signed (see Figure 18-3). Instead it brings up a warning that the driver isn't signed and that the source of the driver cannot be confirmed.

FIGURE 18-2   A signed driver

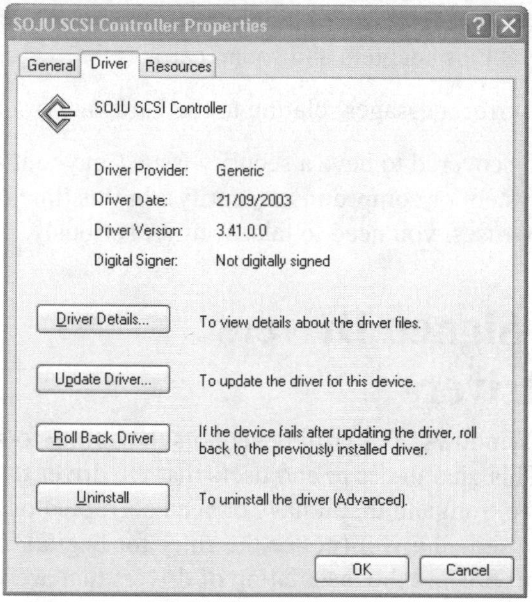

SOJU SCSI Controller Properties

General | Driver | Resources

SOJU SCSI Controller

Driver Provider:	Generic
Driver Date:	21/09/2003
Driver Version:	3.41.0.0
Digital Signer:	Not digitally signed

Driver Details...	To view details about the driver files.
Update Driver...	To update the driver for this device.
Roll Back Driver	If the device fails after updating the driver, roll back to the previously installed driver.
Uninstall	To uninstall the driver (Advanced).

OK   Cancel

FIGURE 18-3   An unsigned driver

The system offers to continue the installation or let you cancel. Most of us simply click the Continue Anyway button, complete the installation, and have no trouble at all. This method works fine as long as you're downloading from a well-known vendor.

From a stability point of view, a signed driver is no different from an unsigned driver. But if possible, use signed drivers, as you can guarantee that these are unaltered and come from an authentic source. However, there may not be any alternatives, in which case, you'll have to use the drivers available.

Installing an altered driver (altered to hold a virus perhaps or a hack tool) or a corrupted driver can cause you no end of problems. The driver might appear to install properly, but there is a good chance it will cause problems later on.

PC DOCTOR'S ORDER! *Be careful about the source of your drivers. Download drivers from the hardware manufacturers' websites if at all possible. And remember, always scan them for viruses before installing.*

Driver Rollback

XP offers driver protection beyond signed drivers, just in case things go wrong. If you run across a problem with a driver once you've installed it, such as unexplained crashes or a device that doesn't work properly, Windows XP can get you out of trouble. To do this it uses the Driver Rollback feature, which allows you to replace your current bothersome driver with the previous working version.

To access Driver Rollback, click Start | Control Panel, and then select Classic View for the Control Panel. The Classic View shows you all of the Control Panel options, as shown in Figure 18-4.

Next, double-click Administrative Tools | Computer Management. In the left-hand list under Computer Management, select Device Manager. Device Manager will display a list of all of your system devices. Double-click the device with which you are having a problem, and then select the Driver tab. On the Driver tab, click the Roll Back Driver button for a list of previous drivers for the device.

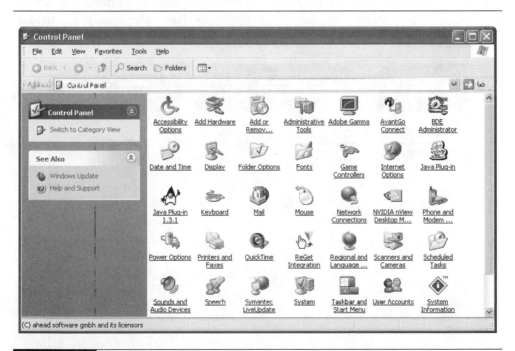

FIGURE 18-4   Control Panel Classic View (Note that you might not have all these icons on your system.)

Windows XP System Restore

You can attempt to repair a driver problem on a PC running Windows XP another way: by using the System Restore feature. System Restore allows you to undo things on your system that are giving you problems. If you install a driver or application and you later find that it causes problems, you can undo the changes and take the system back to the way it was before the installation.

 FIX-IT-YOURSELF HOME REMEDY *Note that Windows Me also has a version of System Restore.*

Before I go any further, I want to make clear that System Restore isn't a "lost document restore" application or "deleted file restore" application. It is not a substitute for a backup. What System Restore offers is a way to take the system back to a previous state (hopefully, a state that was working).

System Restore keeps "restore points" that hold information from past system configurations of the PC system. To access System Restore, click on Start | All Programs (Programs in Windows Me) | System Tools | System Restore. You'll see a welcome screen like the one shown in Figure 18-5. There's an onscreen calendar,

System Restore

Welcome to System Restore

You can use System Restore to undo harmful changes to your computer and restore its settings and performance. System Restore returns your computer to an earlier time (called a restore point) without causing you to lose recent work, such as saved documents, e-mail, or history and favorites lists.

Any changes that System Restore makes to your computer are completely reversible.

Your computer automatically creates restore points (called system checkpoints), but you can also use System Restore to create your own restore points. This is useful if you are about to make a major change to your system, such as installing a new program or changing your registry.

System Restore Settings

To begin, select the task that you want to perform:

○ Restore my computer to an earlier time

○ Create a restore point

To continue, select an option, and then click Next.   [Next >] [Cancel]

FIGURE 18-5   System Restore welcome screen

in which you can choose any date that has a restore point and roll back to it. Dates that contain restore points have bold print.

Restore points are created in several ways and at several times:

- When you start Windows XP for the first time

- Every 24 hours

- When Windows recognizes a program installation using an up-to-date installer, such as InstallShield

- Whenever you allow a Windows Update to install

- When System Restore restores to a prior system state

- When you create a manual restore point using the System Restore Wizard

PC DOCTOR'S ORDER! *I recommend that you create a manual restore point when you've just gotten your system the way you want it, or whenever you're about to make a significant change.*

To create a restore point, open the System Restore Wizard. Choose Create a Restore Point and click Next. Enter a descriptive name for the restore point in the text box, as shown in Figure 18-6. You can't rename restore points, so make sure you give them descriptive names; otherwise you'll have no idea what they mean later! Once you've given the restore point a name, click Create. You'll see the final screen, as in Figure 18-7.

FIX-IT-YOURSELF HOME REMEDY *Don't waste name field space with the date and time. System Restore adds them to the restore point automatically.*

As with most things, not everything always goes according to plan. If things go wrong with a System Restore, you can undo the setting changes and remove all the new files added by going back to System Restore and choosing Undo My Last Restoration. This then takes your system back to the state it was in before you carried out the System Restore—problems and all!

If possible, don't restore the system back to a state that is too long ago—a point created less than 24 hours ago is best. The less time that has elapsed between the last restore point and the problem, the better the restoration will be. If you have to go back days, weeks, or months, be prepared to reinstall all updates made to the operating system that have occurred between the time of the restore point and the restoration.

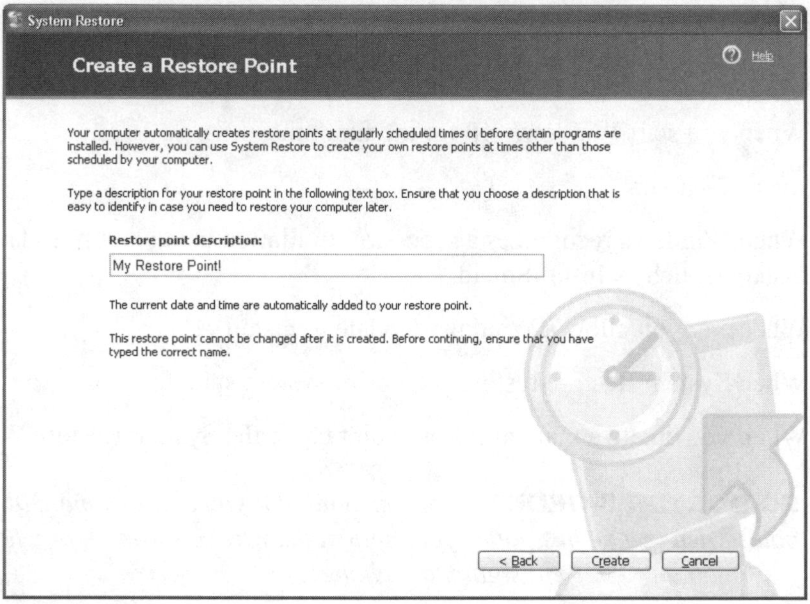

FIGURE 18-6   System Restore Wizard—creating a restore point

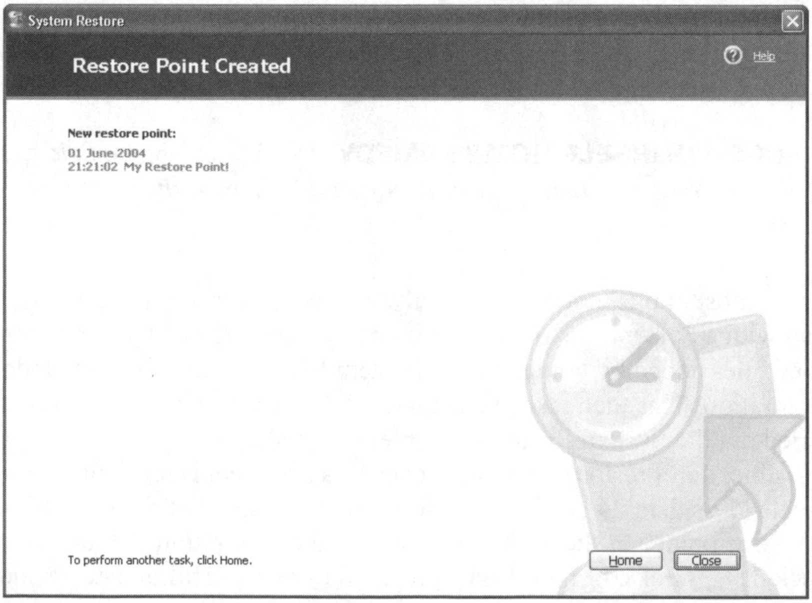

FIGURE 18-7   Finished restore point

WARNING *This is my final warning—System Restore is no substitute for having a proper backup regime in place!*

Windows Update Issues

Windows Update is a great tool that can help keep your Windows operating system in tip-top condition and fully loaded with the latest drivers and security patches. To make sure that you have everything you should have installed on your operating system, I recommend running Windows Update every week or two weeks (sooner if you hear of a report in the media of a security vulnerability). In the following sections I'll cover how to install the controls and troubleshoot some of the common problems.

Installing Windows Update Controls

To install Windows Update controls for Windows 98 and Windows Millennium Edition, first download the controls from http://v4.windowsupdate.microsoft.com/cab/x86/ansi/iuctl.cab and save them to your desktop. Once this is done, extract the *.cab* file following these steps:

1. Go to the desktop (or wherever you saved the file to) and right-click the *iuctl.cab* file.

2. Click Extract To.

3. Point to a known location (like the desktop) and click OK.

4. Go to the location you selected and right-click on the *iuctl.inf* file.

5. Click Install.

For Windows 2000, Windows XP, or Windows Server 2003, again, download the controls from http://v4.windowsupdate.microsoft.com/cab/x86/unicode/iuctl.cab and save them to your desktop. After this, extract the *.cab* file following these steps:

1. Go to the desktop (or wherever you saved the file to) and right-click the *iuctl.cab* file.

2. Click Open.

3. Select all the files listed.

4. Right-click on them and click Extract.

5. Point to a known location (like the desktop) and click OK.

6. Go to the location you selected and right-click the *iuctl.inf* file.

7. Click Install.

Troubleshooting Windows Update

Problems with Windows Update aren't common, but the following is a rundown of some that you might encounter, along with solutions to them.

Windows Update Cannot Connect to the Internet

This is the most common problem with Windows Update and can have a variety of causes:

- Check that you have a connection to the Internet. Try another website.

- The Windows Update website is temporarily unavailable. (It does happen!)

- A firewall is blocking your connection to the Windows Update website. Check your firewall logs for details.

Windows Update Won't Display or Download New Updates

There are two possibilities if you encounter this problem. First, make sure that the system clock is right. If it is wrong, Windows Update may not work correctly. If the clock is OK, follow these steps to repair Internet Explorer:

1. Open Control Panel and click on Add/Remove Programs.

2. Select Microsoft Internet Explorer and Internet Tools.

3. Click Add/Remove.

4. Click Repair.

5. Follow the steps provided by the Repair Wizard.

6. Click OK.

The Windows Update Scan for Updates Hangs at 0%

First, install the latest scripting engine 5.6 from http://msdn.microsoft.com/library/default.asp?url=/downloads/list/webdev.asp. If Windows Update still hangs, try repairing Internet Explorer by following the steps in the previous section.

You Get an Error Message About an Invalid Windows Image

The full error message is "C:\WINDOWS\System32\iuctl.dll is not a valid windows image. Please check this against your installation diskette." Download new files from http://v4.windowsupdate.microsoft.com/cab/x86/unicode/iuctl.cab and save them to your desktop. Follow the instructions below to extract the *.cab* file and carry out the installation:

1. Right-click on *iuctl.cab*.

2. Click Extract To.

3. Indicate the location to which you want the file extracted and click OK.

4. Go to the location you selected and right-click *iuctl.inf*.

5. Click Install.

You Get a Message Saying an ActiveX Control on the Page Is Not Safe

You get this message when your security settings in Internet Explorer are set too high. For Windows Update to work properly, you must change the security settings for the Internet zone to Medium or lower.

1. Open Internet Explorer.

2. Click on Tools | Internet Options.

3. Click on the Security tab.

4. Click on the Internet Zone icon.

5. To adjust your security level, click Default Level or Custom Level.

6. Under Custom Level, try the Low setting, and see if the ActiveX error persists.

Install Process Stops at 0% When Using the AOL Browser

If you encounter a problem when attempting to install an update using the AOL browser, after you have signed on to AOL, click Start, and then click the Windows Update icon. This will fire up Windows Update using the version of Internet Explorer that comes with the operating system.

On the Windows Update Website, You See Text for Windows 98, but You Are on a Windows XP Computer

After upgrading to Windows XP from Windows 98, you may see Windows 98 text on the Windows Update site, even though you are running Windows XP. This will not cause a problem, and I suggest that you leave it alone.

You Get the Error "Script Error Line 1312"

This occurs because of a misconfiguration of the Regional Settings.

1. Click Start | Control Panel.

2. Click on Regional Options.

3. Make sure that your digit grouping is formatted as follows: 123,456,789.

 NOTE *For more information on Windows Update issues, visit http://v4.windowsupdate.microsoft.com/troubleshoot/.*

Doctor's Notes

In this chapter we've looked at how you can increase the performance and stability of your system by keeping your system in tip-top condition. We've looked at two main areas: drivers and updates. Both of these will be unique to your system and vary due to hardware attached, installed software, and what you use your system for.

As you become better at working with and knowing what you have installed on your system, you will become better at knowing what you need to check for and what updates you'll need. Also, as you get more in tune with your PC, you will know when new drivers are needed. Once you've done this, the whole process becomes much easier.

Improving Performance Checklist

☑ In the event of problems, check drivers (especially sound cards and graphics adapters).

☑ If your game uses Microsoft DirectX, check for an update.

☑ Regularly run Windows Update.

☑ Familiarize yourself with the Windows System Restore feature.

Chapter 19

Making More of the Internet

The Internet offers you much more than just the vast repository of information held in web pages that is the World Wide Web. The Internet is much, much more. It is about easily connecting and sending information to other users on the Net in a variety of ways. If you are on the Internet, you should find yourself making fewer phone calls and sending fewer letters and faxes—a move that means your communications with others will not only be faster, but also much cheaper.

But before you can make use of the Internet, you need to be able to connect, and the two main issues that affect Internet users are either being unable to connect or being prematurely disconnected. If you can't connect to the Internet, you can't make use of any of the resources it offers. So, let's take a look at some of the issues that can affect your connectivity.

We'll divide connectivity into two sections, depending on whether you have a dial-up connection using a modem, or an always-on DSL connection.

Connectivity—Modem Dial-Up

When you connect to the Internet using a modem (see Figure 19-1), your computer is making a phone call to a computer run by your ISP (Internet service provider), which is then used to connect you to the Internet as a whole. There are several points along this connection that may cause you trouble, some which are within your control and some that are way outside of your control.

Let's begin by looking at the things that are outside of your control.

Phone Line Quality

When you are using the telephone line to connect to the Internet, you are using technology that was invented well before the computer (and designed purely to carry voices) to make a high-tech connection to other computers. The actual quality of the phone line plays an important part in the connectivity equation.

Because your connection relies on sending and receiving audible computer signals to and from your PC to the ISP's computer, any noise or crackling on the line can affect both the quality and speed of the connection. Errant noise on the line means that data is lost (or masked by the interference), and this means a slower connection, or it can even cause the modem to drop the connection.

If you think that your phone line is particularly noisy, disconnect all the phones you have attached and connect one phone to the main telephone socket, and then check if it is quieter. If not, try a different phone; it may be the phone itself that is generating the noise on the line.

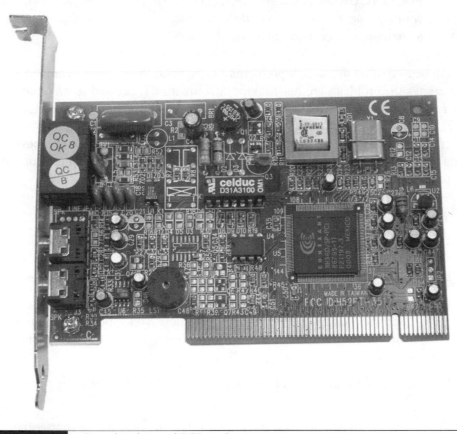

FIGURE 19-1   Complete internal PCI modem

If bypassing all the wiring and other equipment on your phone system helps and the noise disappears, the problems are somewhere in your home or premises. It's then a case of trial and error and testing to find out what is actually causing the problems.

If, however, the problem isn't affected by any changes you make, then it's probably a problem somewhere in the phone system, and it's time to get your phone company involved. It may be a problem with the line to your property or with some other part of the system. The phone company can then carry out tests on the line to check for problems and hopefully correct it.

FIX-IT-YOURSELF HOME REMEDY *Always carry out the checks on your equipment first, as you might be charged for the time that the phone technician spends tracking down the fault.*

Do bear in mind that not all problems can be fixed by the phone company. Sometimes the problems are due to poor infrastructure (lines and so on), and any real solution might have to wait until the lines or the telephone exchange is replaced/upgraded.

If you do find out that it isn't a problem with your telephone line or a noisy phone on your system, it's time to look deeper at your own equipment—from the PC to the phone socket.

The Modem Cable

Start externally, it's easier! Take a look at the length and quality of your modem cable.

- Does it have any breaks in the cable? If so, throw it out and get a new one.

- Does it have knots in it, or does it wrap around other electrical devices? It might be picking up interference from these, so straighten it and move it away from other electrical devices (power supplies, power adapters, and so on).

- Are any of the plugs damaged? If so, that's a sign that the cable needs replacing.

- Check the length—is it far too long for the job? Ideally, the shorter the cable, the better. Preferably you shouldn't buy a cable longer than about one and a half times the distance you want to span.

- Is the cable a thin, poor-quality cable? If so, that might be the problem. It's another bad sign.

The best cable to get is a high-quality shielded cable that's the right length or the next size up. Avoid using cheap phone extension cables, as they are usually far too long, and the cable quality is normally quite poor and only designed for voice.

 PC DOCTOR'S ORDER! *Never cut a cable down to size, lengthen it by adding joints, or twist it too tightly into loops. If the cable is too long, make the loops big. It reduces interference.*

The Modem

Just as a telephone can add noise to the system, so can a modem. There are two ways to check whether your modem is causing the problem: connect another modem on the same line, and see if the problem persists. (If it does, it is unlikely to be the original modem at fault.) Or take the suspect modem to a different location and try it there. (If that place has a good Internet connection, it will make diagnosis easier.) If the problem persists, it is likely to be the modem that is defective and needs replacing.

If the modem is an external one, check the cable connection from the modem to the PC. Also, be sure to check the power connections carefully. If your connection is being dropped regularly, it might be the power supply cutting out or the connection breaking. Undo all connections and redo them.

 FIX-IT-YOURSELF HOME REMEDY *Power supply problems can be hard to track down because most occur intermittently, usually when hot.*

Another thing to check, with an external modem, is that the modem (or its power supply) is not covered with books, papers, or anything else that could obstruct airflow to the devices, as this will cause problems.

If the modem is internal, take it out (safety first, refer to Chapter 6 for details on staying safe), carefully clean it and all connections with compressed air, and replace it in the case. If the slot it is currently occupying is next to another expansion card, move it away if possible, in case there is an interference problem. Make sure the card is properly seated, hand-tighten the fitting screw with a screwdriver, and then test the system again.

 FIX-IT-YOURSELF HOME REMEDY *Moving the card from one expansion slot to another might mean that you have to reinstall the driver afterwards. Make sure you have the files or disc close by, just in case.*

If none of the above help, you might be dealing with a faulty modem. However, before you condemn the modem and get another, take a look at the software controlling it and see if there are any tweaks that might help you get a better connection. Some of the checks we'll look at next might also help if you have a phone line problem that the phone company cannot (or is unwilling to) fix.

Check the Software

Before you get a replacement modem, it is worth checking out the software that controls it in case this might be the problem. It isn't going to completely cure phone line–related issues, but it might help. Checking the software means checking the drivers.

Getting new or updated drivers for a modem can be a hit-or-miss affair. The better brands usually have a fairly comprehensive website with driver downloads, utilities, and a support knowledge base. However, if you bought a generic modem, things may be different. You might have very little information to go on, which makes finding new drivers difficult.

If you have a generic internal modem and you either aren't sure who made it or they don't have a website, your best bet is to find out who made the chipset for the modem (the main modem controller chip). Take the card out and look for the biggest chip. If you are lucky, you will find a name and model number. Type this into a search engine in the following format (using the suffix "+driver" because you are searching for web pages that have the name and model and the word *driver*):

```
+name +model +driver
```

Usually, you will be lucky and find drivers. If not, keep searching, as you often turn up something that will lead you to them.

 FIX-IT-YOURSELF HOME REMEDY *In the long run it is far better to spend a little extra cash and buy "branded" items simply for the support structure they have in place and the continual driver improvement program they carry out. Buying cheap sometimes does mean having to buy twice!*

Operating System Tweaks

Your final port of call should be the operating system. When all else has failed, you might find a solution of sorts here. Here are a few suggestions.

Reduce Speed   One method of making a modem connection more stable is by reducing the maximum speed that is attempted by the modem during the initial stages of a connection. The lower the speed you use on a poor telephone line, generally the more robust the connection you make. This tweak can be found in Control Panel:

1. Click on the Phone and Modem Options icon. (If you are not using Windows XP in Classic style, you will first have to click on the Printers and Other Hardware icon.)

2. Once the dialog box has opened, click on the Modems tab and select your modem from the list. Then click on the Properties button.

3. Another screen will appear, and this time you need to click on the Advanced tab and then click on the Change Default Preferences button.

4. The screen shown here will appear, where you can alter the modem speed by using the Port Speed drop-down box and selecting a lower speed from the list. Test the connection after making any changes.

Toggle Error Control   This setting determines what kind of error correction the modem uses to clean up and correct error in the data. Error correction might sound like a good thing, and usually it is; but if the connection is going via a poor line, it could well be adding to your problems.

There are no hard-and-fast rules here as to whether this will make any difference. Depending on your operating system or modem driver, error control might also be known as "Data Protocol." The options usually available are Standard EC (error correction), Disabled, and Forced EC. The default is normally Standard EC, but you can change to either of the others and try the connection again. Depending on the type and severity of the line problems, many users have found a more stable connection by choosing either to disable error correction altogether or use the forced error correction option.

The normal location for this tweak is also in Control Panel (although some drivers might make it harder to find, in which case you will have to go hunting for it elsewhere—check your documentation). Follow the same steps given previously to reduce speed. In Windows, you will see a Data Protocol drop-down box (as shown in the previous illustration). Note that in some cases this option may be disabled.

Toggle Hardware Flow Control   Just like error control, flow control is another option you can change. Generally, one modem in any connection is going to be able to send data much faster than the other one can receive it. Flow control allows the receiving modem to tell the other one to pause while it catches up with the data.

There are two kinds of flow control. Software (XON/XOFF) flow control and hardware (RTS/CTS) flow control. With software flow control, when a modem needs to tell the other to pause, it sends a certain character, usually Control-S. When it is ready to resume, it sends a different character, such as Control-Q. Software flow control's only advantage is that it can use a serial cable with only three wires. Because software flow control controls the data transmission by sending specific characters, noise in the phone line could generate the character randomly, halting transfer until the proper character is sent again. Hardware, or RTS/CTS, flow control uses wires in the modem cable or, in the case of internal modems, hardware in the modem. This is faster and much more reliable than software flow control.

If you are having a problem, try toggling between hardware (RTS/CTS) flow control and disabling it to see if you get any better results. Again, follow the steps in the procedure under "Reduce Speed," and you will see the options for flow control:

 NOTE *Binary files must never be sent using software flow control, as binary files can contain the control characters.*

Toggle Modem Compression   Most modern modems are capable of a certain amount of data compression in order to speed up the data transfer process. Over a good line, this is desirable and can speed things up (if only a bit), but if the telephone line has noise in it, it can cause more problems than it is worth. This is located in the same place as the previous options. Follow the steps under "Reduce Speed," and you will find the option to enable or disable compression. Toggle the option and see if it helps. Note that in some cases this option may be disabled.

Connectivity—DSL/ADSL/Cable

For the Internet user who wants speed and an always-on connection (at a lower cost than the dial-up user who makes good use of the Web), nothing beats a DSL (Digital Subscriber Line), ADSL (Asynchronous Digital Subscriber Line— *asynchronous* comes from the fact that the upload and download speeds aren't the same), or cable connection.

Not everyone can have a connection like this (it depends a lot on line quality and distance to the phone exchange). And you will need to invest in new equipment (a special modem is needed to connect). If you can get a connection like this (check with your phone company to see if you can) and get a modem and the right package from your ISP, much awaits you:

- Higher speeds (usually at least 10 times that of a modem): the norm these days is 512 Kbps, with speeds up to 2 Mbps possible in many places.

- Increased reliability and performance: because the DSL/ADSL service is carried by the phone company, it does carry guarantees. (The phone company will carry out tests on your phone line before making it available to you.)

- A connection that's always there when you need it and needs no dialing out to use.

- You can still use the telephone line for voice/fax/data while your Internet connection is in use.

Problems with DSL/ADSL/Cable

An always-on connection has many advantages over a dial-up connection, and generally the whole system is more robust. It isn't, however, infallible! The hardware at your end, which is connected to both the phone line and the PC, can go wrong, not to mention software in the form of drivers.

Check All the Connections

In the event of any kind of problem, check the connections: phone socket connection, PC connection, and power connection. Undo them and redo them all, and test again. Check all the cables and connectors for signs of damage.

Switch Off

A good trick with DSL/ADSL/cable modems is to switch them off and unplug them. Leave it unplugged for two to three minutes before reconnecting it to the power supply and allowing it to make a connection. During this time leave the modem connected to the phone line.

This is a trick that works for some modems by allowing the buffers to be cleared, resulting in a better connection.

Check with Your ISP

Sometimes the problem will be with your ISP, and there isn't much you can do about it but wait. Give them a call and see if they are aware of the problem, and ask for an estimate of how long until it is fixed.

Sometimes the problems aren't directly related to your ISP but are a result of the phone company carrying out repairs or upgrades on the system. Usually, the ISPs are made aware of upgrades and repairs that might affect their users.

Noisy Phone Calls

A common problem that many DSL/ADSL users have is a noisy phone line. This is not a problem and is easily cured by the addition of a microfilter to the phone line. This splits the phone line in two, allowing you to connect phones and the modem to the line while filtering out the high-frequency noise of the modem from the phone, enabling clearer calls.

 FIX-IT-YOURSELF HOME REMEDY *The high-frequency sound is that of the modem at work. This is by design, and in order to have clear calls, you will need a microfilter. Note, however, that a microfilter is unnecessary if the phone line is not used for voice calls.*

If you don't have a microfilter installed and you are experiencing disconnections while using the same line for voice or fax, this is the problem. Install a microfilter, and the problems should go away. You might have been supplied one with your modem; if not, they are a few dollars to buy (if you shop around for a good price).

Drivers and Firmware

As with all hardware, we eventually come back to looking at the software that drives it—the drivers. These types of modems will have two sets of software control: the driver and the firmware.

The driver is just like any other driver and allows the device and the operating system to interact. If you are having problems with the equipment, check for an updated driver. It might make the difference.

Firmware is different from a driver in that it is software loaded onto the device, instead of your PC. On a modem of this kind, the firmware takes responsibility for controlling the connection and also providing an interface for you to enter details (username, passwords, etc.) relating to your Internet connection. You'll generally find that new firmware is made available on a regular basis as bugs are fixed, security is improved, and improvements are made.

Take care to follow the instructions relating to firmware installation to the letter. Never take shortcuts, as mistakes can mean your modem will not work, and you may even have to send it back to the maker to be repaired. Print out a copy of the instructions and follow them carefully!

Email

Email has become almost as popular as surfing the Web. The ability to send someone messages and files without leaving your computer and have the messages waiting for the recipient to download is compelling. It is also much faster and a lot cheaper than using snail mail (the postal service) or fax (and not everyone has a fax machine).

Here are a few tips for making the most of email.

Decide on Who You Actually Are!

The days of having just one email address and everything going into one box are long gone. The explosion in free and cheap email accounts means that you can now control which email address you give out to others. So, for example, you could have one account for personal correspondents, one for work, and one that you give out to online merchants and websites that ask for it. This gives you greater control over what goes where and will save you time during the day, enabling you to concentrate on the email that you actually want to see.

Some ISPs allow you to have unlimited email accounts (so you might be something like *youchoose@youraccount.yourISP.com*). If this is the case, you can give each company you deal with an email account. For example, say you deal with XYZ Books; you could give them the email address *xyzbooks@ youraccount.yourISP.com*, keeping their email separate from all the rest.

Another good reason to do this is spam. If a company sells the email address that you gave them (especially if you requested that they not share your details with others), you'll know who did and use that to decide whether you want to deal with them in the future. If they don't respect your wishes, consider whether they respect you as a customer.

Install Antivirus Software

Also, be careful of viruses and worms making their way onto your computer through email. If in doubt, delete the suspect email. Consider the installation of antivirus software as a must if you have an Internet connection, but don't let this be a substitute for common sense and taking care. Many new viruses, worms, and Trojan horses are created and released daily, and there is always a lag between the release of the malicious code and the antivirus software companies coming out with a fix. Sometimes the spread can be so fast that many people will have received (and unfortunately, passed on) the malicious code before the antivirus software receives an update.

With common sense you can avoid becoming a victim and slow down the spread!

Email on Web Pages

Putting your email address on a web page is the fastest, most guaranteed way to get spam email. This is because many of the spammers use programs that trawl the Internet looking for email addresses for harvesting. Once found, an email address is added to a list that is then passed around and sold.

There are many tips to prevent your email address from being harvested, most of which are too complicated to go into here; but two of the best are

- Don't put your email address on a web page in the first place. Consider carefully whether you wouldn't be better off with a feedback form or guest book instead.

- Instead of putting the email address as text, put it on the page as an image.

There are also ways you can hide your email address from harvesters using script on your web page. Fire up your browser and navigate to your favorite search engine, and do a search using the following keywords:

```
email spam buster script
```

You'll find dozens of scripts, along with details of how to use them. Use them wisely, and you will see a dramatic decrease in your daily spam intake!

Web Browsers

After operating systems, nothing causes more outburst of opinions than which web browser is best and fastest. For something that on the surface seems so simple, which web browser you use can, to some, be like which football team you support or which car you drive. Don't get sucked into this; use what you feel best with.

First, there are no rights or wrongs about which web browser you have. Ultimately, as long as it serves you the way you want it to, and you update it as necessary to close any security holes, then pretty much all browsers are the same. The three most commonly encountered browsers are Internet Explorer, Mozilla, and Opera.

- **Internet Explorer**   The free browser built into the Windows operating system is without a doubt currently the most widely used browser on the Internet. Even though it has been plagued by security issues (a good reason to make sure that it is regularly updated), it is fast and convenient, and above all, free! For more information, visit http://www.microsoft.com/ie.

- **Mozilla**   The Mozilla browser is based on open-source code (code that is freely available to others to view and make changes to). It supports all the web standards very well, and it is also available for free, which has helped make it the second most popular browser on the web. For more information, visit http://www.mozilla.org.

- **Opera**   The Opera browser is a fast browser that is available in either a free version (that displays ads while you are browsing) or a paid-for version. Both are identical in terms of functionality and performance, and both do a great job of displaying web pages accurately. They also offer you a vast amount in the way of customization. Despite its overall low popularity, it is still the ultimate geek browser! More information at http://www.opera.com.

There is nothing to prevent you from installing and using multiple browsers simultaneously. In fact, having more than one web browser can speed up how you use the Web, especially if you have a habit of doing more than one thing at once.

Cookies

Most sites you visit will place a cookie on your machine for one reason or another. These cookies are used to personalize your visiting experience, store login information for e-commerce sites, and track your return to the site later.

Cookies cannot contain any malicious or dangerous code, but they can be used to keep track of various sites that you visit (only sites that sign up to be part of certain systems, not every site you visit on the Web). Some people want to delete these cookies on a regular basis just to save on hard drive space or just to make the browser faster. (It's debatable whether it makes much of a difference in speed, but it does "freshen" your browser.) Periodically you might also want to delete your cookies because you are experiencing problems accessing a website or service (sometimes cookies get confused or corrupted). You can either use your browser to do that (covered next) or use special software (see Appendix B) that will delete them separately.

Deleting Cookies

With each browser comes a different way to delete cookies. Here's a rundown of the most popular browsers.

Internet Explorer   Cookies are saved in more than one location on your hard drive, depending on the version of the browser and the version of the Windows operating system that you are using. By far the best way to delete these cookies is to close Internet Explorer and then use your Windows Explorer to do a search for folders called *cookies*. These folders contain the cookies, and you can delete them as you would any other file.

Opera   For Opera 6.0 and 7.0, go to Files on the toolbar, click on Delete Private Data, and select what cookies you want to delete. Usually, a cookie has a name that is the same as or similar to that of the website that provided it.

Mozilla   To delete these cookies, choose Cookie Manager from the Tools menu, and then choose Manage Stored Cookies. Remove any cookie from the list, or remove all cookies.

Mozilla Firebird   This browser is different from Mozilla. Click on Tools, then Options, and select the Privacy icon in the left-hand panel. Now click on Cookies and then on Stored Cookies. To remove a single cookie, click on the entry in the list, and click on the Remove Cookie button. To remove all cookies, click on the Remove All Cookies button.

Netscape Navigator 6.x and 7.x   Choose Cookie Manager from the Tools menu, and then choose Manage Stored Cookies. Remove any cookie from the list, or remove all cookies.

Netscape Navigator 4.x   All the cookie information is stored in one file, called *cookies.txt*. This makes them easy to find and delete. The file can be located by using Windows Explorer to search your hard disk drive for *cookies.txt*.

Proxy Servers

A proxy server is a computer that sits between your web browser and the real server that hosts the website you are visiting. It intercepts all requests to the real server to see if it can fulfill the requests itself. If it can't, it forwards the request to the real server.

There are three advantages to using a proxy server:

- It dramatically improves web performance.

- It allows filtering of the content that is available to the end user.

- It offers you a level of privacy, so that, depending on your ISP, websites will see the proxy server's IP address rather than your own IP address, which could be traced back to your dial-up or cable account. It's not foolproof by far.

If your ISP gives you details of a proxy server, consider using it. What you will be given is what appears to be a web address, and this is used by the browser to access the proxy server.

Using a Proxy Server on Internet Explorer 6.0, 5.5, and 5.0

From the Tools menu select Internet Options, and then click on the Connections tab. If you are on dial-up, now click on Settings. (Click on LAN Settings if you use a network to connect to the Internet.) Make sure that the Use a Proxy Server check box is checked, and enter the address into the box.

Using a Proxy Server on Netscape 6.0, 7.0, and Mozilla (Including Firebird)

Click on Edit from the menu and then Preferences. In the dialog box that appears, navigate to Advanced and Proxies. Click on Manual Proxy Configuration, and enter the details you have been given.

Using a Proxy Server on Opera 6.0 and 7.0

Select Edit, then Preferences from the menu bar in the browser. Select Network from the menu selection on the left side of the dialog box, and then click the button for Proxy Servers. Enter the details as provided by your ISP.

Proxy Issues

If you find that you are unable to see a web page or site on the Internet, this might be a proxy issue. Double-check that the information is correct, and if it still doesn't work, remove the proxy information and try to connect to the Internet directly. If this works, check the proxy information again. If the problem persists, contact your ISP.

Internet Time Sync

Do all your PC clocks say a different time? Would you like a way to update them automatically? If so, then you can sync your PC clock over the Net with one of the many time servers.

To do this you'll either need this ability built into the operating system (it is built in as standard in XP and updates when you are connected to the Internet), or you'll need to get your hands on software to do it. (Consult Appendix B for suggestions, or fire up a browser and do a search!) With some of the paid-for shareware software, you can customize how often the clock is synchronized and even choose the best server to do it.

 NOTE *If you just want the time to be* reasonably *accurate, synchronizing the PC clock once a day should be good enough. If you want more accuracy, then update more often (once an hour should be often enough).*

There are lots of advantages to having an accurate clock. Files and folders will be correctly timestamped, email send and receive times will be accurate, and if you keep appointments on your PC and have a reminder system going, you can avoid the embarrassment of tardiness due to an inaccurate clock.

Doctor's Notes

The Internet is no longer just something you can dip into every so often, but rather a tool you can use to communicate with others almost as if they were on the same network as you are. You can use it to send information and files to others almost as fast as you could send them to someone sitting right next to you. The Internet is now a cornerstone of what many use the PC for. In fact, the explosion of PCs in the home has been driven in part by the desire and need to get onto the Internet and start surfing and using the vast capability that it offers!

This chapter has covered some of the ways that you can make more and get more out of the Internet, from how to get a better connection to the Internet, to speeding up your browser with a proxy server and using time servers to adjust your PC clock automatically. We've only just scratched the surface in terms of what you can do once you are on the Internet, but hopefully we have covered some of the issues that might stop you from getting a connection!

Modem Checklist

☑ In case of any problem, first check the connections from the phone line to the modem and, if present, modem to PC and power to the modem.

☑ Check all cables for signs of damage or deterioration.

☑ Reroute cables away from electrically noisy items (such as fans and electric motors).

☑ Check with your ISP, as they might be having problems.

☑ If the modem appears to be working but the connection is poor or unreliable, have the phone company check out the quality of your line.

☑ Check for updated drivers of software for your modem.

☑ Also check for updated firmware, which may help.

☑ If possible, test the modem on a known good connection (if possible on a known good PC). This isn't always possible, but if it is, it is a powerful diagnostic device.

Part IV

Appendixes

Appendix A

Glossary of Common PC Terms and Abbreviations

10Base-T   An Ethernet network that uses twisted pair (also known as RJ-45) cabling between a network interface card and a hub to connect the network together. This runs at a speed of 10 Mbps.

100Base-TX   An Ethernet network that uses twisted pair (also known as RJ-45) cabling between a network interface card and a hub to connect the network together. This runs at a speed of 100 Mbps.

ACPI   Advanced Configuration and Power Interface is an industry specification for the efficient handling of power usage by both desktop and mobile PCs. ACPI specifies how a computer's BIOS, operating system, and attached peripherals communicate with each other about power usage. ACPI can allow for a variety of power-saving features to activate when required. For example, the user can specify at what time a device, such as a display monitor, is to turn off or on, or the operating system can lower the CPU clock speed during times when applications don't require the full processor clock speed. In order for ACPI to work on your computer, your BIOS must include the ACPI software, and the operating system must be ACPI compatible. ACPI is designed to work with Windows 98 and with Windows 2000 and XP (both Home and Professional).

AGP   Accelerated Graphics Port is an interface specification that enables 3D graphics to display quickly on PCs. The main area that AGP has benefited is the gaming industry, allowing creation of gaming environments that are more realistic and contain real-world elements such as clouds, smoke, and fog.

ANSI   American National Standards Institute is a nongovernment organization that develops and publishes standards for voluntary use in the United States.

ATA   AT Attachment; *see* IDE.

ATX   An industrywide open specification for a desktop computer's motherboard. ATX improves the motherboard design by taking the small AT motherboard that has been an industry standard and rotating the layout of the microprocessor and expansion slots by 90 degrees. Doing this allows space for more full-length expansion cards and also improves cooling. Also specified is a double-height space at the rear of the chassis to allow for more possible I/O arrangements for a variety of devices such as LAN connection and USB ports. The new layout is also cheaper to manufacture and uses fewer cables.

binary   The base two numbering system, where the only digits are 0 and 1. It is used by all computers for internal operations, and data is saved onto hard drives and in memory using this system.

BIOS   Basic input/output system is the program used by the CPU to get the computer system up and running after you turn it on. It also manages data flow between the computer's operating system and attached devices such as the hard disk, video adapter, keyboard, and mouse.

bit   This is a binary digit that can take either the value 0 or 1. The bit is the smallest unit of information that a computer can work with, process, or store. Bits are also used to measure data transfer speeds. This can be noted in bits per second (bps), kilo (thousands of) bits per second (Kbps), and mega (millions of) bits per second (Mbps).

boot-up   This is the process of initializing, testing, and configuring a PC during start-up.

browser   An application used on a PC to view web pages on the Internet. Common browsers include Internet Explorer, Netscape Navigator, Mozilla, and Opera.

bus   The circuitry on the motherboard that carries data from one component to another. The term usually refers to the circuits that connect the components to the CPU and RAM. Another type of bus is the expansion bus that connects expansion cards to the CPU and RAM.

byte   A unit of data made up of eight contiguous bits. A byte is usually the smallest addressable unit of memory. This is considered to be the basic storage for "characters" on a PC. Bytes are used to represent storage size, including memory and hard drive capacities. Thousands of bytes are known as kilobytes, millions of bytes known as megabytes, and a thousand million (billion) bytes is a gigabyte.

cache   The cache (pronounced "cash") memory is special, dedicated, high-speed memory reserved for a particular purpose. Nowadays, hard drives, CPUs, and graphics adapters all take advantage of cache memory.

CD-ROM   Compact Disc-Read Only Memory refers to the disc that stores the media only. The device that reads the disc is called a CD-ROM drive.

Compact Flash   A memory card commonly used in digital cameras and handheld devices.

compressed file   A file that has been made smaller by an application. This is usually done for storage purposes or for making a file smaller for transmission over the Internet. *See* ZIP.

cookie   A small data file stored on your computer by web browsers to help personalize your surfing experience.

CPU   Central processing unit is another term for the processor and microprocessor—the central unit in a computer containing the logic circuitry that performs the actual instructions of a computer's programs.

crash   An unexpected (and usually very annoying) shutdown either of a program or the whole system, which usually results in data loss.

default   The predefined configuration of a hardware device or software application.

DIMM   Dual Inline Memory Module is a type of RAM found in newer PCs.

DOS   Disk Operating System is an operating system designed for early IBM-compatible PCs.

download   The process of transferring a file or data from one PC or device to another. A download can also be carried out over the Internet.

driver   A program that extends the capabilities of a computer by enabling the computer to operate peripheral devices and expansion cards.

DSL   Digital Subscriber Line is a technology that allows high-speed data transmission over ordinary telephone lines.

DVD   Digital Versatile Disc is a standard for storing large amounts of data on a disc the same size as a CD. The advantage that DVD has over a CD is that it can hold almost seven times the amount that a CD can on a single side (4.7GB).

email   Electronic mail sent between network computers via the Internet.

ESD   Electro-static discharge is the discharge of static electricity that has built up on the human body. If this occurs near an electric component, damage may occur.

expansion card   A flat, rectangular circuit board that is inserted into an expansion slot on the computer's main bus. It expands on the existing functions of the PC by adding networking capability, for example, or by updating features included on the motherboard, such as graphics adapters.

FAQ   Frequently asked question—pronounced "fak" or simply "F-A-Q"—is a term you are likely to come across a lot on the Internet. An FAQ is a file (usually a web document) created to answer common questions that a user may have about a certain software application or that a newcomer to a website might have. Beware though; while some FAQs are good, others can be pretty appalling!

FAT   File Allocation Table is a file system that controls access to the files and folders on a hard drive.

FAT32   An upgraded version of FAT present in later versions of Microsoft Windows that supports larger drives.

FireWire   *See* IEEE 1394.

firmware   A program that is embedded in a chip on a device and contains instructions for running that device.

freeware   Software available on the Internet or via email that can be downloaded and used free of charge. Despite being free to use, freeware is still copyrighted to the author.

GHz   Gigahertz, or 1 billion hertz, is 1 billion clock cycles per second and is the measure of a computer's CPU speed. For example, a CPU that runs at 1.4 GHz carries out 1.4 billion cycles per second. Each instruction processed by a computer takes a predetermined number of clock cycles to be carried out; therefore, the more cycles a computer can execute per second, the faster its programs run.

GIF   Graphic Interchange Format is a compressed file format for images. The files in this format have a .gif file extension.

gigabyte   The exact definition of this word often varies with the context. Strictly speaking, a gigabyte is 1 billion bytes. However, in reference to computers, bytes are often expressed in multiples of two, and as such, a gigabyte can also be either 1000 megabytes, 1024 megabytes, or 1,048,576 bytes.

glitch   Unexpected problem or malfunction.

heat sink   A block of metal (usually aluminum or copper) that sits on top of a CPU to carry the excess heat away from it to prevent damage.

IDE   Integrated Drive Electronics is a standard electronic interface used between a motherboard's disk storage devices (hard drives and CD/DVD drives). Also called ATA.

IEEE 1394   Also called FireWire, this is a fast data transfer standard that supports up to 400 Mbps. IEEE 1394 is usually in the form of a port on PCs, and a single port can support 63 devices connected to it.

I/O   Input/output describes any operation, program, or device that transfers data to or from a computer. Typical I/O devices include a printer, hard disk, keyboard, and mouse. Some devices are basically input-only devices (keyboard and mouse), while others are primarily output-only devices (printer), and some provide both input and output of data (hard disk).

ISP   Internet service provider is the company that computer users choose to allow them to connect to the Internet. As well as Internet access, ISPs also provide access to email and newsgroups.

JPEG/JPG . Joint Photographic Experts Group is a popular file format for images. The files in this format have a .jpg or .jpeg file extension.

jumper   A small metal connector that acts as an on/off switch and is used to alter hardware configurations. It is especially common on hard drives and older expansion cards and motherboards.

LAN   Local area network is a group of interconnected computers sharing the resources of a computer or server within a relatively small area (geographically speaking), usually confined to a room, office, or building.

Mbps   Megabits per second is a common measure of data transfer speeds. *See* bit.

megabyte   A unit of measurement frequently used for memory capacity, file size, and other elements. One megabyte is equal to 1,048,476 bytes.

MHz   Megahertz, or 1 million hertz, is 1 million clock cycles per second and is the measure of a computer's CPU speed. For example, a CPU that runs at 800 MHz carries out 800 million cycles per second. Each instruction processed by a computer takes a predetermined number of clock cycles to be carried out; therefore, the more cycles a computer can execute per second, the faster its programs run.

modem   A device that allows you to transfer digital data over telephone lines. This is the way most people connect to the Internet. Modems can be external (outside the PC) or internal (in the form of an expansion card). The word *modem* comes from modulator/demodulator.

motherboard   The largest circuit board in a PC, which contains the computer's basic circuitry and components.

MS-DOS   Microsoft Disk Operating System; *see* DOS.

NIC   Network interface card is another term for a network card or adapter. This is the device that allows you to connect two or more PCs together.

NTFS   NT File System is the file system available in Microsoft Windows NT, 2000, and XP Home and Professional.

operating system (OS)   Every PC must have an operating system to run other programs on the system. Operating systems perform a huge number of basic tasks such as reacting to input from the keyboard, sending output to the monitor, keeping track of files and folders on the hard drive, and controlling peripheral devices such as printers.

parallel port   An interface found on the back of a PC and commonly used for connecting external devices such as printers or scanners to a PC. It uses a 25-pin connector (DB-25) and is rather large compared to most new interfaces.

PCI   Peripheral Component Interconnect is an interconnection system between the CPU and attached cards in the expansion slots. These expansion slots are designed for high-speed operation.

PCMCIA   Personal Computer Memory Card International Association is the name given to an industry group that was organized in the late 1980s to develop and promote standards for a credit-card-sized memory or I/O device that would fit into a personal computer, such as a notebook or laptop computer. These compact memory devices have now found their way into handheld PCs and digital cameras.

peripheral   Short for "peripheral device," this is any computer device that is not a part of the PC itself (the processor, memory, etc.) but is connected to the PC. Peripherals vary depending on how they are connected. Some peripherals are attached to the PC inside the case, such as hard disk drives, CD-ROM drives, DVD drives, and network adapters. Other peripherals are outside the PC case, such as the printer or scanner. These can be attached by a wired or wireless connection, depending on the PC and peripheral in question.

Plug and Play (PnP)   A technology developed by Microsoft for Windows 95 that is still present in later operating systems. PnP gives end users the ability to plug a device into a PC while the system is on and have the computer recognize that the device has been added or is present. PnP can also guide the user through the steps of installing drivers for the device if necessary.

POST   Power-On Self Test is a test run by the BIOS on the PC system (such as memory and CPU) before the system hands over control of the operating system and continues with start-up.

RAM   Random access memory is electronic storage in a PC where the operating system, application programs, and data in current use are kept so that they can be quickly reached by the CPU. RAM has the advantage of being many times faster to read from and write to than the other kinds of storage in a computer, such as the hard drive. The main disadvantage with RAM is that when you turn the computer off, RAM loses all the data that it contains. When you turn your computer on again, your operating system and other files need to be loaded into RAM from the hard drive again.

router   A device used to transmit data between two computer systems or networks.

SCSI   Small Computer System Interface is a high-speed interface that allows the PC to be connected to a variety of hardware devices, such as hard drives, CD-ROM drives, printers, and scanners. SCSI is not commonly found on PCs today, having been replaced by USB.

SD card   A memory card commonly used in digital cameras and handheld devices.

SDRAM   Synchronous Dynamic Random Access Memory is an improvement to standard DRAM in that it retrieves data alternately between two sets of memory. This makes reading and writing data to and from RAM faster and more efficient.

search engine   A web-based tool used to search the Internet for documents containing particular keywords and display them in the browser.

shareware   Software available on the Internet or via email that can usually be downloaded for free, but you have to pay for continued use.

SIMM   Single Inline Memory Module is a type of RAM found in older PCs.

S.M.A.R.T.   Self-Monitoring Analysis and Reporting Technology monitors and analyzes the health of your hard drive and warns you in advance of possible problems with the drive.

text editor   Any word processing application that you can use to type and edit text. One of the simplest and easiest to use, and most widely available, is Windows Notepad.

UPS   Uninterruptible power supply is a backup system that uses batteries to power a PC and peripheral devices in the event of a power failure. This allows you to continue working and save your work, and shut the system down properly.

USB   Universal Serial Bus is a "Plug-and-Play" interface between a computer and add-on devices (such as keyboards, mice, scanners, and printers) that allows you to add a new device to a PC without having to add an adapter card or even having to turn off the computer. USB supports up to 127 devices and data speeds of up to 480 Mbps.

USB hub   A multiport USB connector that allows several USB-compatible devices to be connected to a computer.

VGA   Video Graphics Array is the standard for today's graphics adapters.

WiFi   WiFi is a common term for a high-frequency wireless local area network (WLAN). WiFi technology is an alternative to a wired LAN and is fast becoming the network of choice for home users who don't want to bother with wires.

WLAN   Wireless local area network is a network of computers that does not use wires for data transfer.

ZIF   Zero insertion force is a socket commonly used to attach a CPU to a motherboard.

ZIP   A popular form of file compression. The files in this format have a .zip file extension.

Appendix B

Websites

H ere is a list of websites and resources that I use and recommend.

 NOTE *These URLs were all correct and tested at the time of writing, but be aware that as with all things to do with the Internet, URLs may change or disappear over time.*

Search Engines	
A9	www.a9.com
AltaVista	www.altavista.com
Ask Jeeves	www.ask.com
Dogpile	www.dogpile.com
EasySearcher	www.easysearcher.com
Excite	www.excite.com
Google	www.google.com
Lycos	www.lycos.com
Metacrawler	www.metacrawler.com
MSN	www.msn.com
search.com	www.search.com
Yahoo	www.yahoo.com

Software Vendors	
Adobe	www.adobe.com
Centered	www.centered.com
EA Games	www.eagames.com
Ensemble Studios	www.ensemblestudios.com
Intuit	www.intuit.com
Lotus	www.lotus.com
Macromedia	www.macromedia.com
Maxis	www.maxis.com
McAfee	www.mcafee.com
Microsoft	www.microsoft.com
Mozilla	www.mozilla.org
Opera	www.opera.com
Sierra	www.sierra.com
Symantec	www.symantec.com
V Com	www.v-com.com

Hardware Vendors	
3Com	www.3com.com
3M	www.3m.com
Abit	www.abit.com.tw
Acer	www.acer.com
Adaptec	www.adaptec.com
Agfa	www.agfa.com
AMD	www.amd.com
AMI	www.ami.com
AOpen	www.aopen.com
APC	www.apcc.com
ASUSTek	www.asus.com
ATI	www.atitech.com
Award	www.award-bios.com
Belkin	www.belkin.com
Brother	www.brother.com
Buffalo Technology	www.buffalotech.com
Canon	www.canon.com
Cisco	www.cisco.com
Compaq	www.compaq.com
Conexant Systems	www.conexant.com
Coolermaster	www.coolermaster.com
Creative Labs	www.creative.com
Crucial	www.crucial.com
Disgo	www.mydisgo.com
D-Link	www.dlink.com
Epson	www.epson.com
Freecom	www.freecom.com
Fuji	www.fuji.com
Gigabyte	www.gigabyte.com.tw
Hauppauge	www.hauppauge.com
Hercules	www.hercules.com
Hewlett Packard	www.hp.com
Hitachi	www.hitachi.com
IBM	www.ibm.com

Hardware Vendors *(continued)*

iiyama	www.iiyama.com
Initio	www.initio.com
Intel	www.intel.com
Iomega	www.iomega.com
Kingston	www.kingston.com
Kodak	www.kodak.com
Kyocera	www.kyocera.com
Labtec	www.labtec.com
Lexmark	www.lexmark.com
LG	www.lge.com
Linksys	www.linksys.com
LiteOn	www.liteon.com
Logic 3	www.logic3.com
Logitech	www.logitech.com
Matrox	www.matrox.com
Maxtor	www.maxtor.com
Microsoft	www.microsoft.com/hardware
Microstar	www.msi.com.tw
NEC	www.nec.com
Nikon	www.nikon.com
Nvidia	www.nvidia.com
Oki	www.oki.com
Olympus	www.olympus.com
Panasonic	www.panasonic.com
Pentax	www.pentax.com
Philips	www.philips.com
Phoenix	www.phoenix.com
Pinnacle	www.pinnaclesys.com
Pioneer	www.pioneer.com
Plextor	www.plextor.com
Quantum	www.quantum.com
Relisys	www.relisys.com
Samsung	www.samsung.com
Sanyo	www.sanyo.com

Hardware Vendors *(continued)*

Seagate	www.seagate.com
Sharp	www.sharp.com
Sony	www.sony.com
Surecom	www.surecom-net.com
TDK	www.tdk.com
Thermaltake	www.thermaltake.com
Toshiba	www.toshiba.com
USRobotics	www.usr.com
VideoLogic	www.videologic.com
Viewsonic	www.viewsonic.com
Viking	www.vikingcomponents.com
Westerm Digital	www.wdc.com
Zalman	www.zalmanusa.com

Security

AdAware	www.lavasoftusa.com
Cookie Crusher	www.thelimitsoft.com/cookie
Gibson Research Corp.	www.grc.com
HackerWhacker	www.hackerwhacker.com
Internet Storm Center	isc.incidents.org
McAfee	www.mcafee.com
Microsoft	www.microsoft.com/security
Passwordsafe	passwordsafe.sourceforge.net
PestScan	www.pestscan.com
SANS (Sysadmin Audit Network Security)	www.sans.org
Spybot S&D	www.safer-networking.org
Symantec	www.symantec.com
Window Washer	www.webroot.com/washer.htm

Help Sites

Annoyances.org	www.annoyances.org
AnswersThatWork.com (listing of programs that may run automatically on your PC)	www.answersthatwork.com/Tasklist_pages/tasklist.htm
BIOSCentral.com	www.bioscentral.com
FILExt	www.filext.com
Home PC Firewall Guide	www.firewallguide.com

Help Sites *(continued)*

HowStuffWorks	www.howstuffworks.com
IBM (glossary of computing terms)	www.ibm.com/ibm/terminology/goc/gocmain.htm
Kingsley-Hughes.com (author's website)	www.kingsley-hughes.com
Microsoft support	support.microsoft.com/
Microsoft Technet	www.microsoft.com/technet
Practically Networked	www.practicallynetworked.com
PurePerformance.com	www.pureperformance.com
SysInternals	www.sysinternals.com
WhatIs	www.whatis.com
Windows XP Users	www.windowsxpusers.com
XPTuneup	www.xptuneup.com

Free Software

Download.com	www.download.com
Freeware Home	www.freewarehome.com
FreewareFiles.com	www.freewarefiles.com
LinuxISO	www.linuxiso.org
Mandrake Linux (free operating system)	www.mandrakelinux.com
Open Office (free suite of programs)	www.openoffice.org
Red Hat Linux (free operating system)	www.redhat.com
SuSe Linux (free operating system)	www.suse.com
Tucows Downloads	www.tucows.com

Utilities (Free and Commercial)

Antivirus

AVG Antivirus	www.grisoft.com
Computer Associates	www.ca.com
McAfee	www.mcafee.com
Norton AntiVirus	www.sarc.com
Panda Software	www.pandasoftware.com

Backup

NovaStor	www.novastor.com
PowerQuest	www.powerquest.com
Second Copy	www.centered.com
Veritas	www.veritas.com

Online Backup

@Backup	www.backup.com
First Backup	www.firstbackup.com
IBackup	www.ibackup.com
Iron Mountain	www.ironmountain.com
LiveVault	www.livevault.com
Remote Backup Systems	www.remote-backup.com
XDrive	www.atrieva.com

Boot Disks

| Bootdisk.com | www.bootdisk.com |

CD & DVD Burning

| Nero | www.ahead.com |
| Roxio | www.roxio.com |

Communication

SimpleComTools	www.simplecomtools.com
TestMySpeed.com (modem and DSL speed tester)	www.testmyspeed.com
Vypress (network messaging tool)	www.vypress.com

Compression Tools

7-Zip	www.7-zip.org
Info-Zip	www.info-zip.org
PKZip	www.pkware.com
WinAce	www.winace.com
WinZip	www.winzip.com

Encryption

HushMail	www.hushmail.com
PGP	www.pgp.com
Steganos	www.steganos.com

File/Cookie Shredding

AbsoluteShield File Shredder	www.sys-shield.com/fileshredder.htm
Cookie Crusher	www.thelimitsoft.com/cookie
Eraser	www.heidi.ie/eraser
HandyBits File Shredder	www.handybits.com/shredder.htm
Window Washer	www.webroot.com/washer.htm

Firewalls	
BlackICE	blackice.iss.net
Kerio	www.kerio.com
Tiny Firewall	www.tinysoftware.com
ZoneAlarm	www.zonelabs.com

Tweak Tools	
Microsoft Powertoys for Windows XP	www.microsoft.com/windowsxp/pro/downloads/powertoys.asp

Text Editors	
Crimson Editor	www.crimsoneditor.com
Notetab	www.notetab.com
TextPad	www.textpad.com
UltraEdit	www.ultraedit.com

Timekeeping	
Sync-It with Atom	www.tolvanen.com/syncit

And finally, a bit of fun ...	
Arcadetown.com	www.arcadetown.com
Dilbert	www.dilbert.com
Garfield	www.garfield.com

Appendix C

Tools

Here is a list of the tools that you will frequently need in order to effectively carry out the most common PC repair tasks.

- **Screwdrivers**   You'll need the following sizes. (Alternatively, get yourself a multibit screwdriver set that contains all the different screwdriver heads you'll need.)

    - Crosspoint No. 1 and No. 2

    - Straight-edged 2.5, 5, and 6

    With these screwdrivers, you should be able to tackle most fittings that you come across in PCs. However, some makers are moving to Torx screws (with star-shaped holes in the heads of the screws), and these require different bits. If you buy a good-quality multibit screwdriver, it is likely that you'll either get these or be able to buy them separately.

- **Antistatic wrist strap**   This vital piece of kit prevents ESD damage to sensitive components inside your PC. These wrist straps are cheap and readily available from anywhere that sells PC components. I recommend that you always use one, as prevention is much better (and cheaper!) than cure.

- **Boot disks**   It's a good idea to have boot floppy disks for your operating system (and others if you work on other PCs).

- **Spare floppy disks**   These are handy because you might need to copy files, and this is still the best way to do that.

- **Tweezers**   An important but often overlooked tool is a pair of tweezers. Inside PCs you are normally dealing with loads of small, fiddly parts. Moving jumpers on hard drives, CD or DVD drives, or (older) motherboards is made so much easier with tweezers. Also, tweezers make retrieving screws that have been dropped or that have rolled away into the case much easier.

    Small tweezers are better for working with fiddly jumpers, while long tweezers are better for retrieving screws. If at all possible, find yourself plastic tweezers instead of the more common metal ones, as they pose less of a risk of short-circuiting components.

- **Needle-nosed pliers** Again, these are useful for small, fiddly jobs. They can also be useful for working with wires and connectors.

- **Container for screws and little bits** Screws and fittings have a nasty habit of wandering when you are working on a PC. A missing bit can cause problems and even hold up a job, so take good care of them. Also, keep any spares you might have. You never know when you might need a spare.

In addition to the tools I've listed above, for complete peace of mind and the ability to deal with pretty much everything you come across, you might also want to invest in the following optional tools.

- **Wire cutters/stripper** These are not often needed but handy if you have to fit a power plug or add a phone extension.

- **Torx screwdrivers/bits** As noted earlier, these are becoming more popular. You might never need them, but if you do, you'll be thankful you've got them. You'll want the following sizes:

  T-6, T-8, T-10, T-15, T-20, and T-25

- **Small socket set** Some cases you come across can be held together with small nuts and bolts, and having the right tools can make the job go much smoother. You'll want the following sizes:

  1/4, 5/16, 11/32, and 3/8

- **Allen keys** Allen bolts are another fitting you might come across in some systems, in the following sizes:

  3/32, 7/64, 1/8, 9/64, 5/32, 3/16, 7/32, and 1/4

- **Multimeter** Whether you want or need a multimeter really depends on whether you think it would be useful to you. (Don't worry if you don't know how they work or how to use them; most are quite easy to use!) There are a lot of things you can do with even the most basic multimeter, such as check voltages, check the continuity of cables, check battery levels, and whether electrical fuses have blown.

If you want to spend a little more on a multimeter, you can get some that have really handy features: thermometer function, backlit LCD screens for easy reading, and much more. Multimeters are handy for more than just PC repair, so other things that you might be interested in (such as automotive repair) might help you justify the cost.

- **Loopback plugs**   These are connectors that fit into ports (for example, serial, parallel, and USB ports) and allow special diagnostic software to check that they work correctly. They are very useful for diagnosing port problems, but not something you'll need all that often.

- **POST card**   This is the ultimate tool for the PC doctor. This is a "medical tricorder" for the PC (yes, I do like Star Trek!). You slot the card into a free PCI or ISA slot on the motherboard of a dead machine (there are combo cards that fit both slots), fire up the system, and the card tells you what's wrong with the system. The better the card, the better the level of detail you get from it. If you work a lot on dead PCs, this card can pay for itself quickly in the time you save alone. However, for the home user this is generally overkill, as a high-quality POST card will cost as much as a new budget PC!

- **Power tester screwdriver**   These are really handy because they let you test for live wires safely. If a wire is live, the little neon tube in the screwdriver will glow. It's a handy backup in case someone accidentally plugs the PC back into the power outlet.

- **Plastic ties**   Use these to tie back cables and keep the inside of the case tidy. Never use wire ties for this job, as they can cut through the cable, and the wire can cause short circuits.

- **Insulating tape**   Again, this is handy for keeping things tidy, but limit its use inside the case, as the adhesive collects dust.

- **Soft, lint-free cloth**   You'll want one for wiping down surfaces that collect dust, but don't use it on circuit boards, as this could result in ESD damage.

Appendix D

Common File Extensions

What follows is a list of commonly seen file extensions. It is by no means exhaustive (there are hundreds of them) but these are among the extensions you will most frequently encounter.

Extension	Characteristics
.aam	Macromedia Shockwave
.arc	A compressed file that can be opened with PKZip or WinZip
.asp	Active server page, used to code web pages and connect to databases
.au	Sound file, open with player, used on older web pages
.avi	Audio/video interleaved, movie clip, open with mplayer, Internet Explorer, or Navigator with plug-in
.bak	Used by many applications, often created automatically
.bat	DOS batch file, run by double-clicking in Windows (95 and later), edit these files with a text editor such as Notepad
.bmp	Microsoft bitmap, open using MS Paint or another graphics program
.cab	Microsoft installation archive (cabinet file), similar to .zip archive
.cfg	Configuration file
.css	Plain text file containing web page–style information
.csv	Comma separated variable file, a way of presenting tabular data in a text file, usually viewed in MS Excel
.dat	Used by several applications, do not open these file directly in text editors
.dll	Software used by Windows to provide services to applications
.doc	Microsoft Word file
.dot	Microsoft Word template
.exe	Self-extracting or executable file, run by double-clicking in Windows (95 and later)
.faq	Frequently asked questions, almost always a text file
.fnt	Font file
.gif	Graphic in GIF format, open in web browser or graphics program
.gz	Compressed archive file created by Gzip in the Unix operating system
.htm	Hypertext document (same as .html), open in a web browser, edit in any word processor or text editor
.ico	Open with an icon editor

Extension	Characteristics
.ini	Initialization file
.jar	Java compressed archive file
.jpg	Graphic in JPEG format (Joint Photographic Experts Group), view with web browser or image editing program
.js	Part of web page used to create interactive effects such as mouse roll-overs and pop-up boxes
.log	Created by many applications, usually a text file, edit in any text editor
.mid	Audio file in MIDI format
.mov	QuickTime movie, view using Internet Explorer or Netscape using plug-in
.mp3	Audio file in MP3 format, CD-quality sound, with 10x compression
.mpg	Video movie in MPEG format (Motion Picture Experts Group)
.old	Backup file (generic file extension used by many applications)
.pdf	Portable Document Format, requires Adobe Acrobat reader
.png	Graphic in Portable Network Graphics format, can work on all platforms
.ppt	Microsoft PowerPoint file, used for creating slides and overhead presentations
.pub	Microsoft Publisher file
.ram	Real Audio file, open in web browser with Real Audio plug-in
.rtf	Rich text format, word processor file with formatting codes
.scr	Screensaver file
.sig	Appended to outgoing email messages, editable in a text editor such as Notepad
.sys	DOS system file, device driver or hardware configuration info
.tar	File archive created in the Unix operating system
.tif	Tagged Image File format, graphics file, editable in graphics program
.tmp	Temporary file, used by many programs
.ttf	TrueType font file
.txt	Contains only ASCII code, also called "text file," can be created and edited in any text editor
.wav	Sound file in Waveform format
.xls	Microsoft Excel worksheet file
.xml	eXtensible Markup Language, a plain text file for web pages
.zip	Compressed file, open with WinZip or PKZip

The following table lists filename extensions identified by Microsoft as containing potentially dangerous applications (that is, they can, under certain circumstances, contain malicious code—such as viruses, worms or Trojans that can damage PC systems).

Extension	File Type
.ade	Microsoft Access project extension
.adp	Microsoft Access project
.asx	Windows Media Audio/Video
.bas	Microsoft Visual Basic class module
.bat	Batch file
.chm	Compiled HTML Help file
.cmd	Microsoft Windows NT Command script
.com	Microsoft MS-DOS program
.cpl	Control Panel extension
.crt	Security certificate
.exe	Program
.hlp	Help file
.hta	HTML program
.inf	Setup information
.ins	Internet Naming Service
.isp	Internet communication settings
.js	JScript file
.jse	JScript encoded script file
.lnk	Shortcut
.mda	Microsoft Access add-in program
.mdb	Microsoft Access program
.mde	Microsoft Access MDE database
.mdt	Microsoft Access workgroup information
.mdw	Microsoft Access workgroup information
.mdz	Microsoft Access wizard program
.msc	Microsoft Common Console document

Extension	File Type
.msi	Microsoft Windows Installer package
.msp	Microsoft Windows Installer patch
.mst	Microsoft Windows Installer transform or Microsoft Visual Test source file
.ops	Office XP settings
.pcd	Photo CD image, Microsoft Visual compiled script
.pif	Shortcut to MS-DOS program
.prf	Microsoft Outlook profile settings
.reg	Registration entries
.scf	Windows Explorer command
.scr	Screensaver
.sct	Windows Script Component
.shb	Shell Scrap object
.shs	Shell Scrap object
.url	Internet shortcut
.vb	VBScript file
.vbe	VBScript Encoded script file
.vbs	VBScript file
.wsc	Windows script component file
.wsf	Windows script file
.wsh	Windows script host settings file

Index

INTERNATIONAL CONTACT INFORMATION

AUSTRALIA
McGraw-Hill Book Company
Australia Pty. Ltd.
TEL +61-2-9900-1800
FAX +61-2-9878-8881
http://www.mcgraw-hill.com.au
books-it_sydney@mcgraw-hill.com

CANADA
McGraw-Hill Ryerson Ltd.
TEL +905-430-5000
FAX +905-430-5020
http://www.mcgraw-hill.ca

GREECE, MIDDLE EAST, & AFRICA
(Excluding South Africa)
McGraw-Hill Hellas
TEL +30-210-6560-990
TEL +30-210-6560-993
TEL +30-210-6560-994
FAX +30-210-6545-525

MEXICO (Also serving Latin America)
McGraw-Hill Interamericana Editores
S.A. de C.V.
TEL +525-1500-5108
FAX +525-117-1589
http://www.mcgraw-hill.com.mx
carlos_ruiz@mcgraw-hill.com

SINGAPORE (Serving Asia)
McGraw-Hill Book Company
TEL +65-6863-1580
FAX +65-6862-3354
http://www.mcgraw-hill.com.sg
mghasia@mcgraw-hill.com

SOUTH AFRICA
McGraw-Hill South Africa
TEL +27-11-622-7512
FAX +27-11-622-9045
robyn_swanepoel@mcgraw-hill.com

SPAIN
McGraw-Hill/
Interamericana de España, S.A.U.
TEL +34-91-180-3000
FAX +34-91-372-8513
http://www.mcgraw-hill.es
professional@mcgraw-hill.es

UNITED KINGDOM, NORTHERN,
EASTERN, & CENTRAL EUROPE
McGraw-Hill Education Europe
TEL +44-1-628-502500
FAX +44-1-628-770224
http://www.mcgraw-hill.co.uk
emea_queries@mcgraw-hill.com

ALL OTHER INQUIRIES Contact:
McGraw-Hill/Osborne
TEL +1-510-420-7700
FAX +1-510-420-7703
http://www.osborne.com
omg_international@mcgraw-hill.com